Sociolinguistic Patterns in British English

Contributors

Richard Bourhis, *Department of Psychology, University of Bristol*
Jenny Cheshire, *Department of Linguistic Science, University of Reading*
Ellen Douglas-Cowie, *Department of English, Queen's University, Belfast*
Olwen Elyan, *Department of Psychology, University of Bristol*
Tina Foxcroft, *Department of Linguistics, University of Reading*
Val Jones, *Department of English, University of Newcastle*
Howard Giles, *Department of Psychology, University of Bristol*
G. O. Knowles, *Department of English Language and Literature, University of Lancaster*
R. K. S. Macaulay, *Department of English, Pitzer College, Claremont, California*
James Milroy, *Department of English, Queen's University, Belfast*
Lesley Milroy, *Department of English, Ulster College, Northern Ireland Polytechnic*
John Pellowe, *Department of English Language, University of Newcastle*
Malcolm Petyt, *Department of Linguistic Science, University of Reading*
Euan Reid, *Department of Language Studies, West Midlands College of Education*
Suzanne Romaine, *Department of Linguistics, University of Edinburgh*
Philip Smith, *Department of Psychology, University of Bristol*
Peter Trudgill, *Department of Linguistic Science, University of Reading*

Sociolinguistic Patterns in British English

Edited by Peter Trudgill

University Park Press
Baltimore

© Edward Arnold 1978

First published 1978 by Edward Arnold (Publishers) Ltd, London
First published in the USA in 1978 by
University Park Press
233 East Redwood Street,
Baltimore, Maryland 21202

Library of Congress Cataloging in Publication Data
Main entry under title:

Sociolinguistic patterns in British English.

   Bibliography: p.
   Includes index.
   1. English language—Social aspects—Addresses, essays, lectures. 2.
Sociolinguistics—Addresses, essays, lectures. 3. English language—
Dialects—Addresses, essays, lectures.
I. Trudgill, Peter.
PE1072.S65   301.2′1   78–1763

ISBN 0-8391-1269-6

Printed in Great Britain

Contents

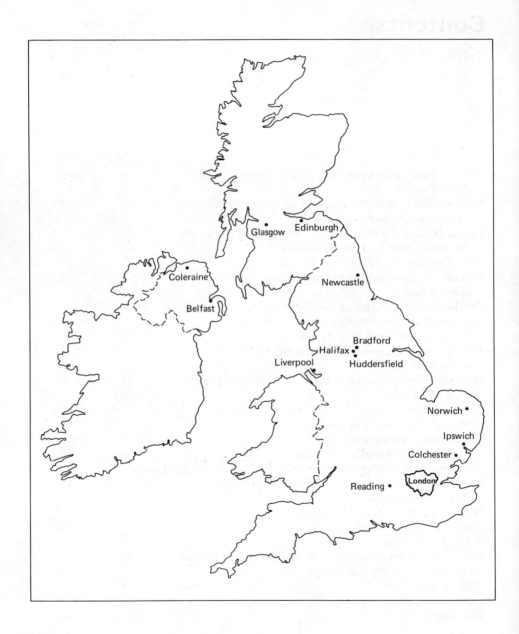

1

Introduction: sociolinguistics and sociolinguistics

Peter Trudgill

We have chosen to employ the word *sociolinguistic* in the title of this book, and it is unlikely that anyone would object to most of the papers in the book being classified under that heading.[1] It is more likely, however, that we shall meet the reverse objection: that we have taken too narrow a view of what constitutes sociolinguistics and that, therefore, the papers that follow are representative of only a small area of the total field. As a result, it could be argued, they give a somewhat inadequate picture of British work in sociolinguistics as a whole.

It is not my purpose in this introduction to defend the book against this objection, since my own feeling is that whether you call something *sociolinguistics* or not does not, in the last analysis, matter very much. I want, however, to attempt to explain briefly why the term *sociolinguistics* causes problems, and where the origins of possible misunderstandings lie. It will then be possible to locate the studies in this volume in relation to other types of work sometimes referred to as sociolinguistic, and in this way point out their own particular relevance and importance.

The difficulty with *sociolinguistics*, then, is that it is a term which means many different things to many different people. This multiplicity of interpretations is probably due to the fact that, while everybody would agree that sociolinguistics has *something* to do with language and society, it is clearly also not concerned with *everything* that could be considered 'language and society'. The problem, therefore, lies in the drawing of the line between *language and society* and *sociolinguistics*. Obviously, different scholars draw the line in different places.

In looking at the field of language and society as a whole, it is useful, if we are considering the drawing of lines, to examine *objectives*. It is helpful, that is, to look at why or to what purpose workers are carrying out studies in this field.

[1]Acknowledgements by contributors to this volume accompany the individual papers. I would like at this point to acknowledge the cooperation of the other contributors; to thank Peter Huxley, Michael Stubbs, J. K. Chambers, Michael Garman, Paul Fletcher and F. R. Palmer for their help with this introduction; and to point out that five of the papers in this volume, those on Belfast, Reading, East Anglia, Tyneside and Glasgow, stem from work financed wholly or in part by the SSRC.

If we do this, we can see that it is possible to divide studies of language and society into three groups: those where the objectives are purely sociological or social-scientific; those where they are partly sociological and partly linguistic; and those where the objectives are wholly linguistic.[2] Like most such divisions, this classification is somewhat arbitrary and not easy to apply in practice, but it may be helpful in dealing with the problem of what sociolinguistics is and is not. We will examine each of these three groups in turn.

Language and society and sociolinguistics

1   An obvious candidate for the first category—studies of language and society which are purely social scientific in intent—is provided by some aspects of the field of *ethnomethodology*. It is not easy for an outsider to give an informed or accurate characterization of ethnomethodology, but ethnomethodologists might not object too strongly to a statement to the effect that it can be regarded as a way of doing ethnography or sociology which studies people's practical reasoning and common-sense knowledge of their society and the way it works. It is:

> an organizational study of a member's knowledge of his ordinary affairs, of his own organized enterprises, where that knowledge is treated by us as part of the same setting that makes it orderable (Garfinkel, 1968 p. 18).

One way in which studies of this type can be carried out is by investigating the use of language in social interaction—*talk* rather than *speech*. Talk is 'a constituent feature of the same setting that it is used to talk about' (Garfinkel, 1968), and its analysis makes it possible to locate those things which a member of a society takes for granted—his 'knowledge of his ordinary affairs'.

Turner (1970 p. 174), for example, quotes the following piece of conversational interaction (somewhat abbreviated here):

> *Bert:* Yeah, that's correct. I really did know him and he was with me in the Alexander Psychiatric Institute. I don't remember his name but we always buddied around together when we were at the hospital. And I saw him about three weeks ago, and I said to'm, 'Hallo, howarya doing?' He said 'I don't know you—who are you?' 'Well, lookit', I said, 'You must know me.' He says, 'No, I don't know you.' Now he was with another fellow there too—waal he didn't want to admit that he was in a mental hospital—he didn't want to admit it to the other fellow that was with him. So he just walked off and that was it. He wouldn't say hallo to me. He wouldn't say nothin'!
> *Rob:* What was your view there? Do you have your own views on that? A touchy point.
> *Jake:* Perhaps he didn't like the idea of being in that place. Maybe he didn't want—

[2] Already one source of confusion suggests itself: different workers may use the same data and the same methodology but with different objectives.

Bert: Well no he had to say it—there was another fellow with him you see—
Jake: Well he didn't want to admit—
Bert: Who hadn't been in a mental hospital probably, and he *was* in the hospital. He didn't want *him* to know.

What is going on in this conversation is obvious. But it is only obvious to us, an ethnomethodologist might say, because we are, as it were, competent members of our society. What remains to be explained is exactly what is required to be 'competent' in this sense.

Turner notes that, in this text, Bert first of all complains and then explains. What is of interest to ethnomethodologists is what it takes to 'do complaining' and 'do explaining' successfully, and how it is that we recognize that that is in fact what Bert is doing. In fact we can say that the complaint is taken as such because Bert establishes that he knew the other party and that he greeted him by saying 'Hello, howarya doing?' It is then taken for granted that, given that two parties are acquainted and one greets the other, a greeting is required in return. Bert indicates that this did not in fact happen. Turner says that:

> assumption of shared knowledge that a greeted acquaintance has an *obligation* to respond with a greeting is both a requirement and a resource for seeing how Bert is entitled to say He *wouldn't* say hello to me, in that he is thus enabling his listeners to find the 'absence of greeting' as a motivated fact.

Similarly, Bert's explanation that 'he didn't want to admit he was in a mental hospital' works as an explanation—we interpret it as an explanation—since we share the common-sense knowledge that greetings in chance encounters open up the obligation (in this case on Bert's friend) to explain (to his companion) the basis of the acquaintance (of himself with Bert). In other words, a greeting in response to Bert's greeting could have led to a subsequent dialogue of the type:

> 'Who was that?'
> 'Someone I was in mental hospital with.'

The competent member of society interprets Bert's 'doing explaining' as exactly that because it is taken for granted (in addition to the potential stigma of having been in a mental hospital) that the participants in a greeting sequence would have taken it for granted that this would have legitimized questions about the acquaintance *and* introduced the obligation to answer these questions.

It may be felt that ethnomethodological studies of this type have a clear link with linguistic studies of topics such as presupposition, pragmatics, and speech acts. Generally speaking, however, work in ethnomethodology, while it may deal with language and society, is fairly obviously not linguistics.[3] Language ('talk') is being employed as a datum, but the objectives are wholly social scientific. The point is to use the linguistic data to get at the social

[3]It has, however, been pointed out (Hymes, 1974, p. 81) that ethnomethodologists might well benefit from a little more linguistic expertise in the analysis of their data.

A*

knowledge that lies behind it, not to further our understanding about language. Ethnomethodology, that is, is not sociolinguistics.[4]

2   The second category, as we saw above, consists of studies of language and society which are, in varying degrees, both sociological and linguistic in intent. This, it will be apparent, is where the main problem with the term *sociolinguistics* lies: some workers would include the whole of this area within sociolinguistics; others would exclude it totally; yet others would include some areas but not all.

Into this second category come a number of fields of study, none of which is wholly distinct from all the others. In discussing these different fields I shall not attempt any definitive analysis or sub-classification of the area as a whole. Such an attempt would be unprofitable and probably impossible. Rather, I shall select descriptive labels employed by scholars working in this area, and attempt a characterization of the kind of work that is typically carried out under these labels, particularly where this is work that has involved the examination of British English. As we shall see, many of these labels overlap, and they are also of widely differing degrees of generality.

(i)   A field which is closely related to some aspects of ethnomethodology is one which is often referred to in a fairly general way as *discourse analysis*. (This cannot be fully identified with 'discourse analysis' where this is understood to mean simply text grammar or the grammatical analysis of units larger than the sentence. The analysis of discourse under the general heading of 'language and society' presupposes some kind of social interaction i.e. *conversational* discourse.)

The data examined in studies of conversational discourse are very often of the same type as those investigated by ethnomethodologists who work with linguistic data. It is therefore not always possible, as indeed was hinted at above, to draw a dividing line between the two: 'doing conversation' is one of the social accomplishments which ethnomethodologists will wish to study. There are, however, many studies in conversational analysis which are concerned not with the social meaning which lies behind conversation but with the organization of conversation: rules, we can say, for conversational interaction. Sacks *et al.* (1974), for example, have pointed out that conversation can be regarded as a kind of speech exchange system which is organized in such a way as to ensure that at a given time only one speaker speaks. It also guarantees that changes of speaker occur. Conversations, that is, are based on a turn-taking mechanism, where a 'turn' consists of the right and the obligation to speak which is allocated to a speaker, as well as his actual utterance. (We can confirm that a 'turn' is an obligation as well as a right. It might, for instance, be reported of a conversation between Mary and John that at one point 'Mary remained silent' when in fact both parties were silent. The point is, obviously, that the onus was on Mary to speak because it was her 'turn'.) There are, further, rules for turn-taking such that it is open to the

[4]Another candidate for this category is the work of Bernstein (in which he himself employs the term *socio-linguistic*). This is work in language and society which has no linguistic objectives, although it has been extended in that direction by Halliday (1973).

current speaker to select the next speaker and that only if this is not done is it then open to any speaker to 'self-select'. And work of this sort is also concerned with rules for interruptions, the introduction of new topics, silences, and so on.

Other workers have looked more specifically at the structure of discourse, and have pointed out that stretches of discourse are no more unstructured sequences of utterances than sentences are unstructured sequences of words. An obvious and trivial instance is provided by the fact that questions are typically followed by answers. A discourse structure of the following form is quite usual:

$$(Q_1 A_1) \ (Q_2 A_2) \ (Q_3 A_3)$$

where Q_1, Q_2 and Q_3 are questions, paired here with their appropriate answers. But it is also perfectly possible for discourse structures involving sequences of this type to involve embedding of the form:

$$(Q_1 \ (Q_2 \ (Q_3 A_3) \ A_2) \ A_1)$$

An example of this is provided by Goffman (1976 p. 259):

Q Have you got the time?
Q Standard or Daylight Saving?
Q What are you running on?
A Standard
A Standard then.
A It's five o'clock.

Schegloff (1968) has also suggested that it is not at all obvious why it should be the answerer of the telephone rather than the maker of a call who actually speaks first, unless the ringing of the telephone itself is interpreted as the *summons* part of a *summons-answer* discourse sequence. (He also points out that *summons-answer* sequences have a number of interesting differences from *question-answer* sequences.) And Sinclair and Coulthard (1974) have examined the structure of discourse in British classrooms. Naturally enough, discourse of this sort differs in a number of revealing ways from discourse in other situations.

Other researchers have examined the nature of the cohesion of conversational discourse in some detail by noting the way in which structure is maintained through the repetition of lexical items across speakers, pronominalization, and the use of signals such as *mm, uhuh, well, you know*, and so on.

Yet other scholars have been concerned with an aspect of the analysis of conversational discourse which deals with what has been referred to as 'rules for discourse'. Studies of this type are concerned with the problem of how it is possible to distinguish between meaningful, coherent conversations and those which are not coherent. Some linguists have resisted the inclusion of studies of this type within linguistics on the grounds that this would involve us in the impossible task of incorporating into descriptions or grammars everything that speakers know about the world. However, Labov (1972b, p. 299) has demonstrated that it is possible to develop rules of discourse which have the required explanatory power without this. We know, he says, that the following is a perfectly coherent piece of discourse:

A: Are you going to work tomorrow?
B: I'm on jury duty.

Now there is no obvious *linguistic* connection between A's question and B's answer. So what is the connection? Labov states that this kind of cohesion can be handled by a discourse rule as follows:

If A makes a request for information $Q-S_1$, and B makes a statement S_2 in response which cannot be expanded by rules of ellipsis to the form XS_1Y, then S_2 is heard as an assertion that there exists a proposition P known to both A and B:

If S_2, then $(E)S_1$

where (E) is an existential operator, and from this proposition there is inferred an answer to A's request: $(E)S_1$

In this case, the proposition known to both A and B, which B's reply can be heard as asserting, is that people who are on jury duty are not allowed to go to work. It is not, however, necessary for linguists to build this information into any linguistic description which attempts to account for the acceptability of this dialogue. It is necessary for linguistics only to be concerned with the form of the discourse rule itself and with the *fact* of the proposition. The *content* of the proposition is not relevant. (Ethnomethodologists, on the other hand, *are* interested in the content of such propositions. It is precisely propositions of this type which are revealed as constituting shared knowledge through ethnomethodological studies of conversational interaction. Typically, of course, the propositions will be rather less obvious than the one discussed here.)

That such rules of discourse exist can readily be demonstrated by breaking them. Wolfram and Wolfram (forthcoming) have investigated informants' reactions to sequences of the type:

A (Wolfram): How old are you?
B (Informant): Thirty-three.
A (Wolfram): How come?

There is a rule of discourse which interprets *how come?* questions as an assertion of the fact that there is a non-obvious proposition known to B which is not known to A. Wolfram here breaks the rule by asserting, in effect, that it is not obvious why someone is thirty-three. Informants' reactions showed very clearly that a rule had indeed been broken. Some laughed and/or were embarrassed, and some responded with a humorous reply. Others were clearly searching for a non-obvious proposition such as, 'I look older than thirty-three because. . .'.

Labov points out that children sometimes have difficulties with discourse rules because they are not aware of the proposition that is being asserted:

> *Linus:* Do you want to play with me, Violet?
> *Violet:* You're younger than me. [Shuts the door]
> *Linus:* [puzzled] She didn't answer my question.

That adults are aware of this fact is confirmed by Wolfram. Where the *how come?* questions were asked by Todd Wolfram (aged 6), adults responded quite naturally: it is clear to them that propositions that are obvious to an adult may be non-obvious to a child:

> *Wolfram Jnr:* How old are you, Uncle Jerry?
> *Informant:* Thirty-seven, think.
> *Wolfram Jnr:* How come?
> *Informant:* 'Cause I was born in 1936.

(A very useful overview of and plea for work of this type in general is provided by Burton and Stubbs, 1975.)

(ii) A further label which refers to a field whose objectives are clearly both linguistic and social is the *ethnography of speaking*. As employed by Dell Hymes (1974, and elsewhere) and others (see Bauman and Sherzer, eds., 1974) the term *ethnography of speaking* is applied to a field which looks at the role of language in the 'communicative conduct of communities'—the ways in which language is actually used in different cultures. It examines the functions and uses of styles, dialects and languages, and looks at the way in which verbal arts and speech acts are interpreted and carried through in particular societies. It involves elements from sociology, social anthropology, education, folklore and poetics, as well as linguistics, and, as a fairly general term, could well be interpreted as including many aspects, at least, of the kind of discourse analysis we have just been discussing. The ethnography of speaking includes, for example, the study of routine, specialized and ritual speech acts in particular communities: there are rules in most communities for activities such as the narration of stories and the telling of jokes; and the now numerous studies of Black American speech acts such as 'sounding' can also be considered under this heading. Labov's 'Rules for ritual insults' (see Labov, 1972b) is a good example of a study of this kind. So far, we have nothing really comparable for any kind of British English.

The ethnography of speaking also tends, as one might expect, to be cross-cultural in emphasis. It is under this heading that we might note that in Japan it is in fact the *caller* who speaks first in telephone conversations; that there are cultures where rules for conversational interaction *do* permit more than one speaker to speak at a time; that silence is much more usual in some cultures than in others; and so on. In fact, work in this field grew in part out of the recognition by ethnographers and others working with alien cultures that it is not enough simply to learn the language of the particular culture under observation. One must also learn how to *use* that language. One needs to acquire, in Hymes's terms, *communicative competence* in that language (in addition to *competence* in the sense introduced by Chomsky), or, as ethnomethodologists might say, the ability to 'do speaking' competently in that community. One has to learn how to use which variety when; which linguistic formulae to employ; and how to be polite, impolite, friendly, unfriendly, and so on, in an appropriate way.

One obvious aspect of the acquisition of communicative competence which often strikes students learning foreign languages involves the use of formulae for greetings, thanks, leave-taking, and other such activities. English speakers, for example, often feel uneasy when they find that there is no real equivalent to *please* in Scandinavian languages, and Europeans are often similarly distressed to find that there is no real English equivalent for *bon appétit*, or that *please* has a much narrower function than *bitte/prego* etc. As an example of the sort of descriptive problems involved, then, we might examine the relatively recent usage in some types of British English of the form 'Cheers!'. Originally a drinking toast, this now functions both as some kind of leave-taking and as some kind of thanking formula. The problems of the ethnographer of speaking in outlining its exact function, however, are the same as those faced by foreigners (including non-British English speakers) attempting to use it correctly: when is it used and when not? It is, we have observed, a kind of leave-taking formula. The following sort of usage, however, does not occur:

A: Well, my dear, take care of yourself, and I'll see you in six months' time.
B: *Cheers!

It is also, we have claimed, a kind of thanking formula. Similarly, however, the following is very unlikely:

A: I'd like to take you out to dinner tomorrow night.
B: *Cheers!

It seems, in fact, that amongst certain sections of the community 'Cheers!' can be employed (a) as a drinking toast, but particularly (b) as a way of thanking whoever has bought a particular round of drinks, and presumably by extension (c) as a way of thanking someone for a minor service that they have just rendered in your presence—the opening of a door, the picking up of a dropped pencil, or something similar. And it *is* also used as a leave-taking formula (perhaps by extension of a 'thanks and goodbye' usage and/or of the 'your good health'-type component of the drinking toast) but only in informal telephone conversations, in familiar letters, or if the leave-taking is a routine or minor one. Other less frequent uses are equivalent to 'Hello!' in fleeting encounters where no further conversation is going to take place; and to 'here you are' (cf. *bitte, prego,* above) in giving someone something.[5]

(iii) *Anthropological linguistics* is another term which refers to a field that is both social scientific and linguistic. It is, if anything, even more loosely defined than the terms we have considered so far. In some of its forms, anthropological linguistics refers to work which is a good deal less linguistic than that carried out under the heading of, say, the ethnography of speaking. For example, anthropologists who study kinship systems and systems of linguistic taboo, through the study of a community's language, are concerned to learn more about the structure and values of that community than about

[5] I am very grateful to J. K. Chambers and Heather Harris for their observations, ideas and data on the use of 'cheers!'

the language itself. On the other hand, there are many studies, such as the componential analysis of kinship systems by semanticists, and investigations into linguistic relativity, which, while they are often considered to be 'anthropological linguistics', are certainly of more interest to linguists than to anthropologists. The journal *Anthropological Linguistics*, too, is aimed more at linguists than at anthropologists, although some of the papers it publishes could equally well be classified, if one were so disposed, under the headings of discourse analysis and/or the ethnography of speaking.

(iv) The label *the sociology of language* also suggests a field which is predominantly social scientific, on a par with the sociology of religion, the sociology of education, and so on. Typically (although not exclusively), however, *the sociology of language* is a label applied to courses taught in linguistics departments, and it is a field which requires linguistic expertise and whose objectives are at least partly linguistic.

The term is most prominently associated with the work of Joshua Fishman (see Fishman, 1972 p. 1). Fishman says that:

> the sociology of language focuses upon the entire gamut of topics related to the social organization of language behaviour, including not only language usage *per se* but also language attitudes and overt behaviours toward language and toward language users.

Characterized in this way, it is clear that the sociology of language is, again, a very general term that can cover discourse analysis, and aspects of anthropological linguistics, as well as the social psychology of language (see sub-section v). It is also not clear from this characterization how the *sociology of language* can be distinguished from the *ethnography of speaking*. In fact, of course, these two areas do overlap quite extensively (see, in particular, Gumperz, 1971). In practice, though, most scholars would probably associate the label *sociology of language* most typically with topics such as bilingualism, diglossia, verbal repertoire, code-switching, language loyalty, and so on. Descriptions in the field of the sociology of language typically concentrate on, in Fishman's words, 'who speaks what language to whom and when and to what end'. MacKinnon's study of Scottish Gaelic (1974), for instance, examines the role of Gaelic in Outer Hebridean society, and investigates the social constraints on the use of Gaelic and English.

(v) The *social psychology of language* is a label which can be used to cover studies of the use of language in social interaction from a psychological perspective, as well as studies of attitudes to languages and varieties of languages. Howard Giles has pointed out (see references to Elyan, Smith, Giles and Bourhis, in this volume) that although it is certainly true, as we have just observed, that there are social constraints on and contextual correlates of the use of linguistic varieties, speakers are not 'sociolinguistic automata' and are also able to select particular varieties in order to influence and manipulate situations (see also Gumperz and Hernandez, 1971). (The use of a formal style in an informal situation, for instance, can be used as a joke or to signal disapproval or social distance.)

Giles, following on the work of Lambert (see Lambert, 1967) and others, has also investigated attitudes to different varieties of British English through the use of *matched guise* experiments (see Elyan *et al*, this volume). These experiments have produced a number of very interesting results. Some, such as the finding that RP-speakers are rated as being more competent and intelligent than non-RP-speakers, are not too surprising. Others, such as the finding that arguments couched in RP are less persuasive for many listeners than the same arguments couched in their local accent, are very revealing. Trudgill and Giles (1977) have also produced evidence, in a comparative study of English, Scottish, Irish, Canadian and American listeners, that apparently aesthetic evaluations of different accents are in fact much more social and cultural in origin than genuinely aesthetic.

(vi) Most of the areas we have been discussing in section 2 have their practical, applied side, in addition to their more theoretical aspects. Studies of conversational discourse, for instance, are currently being applied to the analysis of interaction between, for example, doctors and patients; and we have already noted the educational work of Sinclair and Coulthard (1974). The ethnography of speaking, too, has its obvious applications in foreign-language teaching—the idea of *notional syllabuses* (Wilkins, 1977) depends in part on how to perform particular speech acts in particular ways. And *language planning* is clearly to be regarded as the applied sociology of language.

(vii) All the labels discussed in section 2 cover fields of study which come into the area which presents problems if we are attempting to decide what is sociolinguistics and what is not. This is because their objectives are mixed. The social objectives of these areas are clear. But they also have linguistic benefits and objectives. We have already noted the interest of semanticists in the 'anthropological linguistic' subject of kinship systems. But the study of the other areas also has consequences for linguistic theory. For instance, the study of the structure of conversational discourse is as linguistic a concern as the study of text grammar generally. And students of linguistic change will note Sankoff and Brown's explanation (1976) of the development of relative clauses in New Guinea Tok Pisin through conversational interaction between speakers. Similarly, the sociology of language, in its studies of bilingualism, links with the study of interference between linguistic systems (see, notably, Weinreich, 1963). And the notions of verbal repertoire, from the sociology of language, and communicative competence, from the ethnography of speaking, concern those who are interested in how far it is legitimate to extend grammars and to expand Chomsky's notion of competence. As far as the social psychology of language is concerned, Labov (1963) is one of many who have demonstrated that attitudes to language can be a powerful force in the propagation of linguistic changes, and Giles's (1973b) theory of linguistic accommodation between speakers helps to explain the role of face-to-face interaction in the dissemination of change.

All these areas, then, do have linguistic objectives. But it is because they can be interpreted as having social scientific objectives *as well* that disagreements may arise as to exactly how they should be classified. Ultimately, however, as I have suggested above, the labelling of disciplines and the drawing of boundaries between them is probably unimportant, unnecessary, and unhelpful. As Hymes writes in his Foreword to Fishman (1972 p. viii):

> The parcelling out of the study of man among competing clans may serve petty interests, but not the supervening interest of mankind itself in self understanding and liberation.

We note, in any case, that most of the scholars working in the fields discussed in section 2 would refer to their own work as falling under the heading of *sociolinguistics* (something which most ethnomethodologists would not do). Burton and Stubbs (1975), for instance, claim that 'everyday conversation is ultimately the data with which sociolinguistics had to deal', and Hymes (1974) has the title *Foundations in sociolinguistics: an ethnographic approach*. Fishman, too, entitled an earlier version of his *The sociology of language* (1972), *Sociolinguistics: a brief introduction* (1970).

And we note also that in this book, while we recognize that the label *sociolinguistics* may perfectly legitimately be applied to the areas we have discussed here in section 2, we do not, for the most part, cover topics of this type.

3   Our third category consists of studies in the field of language and society which are linguistic in intent. Studies of this type are based on empirical work on language as it is spoken in its social context, and are intended to answer questions and deal with topics of central interest to linguists. In this case the term *sociolinguistics* is uncontroversial, but it should be clear that here it is being used principally to refer to a methodology: sociolinguistics as a way of doing linguistics.

Much work of this type falls within the framework established first and foremost by William Labov (particularly in Labov, 1966). It consists of work which Labov himself has sometimes referred to as *secular linguistics*, and which I have elsewhere labelled, not entirely facetiously, 'sociolinguistics proper'. Labov has, as is well-known, addressed himself to issues such as the relationship between language and social class. However, his main objective in this has not been to learn more about a particular society, nor to examine correlations between linguistic and social phenomena for their own sake. Rather, he has been concerned to learn more about language, and to investigate topics such as the mechanisms of linguistic change; the nature of linguistic variability; and the structure of linguistic systems. (Indeed, Labov has said that he resisted the term *sociolinguistics* for some time, as this seemed to him to be in danger of opening up the way to a series of correlational and descriptive studies of little theoretical interest.) Empirical work on creole languages by scholars such as Bickerton and Le Page (see References) must also be considered under this heading. All work in this category is aimed ultimately at improving linguistic theory and at developing our understanding of the nature of language, and in recent years has led to the development of 'variation theory': the recognition of 'fuzziness' in linguistic systems, and the problems of incorporating variability into linguistic descriptions (see Bailey, 1973; Bailey and Shuy, 1973; Fasold and Shuy, 1975).

Secular Linguistics

The papers in this book, with one exception, must be considered as representing sociolinguistics in the sense of category 3. (The exception is the paper by Elyan *et al.* ('RP-accented female speech: the voice of perceived androgyny?' which has to be considered an example of work in the field of the social psychology of language). The majority of the papers, that is, consist of studies of language in its social context which are written by linguists for linguists, with linguistic objectives. The influence of the work of Labov, too, is obvious throughout, and it is in recognition of this fact that the title of this work incorporates the title of Labov's own book, *Sociolinguistic patterns.*

This does not mean to say, however, that we are not interested in more sociological issues. One cannot easily work from tape-recorded interviews without being interested in the social psychology of conversational interaction; nor ignore the influence of social networks in urban dialectology (see the paper by Milroy and Milroy); nor neglect socio-psychological factors such as social ambition (the paper by Douglas), or loyalty to the vernacular culture (Cheshire). We do not, that is, wish to overstate the case for a dividing line between studies which have purely linguistic objectives and those which do not. I have drawn such a line in this introduction merely in an attempt to locate the contribution this particular book is trying to make. In practice, however, there can be no such absolute line. In fact, many would argue that there *must* be no such line: an orientation involving the integration of linguistic and social studies, to the mutual benefit of both, is indicated by Le Page (1969), and specifically argued for by Hymes (1974). As Labov has said of the findings presented in his paper 'The linguistic consequences of being a lame' (Labov, 1972b p. 255):

> The findings will be of considerable sociological interest, since it appears that the consistency of certain grammatical rules is a fine-grained index of membership in the street culture. The data should also be of interest to theoretical linguistics, since it appears that patterns of social interaction may influence grammar in subtle and unsuspected ways.

Nevertheless, the papers that follow are predominantly linguistic, and are based on empirical linguistic work carried out in British speech communities. The need for work of this type in linguistics has been ably stated by Labov, who writes (1974b, p. 292) that though 'it is difficult for us, caught up in current linguistic practice, to evaluate the overwhelming reliance of our field on the theorist's own intuitions as data', it is apparent that this kind of methodology has brought with it a number of fundamental problems. Not the least of these is the extent to which it has become possible to base arguments for particular theoretical positions on (invented) examples which other linguists (most often those who oppose the theoretical position in question) find unacceptable.

It is also safe to say that intuition-based work is unreliable in the study of areas of the language which are undergoing linguistic change or are subject to variation of some kind. As evidence in favour of this assertion, we can cite a number of instances of linguistic change or variability, to be found currently in British English, about which we remain rather ignorant because little empirical work has been done, and where linguists' intuitions cannot be relied upon. (These instances are mostly linguistically rather trivial. This is, however, because they are based on casual rather than systematic observation. Doubtless, more significant changes may also be under way, but, because of the lack of empirical work, most of us remain unaware of them.) Among others, we might mention the following changes:

(i) A number of British linguists[6] have observed, informally, that 'something is happening to the perfect'. The observations are, specifically, that increasing numbers of speakers are using constructions such as:

> He's played for us last year
> They've done that three years ago

One's initial reaction to observations such as these is that they are nonsense, and that no one would ever say such things. Having been alerted, however, one notices that native speakers *are* using these forms. They may have their origin in a form of blending: *He has played for us* + *He played for us last year*. The point is, however, that we do not really know how they have arisen, or exactly how they are used; and that, not only are intuitions of no use in this case, they are actually wrong.

(ii) We can also observe that speakers in the south of England tend to use contracted forms such as:

> I won't do it
> I haven't done it

while the further north one goes (and this is truer of the north-west than of eastern areas—see Petyt, this volume), the more likely one is to hear the alternative contraction type:

> I'll not do it
> I've not done it

(Indeed, these forms are quite consistent for most Scottish speakers.) Casual observation, however, suggests that in certain, particularly formal usages the 'northern' forms are on the increase in the south. But whether in fact this is what is happening and, if so, exactly how it is happening, we do not know. Interrogation of informants as to which form they employ in which social and linguistic contexts does not work: they do not know. And we are similarly equally ignorant about the extent and significance of (undoubtedly increasing) usages such as:

[6]Arthur Hughes was the first to bring this to my attention.

> You didn't ought to do that
> We didn't used to do that
> I wish I had've done that
> I would of done that (with unreduced *of*)

and many others.

(iii) It is also apparent that intuitions will be particularly unreliable where linguistic change produces a combination of social, regional and linguistic constraints on linguistic variability. A good example of this is the verb *have*, which varies widely in its treatment in different regions, amongst different age-groups, in different social contents, and in different linguistic environments. In some cases, of course, *have* is clearly an auxiliary, and in others a full verb. There are some cases, however, where it could be regarded as being something in between.

Palmer (1974) provides a good description of the use of *have* in educated 'British' English (as we shall see shortly, *English* English might have been a more accurate label). This work, however, is based on Palmer's own usage, and does not pretend to give information about other varieties. In particular, of course, it gives no indication of current changes, or of differential behaviour in particular environments.[7] Table 1 is my attempt to give some idea of the complexity involved in any attempt to study changes that are taking place in the use of *have*, and naturally represents a gross simplification of the facts. It must be made clear that it is based on casual observation and guesswork, and that the main point of its presentation is to demonstrate that we have no sure way of learning exactly what is taking place without a considerable amount of empirical work. Column 1 gives the usage typical of perhaps most Scottish and Northern Irish speakers; column 2 the usage of many northern (particularly Lancashire, but not Liverpool), and older southern English speakers (as described by Palmer); column 3 the colloquial usage of most younger southern English speakers; column 4 the usage of certain younger educated British speakers, particularly in formal styles— which may show American influence; and column 5 shows what I take to be typical North American usage. It will be seen that American usage treats *have* as a normal verb except where it is clearly an auxiliary, and that this is also possible in all varieties of British English with the past form. In British English there is greater freedom for *have* to be treated as an auxiliary, however, particularly with Scottish, northern and older southern English speakers. Where the *got* form is not available (where no element of possession is indicated) it is only the Scottish variety which permits the auxiliary-type treatment, and here only with the past form.

(iv) That linguistic constraints on variability are so fine as to go unnoticed without systematic observation is demonstrated by the study of a further

---

[7]A good example of the unreliability of intuitions is provided by my own reading of Palmer (1974). I was very surprised to learn that the 'British' equivalent of American 'I didn't have the nerve' was 'I hadn't the nerve'. My first reaction was to think 'who on earth would ever say that?'. I later noticed that both my parents regularly use this form.

Table 1: *have* in modern English

	1	2	3	4	5
Have you been there?	✓	✓	✓	✓	✓
Had you been there?	✓	✓	✓	✓	✓
Have you any money?	✓	✓	X	X	X
Have you got any money?	✓	✓	✓	✓	X
Do you have any money?	X	X	X	✓	✓
Had you any money?	✓	✓	X	X	X
Had you got any money?	✓	✓	✓	✓	X
Did you have any money?	✓	✓	✓	✓	✓
Have you the nerve to do that?	✓	✓	X	X	X
Have you got the nerve to do that?	✓	✓	✓	✓	X
Do you have the nerve to do that?	X	X	X	?	✓
Had you the nerve to do that?	✓	✓	X	X	X
Had you got the nerve to do that?	✓	✓	✓	✓	X
Did you have the nerve to do that?	✓	✓	✓	✓	✓
Have you a good time?	X	X	X	X	X
Do you have a good time?	✓	✓	✓	✓	✓
Had you a good time?	✓	X	X	X	X
Did you have a good time?	✓	✓	✓	✓	✓
Have you your lunch at home?	X	X	X	X	X
Do you have your lunch at home?	✓	✓	✓	✓	✓
Had you your lunch at home?	?	X	X	X	X
Did you have your lunch at home?	✓	✓	✓	✓	✓

feature. This is a feature labelled by Wolfram and Fasold (1974), and Wolfram and Christian (1976) *a-verbing*. This refers to forms such as:

I'm a-comin'

which correspond to standard English *I'm coming*; and which are found in many parts of the English-speaking world.

In conservative East Anglian dialects, the use of such forms is widespread but variable. Comparison of older speakers with younger speakers in the Norwich sample reported on in Trudgill (1974a), and comparison of this sample with recordings made in rural Norfolk by W. Nelson Francis for the Survey of English Dialects, shows that the use of these forms is dying out. Younger speakers use it much more infrequently than older speakers, and urban speakers more infrequently than rural speakers. This much, of course, is also readily susceptible to casual observation. What is *not* clear until close analyses of data obtained in the speech community are carried out is that this old-fashioned form is dying out in a very interestingly structured way.

In carrying out this analysis we have to recognize, first, that there are a number of contexts in which the *a-* prefix on the present participle cannot occur—as Labov has said, knowing what to count is half the battle. For example, the prefix cannot occur before a vowel, or before an unstressed syllable:

> *I was a-eatin'
> *He was a-recoverin'

(There is also an interesting rule which inserts *on* between a transitive verb and an immediately following unstressed pronominal direct or indirect object beginning with a vowel:

> I was just a-doin on it
> She was a-kickin on 'im

This *on* also occurs in questions: *What are you a-doin on?*, and presumably relates to *of*, since it occurs in other contexts such as: *What do you think on it?*)

In those environments where variability is possible, analysis shows that there are syntactic constraints on the use of the prefix. These constraints are: whether or not the prefixed verb has an immediately following direct object; and whether it occurs in a simple verb phrase or a complex verb phrase (one involving a catenative, for instance: *He kept a-doin on it*). As Table 2 shows, these constraints operate differently for rural and for urban speakers (for rural speakers the direct object constraint is probably not in fact a constraint at all). The point is, however, that no amount of intuiting would ever have revealed this rather detailed aspect of what we have probably to consider as part of the native speaker's knowledge of this particular variety of English.

A more complex and interesting example of grammatical constraints on grammatical variation is discussed in this volume in Cheshire's paper 'Present tense verbs in Reading English'. This is a much more striking example of the way in which empirical work can reveal hitherto unsuspected refinements in linguistic variation.

Sociolinguistic patterns in British English

The papers in this book, then, are essays in the field of 'secular linguistics', and consist, in many cases, of developments from and reactions to the initial work of William Labov. In fact, of course, no one has been more active in developing the work begun in Labov (1966) than Labov himself, but the work we present here can be seen as having developed parallel to Labov's own subsequent work, and in some cases representing refinements, in others a narrowing of focus.

We can observe, first of all, that whereas earlier sociolinguistic studies concentrated on segmental phonetics and phonology, more recent studies (e.g. Labov, 1972c) have come to look at grammar as well. In this volume, Cheshire, as we have just seen, looks at present-tense verbs in the vernacular

Table 2: % *ing* participles with *a*- prefix, Norfolk

(a)

%	V+DO		Others	
	Urban	Rural	Urban	Rural
prefix	7	57	44	44
no prefix	93	43	56	56

(b)

Rural		
-ing principles with *a*-	simple VP	*V*+DO 67%
		others 63%
	complex VP, etc.	*V*+DO 14%
		others 11%

(c)

Urban		
-ing participles with *a*-	others	simple VP 46%
		complex VP, etc. 28%
	V+DO	simple VP 13%
		complex VP, etc. 0%

working-class English spoken in the town of Reading. And Petyt ('Secondary contractions in West Yorkshire negatives') examines an interesting morphophonemic phenomenon. Even more recently, some workers have been extending sociolinguistic research into the field of prosodic and paralinguistic features. In this volume, Knowles ('The nature of phonological variables in Scouse') argues for the inclusion of the study of intonation, rhythm, setting and other features in sociolinguistic work, and bases his arguments on data from Liverpool English ('Scouse'), obtained in a 'classical' New York City-type study using face-to-face interviews with a random sample of 100 informants. And Pellowe and Jones ('On intonational variability in Tyneside speech'), using data derived from the large-scale survey of English spoken in and around Newcastle-upon-Tyne, the Tyneside Linguistic Survey, have begun to develop a methodology for the study and comparison of prosodic systems within sociolinguistic research.

Secondly, some of the papers in this book demonstrate developments in sampling and informant selection. Douglas, for instance, ('Linguistic code-switching in a Northern Irish village') has taken sociolinguistic methodology into a rural setting. She also counteracts the charge that sociolinguistics, by grouping and averaging scores, often misses or ignores the speech of informants as individuals (see Bickerton, 1971; and Berdan, 1975, quoted in this volume by Macaulay). Douglas presents her data speaker by speaker rather than for groups as a whole, as does Reid, in his paper on the English of Edinburgh ('Social and stylistic variation in the speech of children'), and Cheshire. A number of the studies, too, following Labov's arguments in favour of concentration on the vernacular, ignore the social class variable, and focus on working-class speech. Cheshire, for example, examines the speech of three different working-class adolescent peer-groups; and Romaine ('Post-vocalic /r/ in Scottish English') compares three age-groups of working-class children. The paper by Milroy and Milroy is also based on a one-class study. Their work in Belfast ('Change and variation in an urban vernacular'), which deserves the admiration of all those of us who work in less troubled areas, compares the speech of informants from three different areas of the city. Other studies are of a wider scope: Petyt's work covers three neighbouring Yorkshire towns; and the study by Trudgill and Foxcroft ('On the sociolinguistics of vocalic mergers') incorporates data from six urban centres.

Thirdly, there are several methodological developments to be noted. Reid, for instance, goes after the vernacular by using radio-microphones in school playgrounds. And, while Knowles points to a number of important difficulties in the use of linguistic variables and indices of the type developed by Labov, both Macaulay ('Variation and consistency in Glaswegian English') and Douglas have found the use of composite linguistic indices to be revealing and helpful. Pellowe and Jones, moreover, work in the opposite direction to that taken by most sociolinguists, and group speakers linguistically before examining the social correlates (if any) of these groupings while Macaulay actually argues against this type of procedure.

Fourthly, we can note some developments in the social variables dealt with. Milroy and Milroy look at the role of social networks; while Romaine and Reid both examine the age variable and give quantitative evidence to demonstrate the growth of social and stylistic variation in the speech of young children. Douglas looks to socio-psychological factors, in particular social ambition, in an attempt to account for linguistic differences between socially similar individuals (cf. Labov's, 1966, discussion of Nathan B.). And Elyan *et al.* look at the differential perceptions of the social meaning of accents as they are used by men and women.

Finally, in earlier work, sociolinguistics tended to concentrate on social and stylistic constraints on linguistic variability. More recently, work of this kind has come to focus more on the perhaps more interesting *linguistic* constraints on linguistic variability, as we did briefly with the *a-verbing* example above (see also, for example, Labov, 1969; Sankoff, 1974). In this book, Romaine discusses phonological constraints on the deletion of post-vocalic /r/ in Scottish English; the Milroys examine the patterning of Belfast vowels in different phonological environments; and Cheshire describes syntactic constraints on the presence and absence of present tense –*s*. Many of the writers in this volume, too, are concerned to examine phenomena such as the nature of linguistic variability and the mechanisms of linguistic change. Macaulay, for example, takes issue with Bickerton and Bailey over the nature of variation in linguistic systems; and Romaine, Milroy and Milroy, and Trudgill and Foxcroft all use sociolinguistic techniques to examine different aspects of sound change.

It is our intention that the papers presented here will help to fill a gap in the sociolinguistic literature by complementing North American work with data from the English of the British Isles, and that they will in some measure lead to progress in the development of linguistic and sociolinguistic theory.

2

Belfast: Change and Variation in an urban vernacular

James Milroy and Lesley Milroy

Introduction

This paper is concerned with different kinds of variability observed during the first year of our study of Belfast working-class speech, and with interpretation of the data that has so far been analysed.[1] The scope and aims of the work differ in certain respects from those of previous urban studies, particularly in our deliberate decision to study three geographically differentiated working-class communities in comparable inner-city areas. This means that, although we are prepared to recognize status differences between the communities and within them, we have ruled out the social class dimension in the design of the project and do not as yet present data on the full range of classes within the city.

One reason for this is our initial interest in the rise of urban *vernacular* speech in relatively young industrial cities. Belfast's major expansion as an industrial city took place very recently, as a result of an influx after the Great Potato Famines of the mid-nineteenth century and with the subsequent development of the linen and ship-building industries in the late nineteenth century. Many older residents of the city were born in the country, and many of our middle-aged informants are first-generation Belfast people. The geographical differences in our samples reflect a historical difference in that the communities as a whole are of different ages. The West Belfast communities studied are of more recent development than the East Belfast community, and Catholics, on the whole, are more recent immigrants to the city than Protestants. Furthermore, the immigrants have come from two quite sharply differentiated dialect areas (Gregg, 1972), with the Catholics on the whole originating from central, south and west Ulster and the Protestants proportionately more from the 'Ulster Scots' areas of the east and north. In

[1]The data here presented arise from work in progress on a project entitled 'Speech Community and Language Variety in Belfast', supported by the Social Science Research Council. We are indebted to Rose Maclaran and Domini O'Kane for very considerable help, chiefly in analysing and quantifying data. Statistics mentioned in this paper have been carefully checked, but will be subject to further checks in the course of this as yet unfinished project.

short, we are interested in the nature of the rapid language mixing believed to characterize the growth of cities (Labov, 1972a, p. 300). Since traditional scholarship (Wyld, 1920) tends to assume that the speech of cities is a 'modified standard', it is worth concentrating on working-class speech (characteristic of the majority of city-dwellers everywhere) in order to illuminate the social and attitudinal reasons for the persistently *non-standard* nature of urban vernacular *phonology*—for generations and, in some cases centuries.[2] Patterson's (1860) Belfast evidence, when compared with our own, suggests that movement towards the 'standard' can indeed be said to have occurred—but mainly in the reclassification of particular lexical items in the vernacular equivalents of 'standard' lexical sets. Patterson's *breek* (brick), *rid* (red), *git* (get), *wud* (wood) and others, are now usually relexified in standard classes. We have no definite evidence, however, that phonetic realizations of vernacular phonology have moved significantly towards the 'standard'. On the contrary, we have observed some changes which appear to have deviated from standard pronunciations more markedly than in Patterson's day.

The situation is, therefore, complex, and we have been aware from the start of the existence of types of variability *not* found in sufficient quantity to analyse statistically in those studies that cover the full range of social classes. Everything that we have observed tends to justify the hypothesis, based on the history and ethnography of the city, that Belfast exhibits a relatively early stage in the development of an urban vernacular. There is very great variability in lexical classification or sub-classification of items, owing to the occurrence of relic and residual forms, some of them apparently of great antiquity. In one such case at least (see Maclaran, 1976 and below), the data can be quantified, and in all such cases we encounter binary sets in which speakers may choose one of two clearly differentiated forms, which may often be regarded as belonging to different 'phonemes'.

However, while encountering complexity of this kind, we also observe a seemingly paradoxical trend towards *simplification* of phonological distinctions. This is clearly observable before /r/, in which some younger speakers appear to merge *fir, fair* and *fur* although older speakers make at least one distinction here; *our/are, wine/whine*, are merged, although distinct in much of the hinterland; similarly *sort/port* are rhymed, and /ɔ:/ as in *caught* is now distinct from /ɔ/ as in *cot* only when followed by a voiceless stop. Thus, we may view the rise of this urban vernacular as a dialect-contact situation in which, to quote Herzog, there is a

> classic structural reductionism, and it would not be difficult to argue that it is a sub-type of the same process that produces contact languages. . . . One of the

[2]This is suggested by the persistence of some stereotypes such as the Brooklynese *dem, dese, dose* discussed by Labov, and also characteristic of much Irish speech (not Belfast). For the city which has the richest historical data available (London), *The Diary of Henry Machyn* provides almost unassailable proof of a recognizably 'Cockney' sixteenth-century speech. On Henry Machyn, see Wyld (1920). For an incorrect argument that he was a northerner, see Axel Wijk *The Orthography and Pronunciation of Henry Machyn* (1937) and for a rebuttal of Wijk, see R. M. Wilson, 'The Orthography and Provenance of Henry Machyn', in A. Brown and P. Foote, eds., *Early English and Norse Studies* (London, 1963).

universal constraints on change seem (*sic*) to be operating here—that in contact situations, mergers expand at the expense of distinctions (quoted by Labov, 1972a, p. 300).

To sum up: it appears that since we are dealing with a relatively early stage of an urban vernacular, we are likely to find clear binary choice systems (probably resulting from dialect contact) in which one item in the pair is recessive and more often found in relatively casual styles or particular groups of speakers. We are also likely to find neutralization of distinctions in certain environments or obliteration of whole phonemic classes, such as /ʍ/. Finally, we may be able to discern innovations in phonetic realizations, which appear to be changes now in progress. Such changes may or may not move in the direction of what is normally considered to be the standard; it is not possible to give the fullest account of such changes and their probable social or attitudinal motivation until the language of other social groups in the city has been studied. For the moment we confine ourselves to a study of change and variation within and between our three working-class communities, and give such explanations for the motivations of these changes as are suggested by our method and our data so far. In particular, it is clear that the display of quantified information in graph form shows not only patterns of change in progress, vernacular norms and differences between styles and social groups; it is also a valuable indicator of speakers' *evaluations* of different forms. In other words, such graphs can be interpreted as displaying *attitudes* to the forms in question. This needs some emphasis, since the point has not always been clearly understood from previous work.

Since the methods employed may have a bearing on the results achieved and their interpretation, we now proceed to an account of our methods of investigating city vernacular speech.

Networks and the Urban Sub-Culture

The project investigates three communities in the inner city: a Protestant area in Ballymacarrett (East Belfast), the Protestant Hammer area of the Shankill Road (West Belfast), and the Catholic Clonard area of the Falls Road (West Belfast). All three are decayed 'core working-class' areas with a high incidence of unemployment and other kinds of social malaise (see Boal *et al.*, 1974). For some years local authorities have been actively encouraging residents to leave these areas. The majority of those who are socially mobile have long ago moved out of the city to more 'desirable' council estates in the suburbs. Each community is unambiguously Catholic or Protestant, occupying a central position in an area segregated from its neighbours along sectarian lines. For a number of reasons (see L. Milroy, 1976) including a desire to reach central community networks where loyalty to vernacular norms is likely to be strong, we approached our communities through informal contacts with people who had no institutional status in the communities but were core members of them. By mentioning names mutually known, the interviewer was able to associate herself with the community networks of kith and kin, and was received with

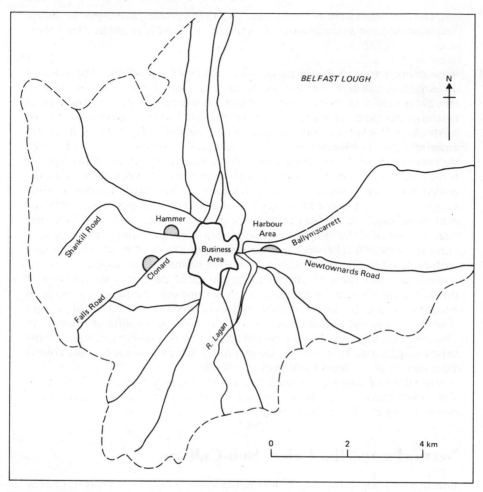

Map of Belfast showing location of the inner city areas studies (shaded areas.)

warmth, friendliness and trust. In long interviews, extending sometimes to three hours or more, she moved from one person to another in his family or group until the quota sample of sixteen persons in each area was filled. Each quota sample consisted of eight young people (aged 18–25) and eight middle-aged people (aged 42–55), equally divided between males and females. Data were also collected from numerous network members who fell outside the core quota.

The method employed has the most important bearing on the results. Sociological and anthropological literature on networks and urban sub-cultures (Bott, 1971; Fried, 1973; Boissevain, 1975) amply justifies the psychological importance of an informal approach. In our case, even a mildly formal approach would certainly have meant that mainly standardized, relatively literate, socially mobile speakers would have responded without suspicion (the politically troubled state of Belfast makes this even more likely than elsewhere). One of the more obvious results of this would have been that we could not have presented quantifiable data on such stereotyped vernacular forms as the relic (ʌ) variable (see below), since standardized WC speakers with loose allegiance to the sub-culture avoid the unrounded stigmatized vowel in *pull, put*, etc.

In the course of the research, it has become evident that the concept of 'network' is of the greatest importance in interpreting results (Bott, 1971; Boissevain, 1975). Like core working-class areas in other large cities (Frankenberg, 1969; Fried, 1973), the Belfast communities are characterized by dense overlapping kin and friendship networks which tend not to cross the territorial boundaries of 'our' area as intersubjectively perceived by the residents. These dense close-knit networks are maintained by a number of mechanisms such as extended visiting, corner-hanging, and (most important of all) a homogeneous traditional form of employment located within the area. The main importance of this last is that it tends to reinforce dense multiplex network ties, enhancing male solidarity and segregation of sex roles (see Bott, 1971; Frankenberg, 1969). Of our three communities, only Ballymacarrett is now provided with traditional, locally based employment (the shipyard). The other areas were formerly dependent on the linen industry, but this has now declined, with the result that many men are unemployed or travel out of their areas to work. In addition to this, one of the communities (The Hammer) is in the process of redevelopment. It appears to be a consequence of this that the distribution of our linguistic variables in terms of age and sex is much less regular and symmetrical in The Hammer than elsewhere (see below).

Moreover, the degree to which *individuals* approximate to a vernacular speech norm seems to correlate to the extent to which they participate in close-knit networks. It should not be surprising that a close-knit group tends to be linguistically homogeneous, or that a loose-knit one should be more variable. A close-knit group has the power to impose behavioural norms of all kinds on its members (dress, political attitudes, moral standards, for example), while conversely the person on the fringe of the network may look to the wider social group outside his immediate community for speech and behavioural norms.[3] It is tempting to conclude from this that one of the mechanisms of phonological standardization is a negative one: the collapse, as a result of urban redevelopment or social mobility, of localized close-knit networks.

We have made some tentative progress towards a quantitative statement of relative standardization of phonology by examining the (a) variable (see below) in the speech of our most 'corrected' informant and comparing it with others. It was noted in exploratory work that MC speakers tend for this variable to converge on [a] with little phonetically conditioned variation in vowel height or backing. If a score of zero is assigned for [a], two points for front-raised [æ] and for back [ɑ], and four points for [ɛ] or closer and also for back-raised and rounded [ɔ], a MC speaker scores about 0.5, whereas a

---

[3]For a parallel, see Labov's (1972b) discussion of *lames*. Those individuals in the three Belfast communities whose localized network ties showed least density were most prone to accept institutional values in, for example, dress, visiting and entertainment habits, and speech.

strongly vernacular speaker, with fronting in velar environments and extreme backing and raising mainly in nasal and labial environments, scores 2.00 or more. Our most 'corrected' speaker was a Clonard woman of mixed Protestant-Catholic parentage, whose husband (unlike most) was employed, who showed the interviewer into the parlour and gave her tea and cakes on the best china, who, having no kin in the area or children, was cut off from kin groups, and who did not display typical community interaction patterns. This woman had a score of deviation from [a] of 0.45. On the other hand, speakers with close-knit networks (chiefly males with strong adolescent peer-groups, or with local employment and social life in working men's clubs) showed most markedly the typical allophonic variation of the vernacular and scored 2.00 or more. Such a score means that virtually all the possible deviations from the 'standardized' [a] were exhibited. (An 'ideal' score of 4.00 is impossible, since some phonological environments do not allow considerable backing or raising.) Crude as such an index is, it does appear to make a generally valid statement about the complexity of the vernacular, and may have implications about the typology of urban vernaculars as against that of 'institutional' standards. For other vowels also (see below on (ε)), we have noted extensive predictable allophonic variation involving considerable raising, lengthening, diphthongization and rounding, (see J. Milroy, 1976), contrasting most markedly with the tendency for 'standard' speakers to level out such distinctions. The idea that the institutional standard is characterized by relatively few rules of allophonic variation in vowels, and by relatively successful aiming at psychologically 'ideal' target vowels (probably in order to avoid stigma) does not now seem to us as unacceptable as it once appeared to be.

Quantification and Analysis of Variables

Quantification is a necessary part of all investigations that claim to make valid general statements about linguistic change and geographical variation in urban vernaculars. It also appears to be the best way of assessing attitudinal factors such as the effects of stigma and prestige in linguistic change. This is not to say that all relevant factors *can* be quantified or that other methods are not to be used. Methods based on the technique of *scaling*, for example, may be used as a means of displaying the phonetic range of a variable and the progress of a change through different phonetic environments (cf. Bailey, 1973a).

So far we have extensive quantified data on the seven variables (th), (ʌ), (a), (ε), (ɔ), (t) and (ai). Of these we have treated (th) and (ʌ) as simple binaries and have scored them as percentages of occurrence or non-occurrence of medial [ð], or of [ʌ], in the appropriate lexical items. The others are more complex in that there is considerable variation according to phonetic environment. For this reason, we have listed the tokens in columns representing degrees of frontness, centrality or backness, and height (for the vowels), and presence of dentality, glottalization and so on (for the consonant). This means that the tokens are recoverable, and valid generalizations about allophonic constraints can be made on the basis of rich data, not only for sex, age and geographical groups as a whole, but for individuals. Similarly it is possible to exclude certain environments from quantification for many purposes, for the reason that they are observed *never* to vary in the manner that is being investigated. We can also isolate environments that are particularly variable and in some cases show that innovation is taking place in one particular sex/age group. In this paper, we report on the five variables (th), (ʌ), (a), (ɛ) and (ai).

Variable 1 (th)

Vernacular speakers variably delete the interdental voiced fricative intervocalically in such words as *together, mother, bother, other*. Such pronunciations as [mɔ·ər] are avoided by people outside the sub-culture, but (th), unlike (ʌ), does not seem to constitute a conscious symbol of the vernacular for those within the communities. Although all speakers corrected in formal styles (often with 100 per cent occurrence of [ð] in word-list style: a formal 'reading' style) nobody remarked on [ð] deletion during our long and lively discussions of *sleng* (Belfast vernacular). The striking feature of the (th) data as displayed graphically in Figure 1 is the extent to which all three communities appear to exhibit the same attitude to (th). There is a very clear sex difference in the distribution. The individual figures are even more revealing—for in none of the communities do the male and female scores overlap. In other words, the men who delete least still delete more than the women who delete most. Nor is there any evidence of shift taking place here; the distribution patterns are similar in both age groups. It is the extremely symmetrical character of the (th) data and the lack of any evidence of change which is interesting here, for we are able to contrast this pattern with others to help us infer existence and direction of shift.

Variable 2 (ʌ)

A limited lexical set in which we can recognize twenty-two items (containing, e.g. *pull, took, look, would*, but not *wool, cook, book, wood*) has alternative [ʌ ~ ʉ] realizations in Belfast vernacular. Both within and without the sub-culture, the [ʌ] variant is consistently perceived as stigmatized, and outside the sub-culture at least, this has been so for at least a century (Patterson, 1860). This set differs from the intervocalic (th) set in that its membership is not predictable on phonetic grounds; at least three different historical classes seem to be involved (Maclaran, 1976), and the class has declined in membership since Patterson's time.

   As also for (th), the young male peer groups across the city seem to agree in their evaluation of (ʌ) (see Figure 2), but their elders, who unlike them have in the past been members of loose networks extending across community boundaries, do not agree. In the Clonard, the expected sex pattern is reversed; it is the older *women* rather than the men who make extensive use of [ʌ] in these words. There can be no doubt that the [ʌ] variant has conscious vernacular prestige; it is almost *prescribed* amongst adolescent and other close-knit male

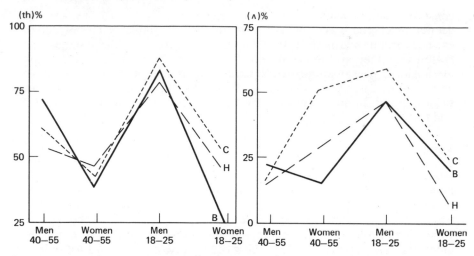

Figures 1 and 2. Distribution of two phonological variables by age and sex in the Ballymacarrett (B), Hammer (H) and Clonard (C) communities. High scores indicate high incidence of vernacular variants.

peer groups. Two Hammer men in their late twenties remarked that they used less *sleng* as they got older, and one spontaneously picked out the [ʌ] variant as particularly characteristic of his previous speech (see also Maclaran, 1976). Why, then, do the Clonard women show a high incidence of this variant which, in the young male peer-groups carries 'covert prestige'?

The answer to this appears to depend fundamentally on the linguistic conservatism and low status-ranking of the Clonard community. This conservatism is exhibited in the retention of older 'country' pronunciations for other variables (the palatal glide on /k/ in e.g. [kja:r] *car*; dentality of /t/ allophones; relative failure of /a/ backing, etc). It is the young women in the Clonard who appear to introduce changes in the direction of higher ranked communities (see below). In a previous generation, young women, who are now older women, may well have introduced or spread the [ʌ] variant in this class, perceiving it as carrying the status of some higher-ranked community. (The [ʌ] variant is far commoner in *word-lists* in the Clonard than elsewhere.) Thus, in the figures for (ʌ), we perceive two tendencies at work: the residue, amongst older women, of a former linguistic change that they were leading, and the covert prestige of a vernacular variant amongst young males throughout the city (despite strict territorial segregation).

Finally, as in the case of (th), we are not witnessing here a large-scale phonological shift. The (ʌ) system involves a *lexical* set in which a binary choice between [ʌ] and [ʉ] is involved. Many other words, for which there is no binary choice, are classed in the dialect as either invariable /ʌ/ or invariable /u/ words. Furthermore, there is no doubt that since Patterson's time, the binary set has shrunk in membership, and evidence from present day hinterland dialects (e.g. [wʌd, wʌl]: *wood, wool*; South Donegal, but not Belfast) supports this. What we are observing, therefore, is analogous to the shifts away from extreme fronting of /a/ in velar environments and from the stigmatized low front realizations of /ɛ/ and /ɔ/ (see below). For these reasons, it seems unlikely that the tendency of the young men to perceive the [ʌ] variant as carrying vernacular prestige will lead to permanent systematic linguistic change. It is a recessive variant, like the /e:/ variant in the *meat, beat* class (see Maclaran, 1976).

Variable 3 (a)

Whereas (th) and (ʌ) are distributionally restricted and binary, (a) is complex. Vernacular and MC speakers contrast very markedly in their realizations of the vowel in such words as *bag, back, fat, man*. While the MC vowel typically falls around cardinal 4 [a] with relatively little variation conditioned by phonetic context, the vernacular vowel may be considerably fronted and raised before velar consonants: [bɛg] *bag*, but variably backed and back-raised in other environments often with some rounding and/or a centring glide, e.g. [mɔ·ən] *man*, [fɔ·əst] *fast*. It is of considerable interest to note that the front-raising rule appears to be regressive and there are clear indications that it is the trend towards *backing* of /a/ that is in progress. This contrasts with the findings of American scholars, particularly Labov (1966), Labov *et al.* (1972), Callary (1975). Indeed, the last-named has been able to say (1975, p. 155) that 'in all English dialects where there is /a/ activity the direction of movement is toward high front position'. Although we have studied both backing and fronting of /a/ and are at present treating the whole range of variability in this vowel by means of implicational scaling (on which see Bailey, 1973a; Bickerton, 1975a), the data here presented are concerned only with variable *backing* of /a/; velar environments, which *cannot* be fully backed, are excluded. Thus, the graphs measure backing before /p,t/ (as in *map, that*), before fricatives, /b/, /d/, /m/ and /n/. Of these environments voiceless stops are the least likely to back and nasals the most likely (with many additional subtleties which we cannot discuss here). Note that the graphs here presented (Figures 3, 4, 5 and 6) are based on conversational styles only.

Scrutiny of the graphically presented data in Figure 3 reveals an apparently chaotic distribution across the communities. There is neither the symmetrical convergence associated with (th), nor the cross-community consensus on norms of a single sub-group characteristic of (ʌ). Examination of the curves for each area in turn reveals the following:

1   There is some kind of sex grading in all areas. This is so clear in Ballymacarrett that the curve resembles the (th) curve, suggesting a stable sociolinguistic marker. Further (Figures 4–6), Ballymacarrett alone shows clear *stylistic* differentiation of (a) throughout the community.

2   Outside Ballymacarrett, (with the notable exception of the young Clonard women) there is little evidence that (a) is a particularly stable or significant marker. Sex grading in the Hammer is much less clear than in Ballymacarrett. Although Clonard has sex grading in the older groups, the young women reverse the expected pattern: for on the basis of the Ballymacarrett and Hammer scores and those of the older Clonard residents,

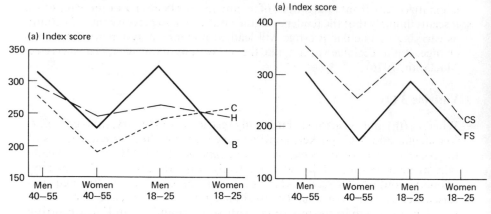

Figure 3. Backing of /a/ in the three communities.   **Figure 4.** Ballymacarrett.

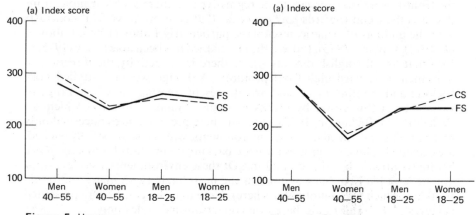

Figure 5. Hammer   **Figure 6.** Clonard.

Distribution of (a) by age, sex and conversational style in three WC communities. CS = casual style; FS = formal (i.e. careful) style.

we would predict for the young Clonard women a *low* score relative to the young Clonard men.

3   The young Clonard women not only score higher than the young men, but also higher than the young Ballymacarrett women. This is surprising if we note that for the men at least, scores are very much higher in Ballymacarrett than in the west. Backing of /a/, then, appears to be a characteristically Ballymacarrett and characteristically male feature, strongest in the Protestant east, weakest in the Catholic west, with the Protestant west intermediate. The Clonard girls appear to be introducing an innovation borrowed directly or indirectly from a higher-ranked community (for in Belfast the terms *Protestant* and *Catholic* function as rank dimensions as well as ethnic labels). A crossover pattern is produced by the relatively low score of their Ballymacarrett counterparts who are relatively 'corrected'. (Every individual

in the 18–25 Clonard female group shows a high score on (a) together with clear style-shifting in a manner characteristic of Ballymacarrett. No other individual in the Clonard style-shifts unambiguously on this variable).

Thus, it appears that an innovation originating with a stable, highly ranked community *within* the WC is being spread into another community by a homogeneous group[4] who simultaneously adopt it as a stylistic marker. The other interesting point is that the Clonard (a) norm (with relatively little backing) is relatively close to the MC norm. In the course of their innovation, the Clonard girls appear to be acting independently of the institutional prestige pronunciation.

The data presented in Figures 3–6, suggest (unlike Figures 1 and 2) that, quite independently of the prestige norm, a change in the form of a tendency to back /a/ is spreading through the community, and that the direction is from east to west, from the highest to the lowest ranked WC community. We may therefore look for further evidence to support our conclusions on the existence and direction of this sound-shift.

There is in fact nothing in Patterson's *Provincialisms* to suggest that /a/ was normally backed in 1860. On the contrary, he provides lists of words in which /a/ was fronted and raised. It was raised before velars, before nasals (*Jenuary, Entrim, brench,* for *January, Antrim, branch*), and after velars even before a following /r/ (*car* pronounced like *care*), which we do not now find in Belfast. Front-raising is now regularly found only *before* velars and variably after initial /k/ before obstruents and nasals. Otherwise, we have observed only sporadic and residual cases, such as [flɛt, trɛp] for *flat, trap,* always in the west of the city. Thus, the linguistically conservative character of West Belfast is confirmed, and the inference supported that the direction of change is geographically from east to west and phonetically from front to back.

Variable 4 (ε)

In Belfast vernacular, the low-mid vowel /ε/ is realized in monosyllables closed by a voiceless stop as a slightly retracted vowel near [æ], as in *bet, peck, slep* (vernacular 'slept'), etc. We symbolize this environment as −T. Before all other single consonants, it is realized as a mid vowel (usually above [ε]) tending to glide to centre and considerably lengthened. Thus, there is a dramatic contrast in vowel height and length between *bet* [bæt] and *bed* [bɛ·əd]. Female speakers variably 'correct' the low vowel before −T to a somewhat higher *short* vowel around [ε], but amongst males this is rare. However, before clusters consisting of liquid or nasal + voiceless obstruent, −ns, −nt, −ls, −lt etc. (symbolized as −NT), where a low vowel is again

---

[4]The Clonard girls constituted a homogeneous group in that they worked, lived, and amused themselves together, and were therefore connected by strong multiplex network ties. They contrast with the older Clonard men whose network ties, owing largely to unemployment, were based almost entirely on shared territory. It does appear that homogeneous groups (e.g. the Clonard girls, the Ballymacarrett boys) tend also to be linguistically homogeneous. More loose-knit groups such as the Clonard men (and the entire Hammer community) show a greater range of variability within the group.

expected, there is a different kind of variation. Whereas the range in which [ǽ] is 'corrected' in −T environments is a continuum and can be seen as a *gradual* tendency to raising, 'correction' before −NT is overwhelmingly a binary choice system in which *either* [ǽ] *or* the long mid vowel may be chosen. There is seldom, if ever, any doubt at all whether the vowel is low or mid, and length distinction is usually also quite plain. Thus, whereas words like *set* vary only within a narrow range between [æ] and [ɛ] and then chiefly among females, words like *went, help* exist in two rather widely separated alternants involving a phonetic distance just as great as is usually involved in a choice between two distinct phonemes. This kind of alternation has not been widely discussed in

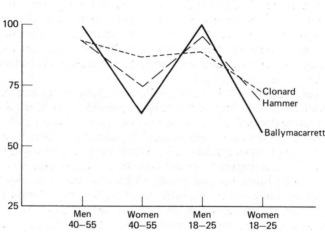

Figure 7. % low vowel in variable monosyllables and prefixed and inflected disyllables.

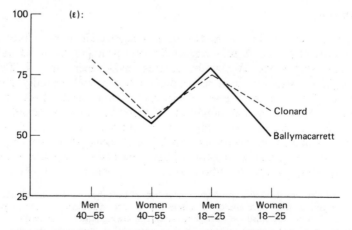

Figure 8. % low vowel in all other disyllables. The Hammer figures (which have been excluded) correspond closely to those of Ballymacarrett.

published work. It may well be a characteristic of urban vernaculars which have a historical mixing of widely divergent dialects.

In disyllables and polysyllables, this binary choice system is even clearer than in monosyllables. But these differ in one important respect. In most environments (e.g. $-s$, $-z$, $-n$, $-l$) where [ɛ:] would be predicted for monosyllables, the disyllables and polysyllables have the low *short* vowel [æ]. This leads to alternation in some grammatically related sets, e.g. first names such as *Ed/Eddy*, *Ben/Benny*, which are [ɛ·əd, bɛ·ən] but [ædɪ, bænɪ]. Generally, if we exclude prefixed derivatives and inflected forms, the great majority of di/polysyllables prefer the low, short vowel [æ] in almost all environments, whereas [ɛ:] is regular in monosyllables except before $-T$, $-NT$.

This variable and complex low-mid alternation (which is so sensitive to phonetic environment) is markedly sex-graded throughout the city. For most males the low vowel [æ] is categorical in the variable monosyllabic environment $-NT$ (as in *went, self*), whereas for females there is a tendency to transfer such items into the long mid class. Similarly (see Figures 7 and 8), there is clear sex-grading for di/polysyllables, with the women in advance in transferring to the mid vowel. The following data from an older male speaker, chosen at random from our Clonard informants, show the categorical nature of the distinction for this one individual. For monosyllables, $-T$ and $-NT$ environments are categorically low, short, whereas other environments are categorically mid, long. *All* the di/polysyllables that occur are low, short.

Including *myself, yourself* as 'monosyllabics' (prefixed derivatives, compounds and inflected forms follow monosyllable rules) the figures for M.C. senior for all tokens recorded are: monosyllables—33 per cent low vowel; di/polysyllables—100 per cent low vowel. On the other hand, M.M. (younger female, Clonard) has only 22 per cent low vowel for *all* monosyllables and only 72 per cent low vowel for *all* di/polysyllables. The general sex differentiation displayed by the graphs is repeatedly confirmed in figures for individuals.

Recording tokens so that they are 'recoverable' for further analysis is seen here to be of great importance. Clearly, it is possible to define very accurately, from lists in which thousands of tokens are recorded, those environments which never vary in the manner being investigated and pinpoint those

Table 1: MC Senior (53) 'Formal' Style

| Monosyllables | | | All Disyllables/polysyllables | |
Low	Mid	Mid	Low	
went (4)	left (5)	—	electric	centre
get	men (2)		heavy	Wednesday
set	then (4)		textile	fellows
met	well (3)		very (8)	definition
next	them		terrible (3)	fundamentals
	less (5)		Devlin (2)	yourself+
			reckon	fundamental
			twenty	myself+
			generations	Grenville
			general (2)	intellectual

environments that are especially sensitive to variation. Within one variable many different kinds of study can be carried out; it is not necessary to assume that study of phonological variation must always be confined to the sort which can be analysed along a phonetic continuum like (a), or as a simple binary, like (th). We shall find that similar considerations apply to (ai).

Variable 5: (ai)

The diphthong /ai/ as in *night*, *wine*, etc., is raised and fronted to [ɛɪ ~ ei] in all environments in some parts of Ulster, and is phonetically similar to its equivalent in some dialects of Wales, the West Midlands and the North of England. In Belfast, as the graphs (Figures 9–11) show, the variable functions as a clear stylistic marker. The vernacular vowel is characteristically [ei], and for some speakers higher and almost monophthongal before obstruents. Although this variation can be seen as a continuum, three variants have been distinguished for our purposes: approximately [ei] [ɛɪ] and [əɪ], and, as for (a) an index score produced in which [əɪ] = 0, [ɛɪ] = 1 and [ei] = 2. The scores are then multiplied by 100, but for reasons which will appear below, pre-vocalic, word-final and − /r/ environments are excluded.

Since a score above 100 represents considerable incidence of fronting and raising, it is evident from the graphs that in all three communities casual style is distinguished from more monitored styles by marked fronting and raising. But the stylistic differentiation is quantitatively less in Ballymacarrett than in West Belfast. In this community, *word-list* style has a fronting/raising score averaging about 50 for all groups, whereas several groups elsewhere have zero

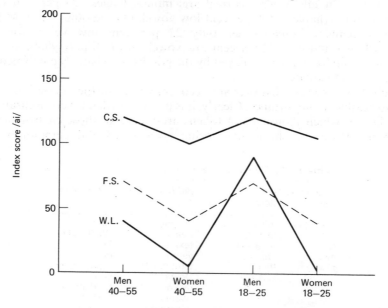

Figure 9. Clonard—all styles /ai/.

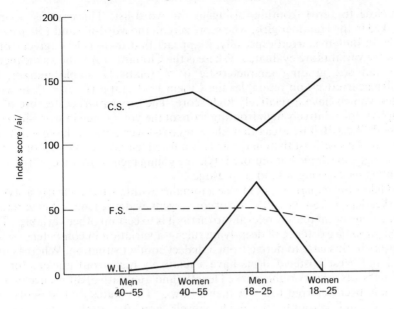

Figure 10. Hammer—all styles /ai/.

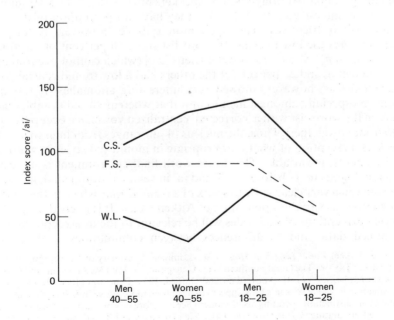

Figure 11. Ballymacarrett—all styles /ai/.

(or close to zero) fronting/raising in the word-list. The contrast is most marked in the Hammer girls, who score zero in the word-list and 150 in casual style. In Ballymacarrett especially, it appears that there is less agreement on how the variants are evaluated. Whereas the Clonard graph shows the regular age and sex grading characteristic of a relatively stable marker, the Ballymacarrett graph resembles the Clonard (ʌ) graph (Figure 2), in which older women have a relatively high score. The other marked feature of the graphs is the relatively high fronting score of the young men in word-list style: in both West Belfast areas they show a cross-over pattern, having a higher score in the word-list than in the less monitored 'careful' conversational style. Seemingly, in the most monitored style the young men consciously (?) perceive fronting as carrying a kind of prestige.

While a full explanation of these anomalies within what is clearly a stylistic marker depends on the collection of convergent evidence from other variables, there is one point plainly relevant to (ai) as it is to certain other variables. That is the *variable* existence of deep-lying rules—a variation in competence which appears in this case to derive from a dialect contact situation. Whereas most Mid and West Ulster dialects have a relatively high front nucleus for /ai/, 'Ulster Scots' observes the marked length (and qualitative) difference that has recently been referred to as 'Aitken's Law'.[5] This states that in Scots most vowels (and certainly the high vowels and the diphthong /ai/), are short, except that before the voiced fricatives, −/r/, and finally, a markedly longer vowel occurs. Furthermore, in the case of /ai/, there is a marked qualitative difference; thus, *drive* in Scots has [aˑe], but *ride* has [ʌɪ] or something similar. Although Belfast speakers have Aitken's Law variation in their three highest vowels :/i/ /u/ /o/, they have no perception of it for /ai/ before voiced fricatives. The open monosyllable, however, is long and frequently *has* the low nucleus. In word-list style, 50 per cent of informants read the item *pie* with a low vowel nucleus [aˑɛ] (which cannot occur in other environments), and 28 per cent of the others had a low to mid central vowel. Individual lists, however, showed very interesting anomalies. It was quite common especially amongst men to find that whereas closed syllables might occur in the word-list with a 'corrected' centralized vowel, *pie* occurred with a *high* front vowel: [pei]. Thus, the nucleus of /ai/ ranges from high to low, and speakers' perception of what is appropriate in monitored styles in word-final environments, is variable. The /ai/ in word-final environment is a sensitive area (analogous to /ɛ/ before −NT and /a/ in velar environments), in which it is possible in a very clear sense to speak of a *variable rule*, which in this case can be described as variable application of Aitken's Law. It is likely that speakers' varying perceptions of such rules will be relevant to the interpretation of our quantified data, and to differences between communities. Aitken's Law

[5] See A. J. Aitken, *Vowel Length in Modern Scots*, mimeo, University of Edinburgh, 1962; and Mary Vaiana Taylor, 'The Great Southern Scots Conspiracy' in John M. Anderson and C. Jones, *Historical Linguistics* Vol. II, Amsterdam and Oxford, 1974. Patterson (1860) presents a 'real time' situation in which Aitken's Law appears to have been more active in Belfast than it is now. He shows the distinction operating, as in Modern Scots, before morpheme boundaries within the syllable, differentiating *tied* [aˑe] from *tide* [ɔɪ], *I'll* [aˑe] from *isle* [ɔɪ]. This distinction appears now to have been obliterated in working-class speech, as has the lexical split between *eye* [ɔɪ] and *I* [aˑe] (and others) noted by Patterson.

variation may partly account for the less clear stylistic distinctions in Ballymacarrett, in that this community is not only Protestant, but historically of East Ulster, and therefore Scots, heritage.

General Conclusions

A one-class study of this kind cannot claim to reveal all large-scale shifts and trends, many of which may be best examined in the speech of other social classes, and which in any case require a multi-class framework if they are to be clearly shown. What can be claimed is that an in-depth working-class study allows a gain in subtlety. When the extent to which the above conclusions are valid outside the three communities has been more definitely established by a rapid, less detailed survey, we shall be in a position to offer a full description of Belfast working-class speech, its variations, and speakers' differential evaluations of such variations.

The data discussed in this paper suggest that changes are taking place, in so far as both general and restricted shifts are revealed by age, sex and areal patternings. We have also pointed out very great variability in the vowels, of a kind that is normally called allophonic. Thus, the (a) system displays a range from mid-front to mid-back, the (ε) system from low-front (short) to mid-front (long), and the (ai) system ranges from high-front to fully low. Other vowels (discussed in J. Milroy, 1976) display an equally wide range. Such wide-ranging variation, which is seemingly phonetically conditioned, is here greater in degree than in the 'standard' language. Quantification of such variation at a sub-phonemic level may be useful in demonstrating degrees of convergence towards 'standard' vowels.

Comparison of our own 'apparent time' data with Patterson's 'real time' data suggests that gradual shifts are taking place in degrees of fronting, backing and raising—at least in the case of (a) and (ai), the latter having obliterated many of the lower-vowel tokens required by Aitken's Law rules. Similarly, as Figure 12 shows there is no doubt that the dental [t] recognized by Patterson is receding.[6] Within general classes, and sometimes as between two phonemes, (e.g. /u/ and /ʌ/), we also observe more restricted shifts, which typically reveal themselves as binary alternations. Here, in the case of (ε) for example, it appears that a general tendency to raise a rather low vowel has worked through a number of environments and has now reached environment −NT and disyllables, where binary alternation patterned by sex, age and style, is now observed.

Where stylistic variation is observable, the identity of a stigmatized variant is usually clearer than that of any supposed 'prestige' target. The 'corrected' variant observed in more careful styles is not necessarily noticeably nearer the 'standard' or 'middle-class' norm; we have no evidence to suggest that speakers from these core working-class areas use middle-class speech as a model in any real sense—on the contrary, those subjective reaction tests which

---

[6]Patterson presents hundreds of words in which /t/ and /d/ in the proximity of /r/ are realized with dentals: these he represents as *tth*, *dth*: *watther*, *thundther*, etc. For his /ai/ data see note 5.

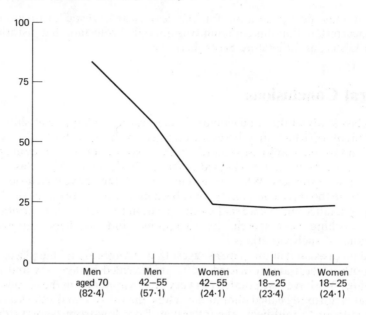

Figure 12. Recession of dentality of /t/ in Clonard, W. Belfast (conversational styles conflated). % dentality of initial [t] and [t] in proximity of [r], as in *train, tree, water, butter.*

have been carried out so far suggest that speakers have difficulty in recognizing and identifying middle-class accents. The diachronic model of dialect contact appears for the moment to offer a more powerful general explanatory framework for the kind of variation so far observed. The conclusion is that this, together with the development of a refined theory of sociolinguistic markers, seeking to link them in a coherent way with different social groups, will be most relevant to further work on vernacular speech in this city. Work carried out within such a broad framework will surely have wider implications.

3

Linguistic code-switching in a Northern Irish Village: social interaction and social ambition

Ellen Douglas-Cowie

The Social Context of the Investigation

Studies of sociolinguistic patterns in British English tend to concentrate on urban speech communities (e.g. Macaulay and Trevelyan, 1973; Trudgill, 1974a; Milroy, in progress). Many present-day rural communities, however, through their social heterogeneity and exposure to outside linguistic influences, may also provide important sociolinguistic data. Despite some reference to the changing sociolinguistic character of rural areas (e.g. McIntosh, 1952, p. 30; Orton, 1962, p. 15), most investigators of rural speech communities in the British Isles have paid no attention in their actual studies to the possible correlation between social factors and linguistic varieties.

This study examines social aspects of bidialectalism in the village of Articlave, situated some four miles from the town of Coleraine in County Londonderry, Northern Ireland. Attention is given to the social factors which promote bidialectalism in villages such as Articlave, to the social situations which determine a bidialectal's choice of linguistic code, and to the varying abilities of different social groups to switch or maintain the switch from non-standard to more standard speech varieties.

Better means of communication, an increase in educational opportunities for all, and the industrial expansion of the neighbouring town of Coleraine have all helped change the sociolinguistic situation in Articlave from what it was several decades ago. In this new situation bidialectalism is likely to emerge. Better means of communication, both by road and through the broadcasting media, have removed the villagers from their comparative isolation, bringing them into contact with new outside linguistic and social influences. They are probably apt to find less satisfaction in their former limited way of life and more anxious to seek the possessions and opportunities that others have. In their general social ambition in the spheres of education and occupation, they show a keenness to 'get on in the world', some inhabitants attending night classes for O-level exams to further their job opportunities. Many villagers of both low and high educational and occupational status attend elocution classes to learn to speak 'more correctly' or 'not so country'.[1] Better means of communication have therefore probably helped to give the villagers a new sense of higher social values and a social unease at the disparity between their own linguistic behaviour and that of outsiders. In more formal situations, for example in the presence of an outsider, they may show their new sociolinguistic awareness by switching from their everyday linguistic behaviour in informal village circumstances to a more standard and hence more socially acceptable linguistic code. With better means of communication through the BBC one might expect all villagers, not just those who attend elocution classes or who are in direct daily contact with outsiders, to be aware of more standard linguistic forms.

The advent of educational opportunities at higher levels for everyone means that the villagers no longer leave the local school at the age of fourteen to enter local employment, but continue their studies in Coleraine at secondary modern, technical or grammar school level. Younger present-day villagers are thus subjected to outside linguistic influences in Coleraine. They are also divided at the level of educational attainment. Better educated villagers might feel a need to switch from a fairly non-standard linguistic code used in relaxed circumstances to a more standard speech variety in the presence of their educational equivalents. Villagers' achievement in the sphere of education, however, is not always synonymous with their ambition and many who fail to achieve their goal try again in night classes (see above) or have higher aspirations for their children.[2] The villagers are therefore divided at the level of educational ambition. As a result of their ambition, some might feel the same need as better educated villagers to signal their desired social status by switching to a more standard linguistic code in the presence of educational superiors. Code-switching in Articlave may be fostered in the local primary school where linguistic pressures seem to help establish in villagers a linguistic awareness and sense of shame at their non-standard speech forms.[3]

The industrial expansion of Coleraine gives the Articlave people a greater choice of jobs than in former times when they were mainly employed in local scutching mills or on the surrounding farms. Most of the villagers, with the exception of a few remaining farmers, now travel to Coleraine or further afield to work in different types of jobs according to their capacities. Of the existing population no one is now a farm labourer. The industrial development of Coleraine also means that outsiders are finding employment in the surrounding area. Some make their homes in Articlave, among them quite a few English families. Villagers, whether they work in Coleraine or in Articlave, are thus likely to come into contact with outside linguistic influences. When speaking to their Coleraine employers or to the English families in the village, the inhabitants of Articlave may switch from a fairly non-standard to a more standard linguistic code.

Articlave is hardly an exceptional village. Better means of communication have brought many villages into contact with outside social and linguistic

---

[1]Questions put to elocution teachers in the neighbouring town of Coleraine and elsewhere in Northern Ireland revealed that they teach pupils an accent approximating RP.

[2]Some children are sent to private tutors before the eleven-plus exam.

[3]Elocution is taught in the local primary school.

influences, and increased educational opportunities for all have helped split the former social unity of many rural areas. There is evidence to suggest that there is a keen interest in elocution and 'correct' speech in other rural communities in Northern Ireland as well as Articlave, doubtless encouraged by an element of humorous scorn in the province towards rural dialects.[4] It is therefore likely that inhabitants from other villages in Northern Ireland, depending possibly on their educational backgrounds or aspirations, will switch linguistic codes in certain circumstances. A study of bidialectalism in Articlave may consequently have wider relevance.

From previous observations in Articlave, it seemed that villagers would be most likely to switch to a more standard linguistic code in the presence of a stranger, particularly if he was a well-educated Englishman with an RP or modified regional accent. The investigator, who is a native of Articlave and lives there, asked a colleague answering to this description if he would cooperate in a sociolinguistic experiment (Experiment Two) by coming to her home and talking to each of ten selected villagers for a considerable length of time.[5] He kindly agreed. Informants' linguistic behaviour in his presence could be compared with their speech in more informal situations (recorded in Experiment One).

While the main purpose of introducing an English outsider was to test the existence of bidialectalism in Articlave, the secondary purpose was to reveal the possible linguistic limitations of being a well-educated English investigator in a Northern Ireland rural community. This secondary purpose arose from suspicions that Englishmen who were engaged in planning The Hiberno-English Dialect Survey might also be planning to carry out some of the fieldwork themselves, and might obtain from bidialectal informants their more standard linguistic codes. The survey, intended to test the survival of older dialect forms among various age-groups, would suffer if its fieldworkers were likely to elicit standard speech counterparts. Since the English colleague used in Experiment Two was one of the people involved in the survey, the results of this experiment would have a very direct relevance for its organizers. The dialectologists in charge minimized their chances of obtaining standard speech forms by selecting informants who were least likely to be bidialectal— people from the most isolated and least educated social groups, farm labourers, for example. Better means of communication, however, probably mean that no one in a rural community today is entirely free from outside linguistic influences. It must be added that after research in Articlave began, the organizers of The Hiberno-English Dialect Survey appointed two Irish people to do much of the required fieldwork. Some of the fieldwork, however, is being carried out by English investigators with strongly modified regional accents.[6]

In Experiment One the ten adult informants, who represented a social cross-section of the Articlave community, were brought on separate occasions in self-elected groups of two to the investigator's home. Each group was

[4]The province's evening newspaper has a humorous column on Ulster dialects, and humorous talks on dialects are given to Women's Institutes.
[5]The colleague used was P. M. Tilling, who worked on The English Dialect Survey.
[6]One of the English investigators is P. M. Tilling.

secretly tape-recorded chatting for a period of two hours, permission for tape-recording having been obtained at a much earlier date. The tape-recorder and microphone were hidden, the microphone placed in a hole and surrounded by flowers in a specially made coffee table. Refreshments were served. Since the informants were good friends of the investigator, they were all very familiar with her home. Most did not ask what the nature of the experiment was but agreed to participate saying 'Aye, if it's any help to you'. The situation was sufficiently informal to encourage the elicitation of informants' more non-standard speech codes.

In Experiment Two the informants were asked to come singly to the investigator's home and were tape-recorded for two hours in one-to-one interaction with the English outsider. The microphone was hidden and refreshments served. The outsider was thus given a good chance to obtain informants' non-standard speech codes. If he failed, his presence and not the physical surroundings would be responsible. Though asked to come singly,[7] two informants, on hearing rumours of the content of Experiment Two, begged to be allowed to come together. Their linguistic behaviour in Experiment Two provides sociolinguistic comparisons with that of other informants interviewed singly. The two-hour recording period provided an opportunity to test whether the stranger would be obtaining a less standard linguistic code at the end than at the beginning.

Variables and Linguistic Contexts

A comparison of informants' treatment in Experiments One and Two of certain major linguistic variables in Articlave shows that the presence of the English outsider very often initiates a switch to more standard speech codes.

Each informant, known by one of the alphabetical letters A–J is given a linguistic index for linguistic Code 1 (informal speech of Experiment One) and an index for Code 2 (speech to English stranger in Experiment Two). Indices are calculated as in previous sociolinguistic research on the basis of a numerical value scale established for each variable (cf. Trudgill, 1974a, p. 82). The lower the number, the less the deviation from more standard speech. Informants' indices for five phonological and one lexical variable are given below in Tables 1 to 6. Informants' names are arranged in order of least deviation from standard speech for Code 1.

The variable (ng)

The variable (ng) is the consonant in the -ing suffix attached to verbs, for example, *walking*, *running*. This variable also concerns the final consonant in

---

[7] Informants were asked to come singly for Experiment Two, since there is one-to-one interaction between subject and interviewer in traditional studies of rural dialects. The situation established in Experiment Two would thus parallel that of other studies and the results would be comparable.

compound nouns such as *anything*, *something*, and other nouns, for example *morning*, *ceiling*. It has two variants, allotted the following values:

$$(ng) - 1 \ [\eta]$$
$$(ng) - 2 \ [n]$$

The linguistic index range for (ng) is 000–100.

Table 1: The Variable (ng) in Experiments One and Two

Name of informant	A	C	B	D	H	E	F	G	I	J
Code 1 (Experiment One)	015	025	049	075	084	091	094	098	100	100
Code 2 (Experiment Two)	004	005	005	035	075	042	075	084	097	100

The variable (ɪ)

The variable (ɪ) is the vowel in, for example, *bit*, *thing*, *live*. It has three variant pronunciations ranging from an almost RP realization to one which is much lower and further back.

$$(ɪ) - 1 \ [ɪ]$$
$$(ɪ) - 2 \ [ə]$$
$$(ɪ) - 3 \ [ʌ]$$

The linguistic index range for (ɪ) is 000–200.

Table 2: The variable (ɪ) in Experiments One and Two

Name of informant	A	C	B	E	D	G	F	J	H	I
Code 1 (Experiment One)	091	142	182	190	200	200	200	200	200	200
Code 2 (Experiment Two)	072	126	160	164	162	193	200	200	200	200

The variable (aɪ)

This variable concerns the degree of centralization present in the first element of the diphthong /aɪ/ in, for example, *bright*, *side*, *cry*. Starting points for the diphthong range from an open tongue position close to that of some RP speakers for /aɪ/ to a very centralized first element. Analysis of tapes showed that where the first element of /aɪ/ was long in informants' speech (cf. long *dye* and *sighed* with short *die* and *side*), they consistently used fairly uncentralized starting points. No counts were made of /aɪ/ with a long first element. The variable (aɪ) has three variant pronunciations.

$$(aɪ) - 1 \ [a̠ɪ]$$
$$(aɪ) - 2 \ [äɪ]$$
$$(aɪ) - 3 \ [əɪ]$$

The linguistic index range for (aɪ) is 000–200.

Table 3: The Variable (aɪ) in Experiments One and Two

Name of informant	A	C	B	D	E	H	J	G	F	I
Code 1 (Experiment One)	048	084	106	152	184	190	194	196	200	200
Code 2 (Experiment Two)	026	068	060	061	158	186	192	190	195	200

The variable (aʉ)

This variable concerns the pronunciation of the first element in the diphthong /aʉ/ in, for example, *ground, about, house*. There are four variant pronunciations ranging from an open tongue position through varying degrees of centralization to a zero first element.

There is also some difference in informants' pronunciations of the second element of the diphthong which varies from a half close fairly back to half close mid vowel. Informants with the more open rather than centralized tongue position for element one tend to use the half close back position in element two.

(aʉ) — 1 [aʉ] or [aʊ]
(aʉ) — 2 [ʌʉ]
(aʉ) — 3 [aʉ]
(aʉ) — 4 [ü]

The linguistic index range for (aʉ) is 000–300.

Table 4: The Variable (aʉ) in Experiments One and Two

Name of informant	A	B	C	D	E	H	F	J	I	G
Code 1 (Experiment One)	067	089	132	135	185	185	200	200	203	213
Code 2 (Experiment Two)	035	042	102	039	130	180	195	200	200	200

The variable (ɔ:, ɒ, ʌ—a)

This variable concerns the total or partial replacement by some informants of /ɔ:/ or /ɒ/ by /a/, especially in words where /ɔ:/, or /ɒ/ are preceded by /w/ or followed by /l/, though by no means exclusively in such contexts, /a/ occurring, for example, in the words *all, wander, was* and *watch* but also in *soft* and *top*. The variable also involves the replacement of /ʌ/ by /a/ in the words *one* and *none*. There are three variants of this variable.

(ɔ:,ɒ,ʌ–a) — 1 [ɔ:] [ɒ] [ʌ]
(ɔ:,ɒ,ʌ–a) — 2 [ɔ:→a] [ɒ→a] [ʌ→]
(ɔ:,ɒ,ʌ–a) — 3 [a]

The linguistic index range is 000–200.

Table 5: The Variable (ɔ:, ɒ, ʌ–a) in Experiments One and Two

Name of informant	B	D	C	E	H	A	F	J	I	G
Code 1 (Experiment One)	000	000	002	002	021	022	062	083	092	097
Code 2 (Experiment Two)	000	000	000	000	010	000	018	047	066	022

The variable (yes, aye)

This variable concerns the alternative use of *aye* for *yes* in response to a question or as an affirmative comment when someone else is speaking. *Yes* is given value 1, *aye* value 2. The index range for this variable is 000–100.

Table 6: The Variable (yes, aye) in Experiments One and Two

Name of informant	A	B	C	D	E	G	J	H	F	I
Code 1 (Experiment One)	000	000	000	000	071	082	087	091	098	100
Code 2 (Experiment Two)	000	000	000	000	036	031	003	090	069	100

Linguistic code-switching and the factor of time

Further analysis of informants' linguistic behaviour in Experiment Two (Code 2) shows that all informants who adjust their speech for the English outsider tend to return to a less standard speech code in the second half of their conversation with him—hence higher indices.

Table 7 (see also Figure 1) and Table 8 (see Figure 2) for the variables (ng) and (aɪ) respectively, illustrate the above tendency.

Table 7: Comparison of informant's indexes for (ng) in first and second hours of Experiment Two
Index Range 000–100

Name of informant	A	B	C	D	E	F	H	G	I	J
Overall index for Experiment Two (Code 2)	004	005	005	035	042	075	075	084	097	100
Index for Hour 1 of Experiment Two	003	004	004	033	036	058	067	078	095	100
Index for Hour 2 of Experiment Two	005	006	006	037	048	092	083	090	099	100

Linguistic code-switching and topic of conversation

Certain topics of conversation, in particular the discussion of occupation and education, can reinforce informants' tendencies to switch to more standard linguistic codes in Experiment Two. Table 9 compares several informants' indices for three major variables during a short discussion of their occupations in hour one of Experiment Two with their overall indices for that hour. Informants may be used to switching to more standard speech forms in the formal situation of work. When discussing their occupations, they may be reminded of values associated with the work situation and adjust their linguistic behaviour accordingly.

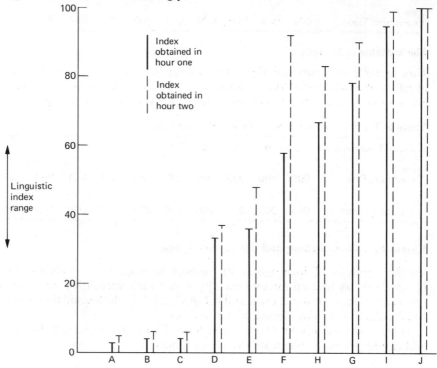

Informants' code names in order
of lowest index obtained in
first hour of experiment two

Figure 1. Comparison of informant's indices for (ng) in first and second hours of Experiment Two.

Table 8: Comparison of informants indexes for (aɪ) in first and second hours of Experiment Two
Index Range 000–200

Name of informant	A	B	C	D	E	H	G	J	F	I
Overall index for Experiment Two (Code 2)	026	060	068	061	158	186	190	192	195	200
Index for Hour 1 of Experiment Two	022	055	062	057	150	179	183	186	191	200
Index for Hour 2 of Experiment Two	030	065	074	065	166	193	197	198	199	200

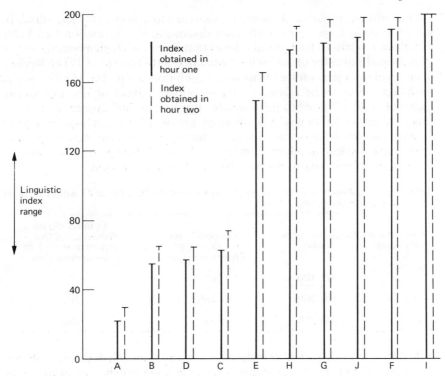

Linguistic index range

Informants' code names in order
of lowest index obtained in
first hour of experiment two

Figure 2. Comparison of informants' indices for (aɪ) in first and second hours of Experiment
Two.

Table 9: Comparison of informants' overall indices in Experiment Two (Hour 1) with their
indices during discussion of Occupation

Three Major Variables	Linguistic Index Range	Overall indices of D, E and H for Hour 1 of Experiment Two	Indices during short discussion of Occupation in Hour 1 of Experiment Two
(ng)	000–100	D 033 E 036 H 067	D 019 E 022 H 035
(aɪ)	000–200	D 057 E 150 H 179	D 024 E 082 H 141
(aʉ)	000–300	D 034 E 126 H 177	D 011 E 058 H 076

One informant, farmer I, however, switches to a noticeably less standard speech code in Experiment Two when discussing his occupation (see Table 10). Research into I's background shows that despite his high income level and educational status (grammar-school educated until the age of 17) he has low social ambition (for rating of his social ambition see p. 48). His low social ambition seems to be related to the unrefined nature of his occupation, summed up by I himself in these words, 'I'm only an oul' farmer workin' wi' muck an' beasts an' things.' I is not an exceptional farmer in his contempt of farming as an occupation. Other farmers in Articlave express similar sentiments. I's less standard linguistic behaviour during the discussion of farming may be linked to his base image of this occupation.

Table 10: Comparison of I's overall indices in Experiment Two (Hour 1) with his indices during discussion of farming

Three Major Variables	Linguistic Index Range	I's overall index for Hour 1 of Experiment Two	I's index during discussion of Occupation in Hour 1 of Experiment Two
(ng)	000–100	095	100
(aʉ)	000–300	195	202
(ɔ:, ɒ, ʌ–a)	000–200	063	090

The shift to more formal speech caused by the topic of education is shown below in Table 11. The effect of discussing education may be similar to that of discussing work: subjects are reminded of values associated with the school situation, and in this case, perhaps of positive linguistic training. Some informants with high educational aspirations (see particularly A, who talks of attending night classes) may try to project high educational images of themselves to the English outsider through their linguistic behaviour.

Table 11: Comparison of 3 informants' overall indices for Hour 1 of Experiment Two with their indices during discussion of education

Three Major Variables	Index Range	Overall indices for A, C and D in Hour 1 of Experiment Two	Indices for A, C and D during discussion of education in Hour 1 of Experiment Two
(ng)	000–100	A 003 C 004 D 033	A 000 C 001 D 012
(aɪ)	000–200	A 022 C 062 D 057	A 010 C 047 D 035
(aʉ)	000–300	A 027 C 096 D 034	A 013 C 066 D 014

Linguistic code-switching in a group interview

Two informants, C and E, were interviewed together in Experiment Two (see p. 40). When talking to each other in the presence of the English outsider they tend to use their less standard speech codes of Experiment One. When addressing remarks to the English outsider, however, they switch to a much more formal code.

C and E's indices for Experiment Two are calculated on the basis of their remarks both to each other and to the English outsider. As can be seen from Tables 1 to 6 there is a considerable numerical gap between C and E's indices for Experiment One and for Experiment Two. Table 12 below, however, shows that there is a significant difference in their indices based on their remarks to each other in Experiment Two and their indices based on remarks directed to the English outsider.

Table 12: Linguistic code-switching in a group interview

Three Major Variables	Index Range	C and E's overall indices for Experiment Two	C and E's indices for Experiment Two based on their remarks to each other	C and E's indices for Experiment Two based on their remarks to the English outsider
(ng)	000–100	C 005 E 042	C 007 E 054	C 003 E 030
(aɪ)	000–200	C 068 E 158	C 082 E 184	C 054 E 132
(aʉ)	000–300	C 102 E 130	C 127 E 169	C 077 E 091

Linguistic code-switching and Social Ambition

It has been suggested that many villagers in Articlave, even those of low educational or occupational status, show a keenness to 'get on in the world', some attending elocution classes, some going to night classes, some having high social aspirations for their children (see pp. 38–39). Since the linguistic indices of many informants are not obviously related to their social status in terms of educational or occupational attainment, it was decided to test the hypothesis that villagers' linguistic behaviour may be more clearly linked to their social aspirations than to their achievements.

Attempts were made to measure informants' social ambitions in Experiment S. Each informant was asked how keen the others were 'to get on in the world'. No one found much difficulty answering this question, since all were members of a tightly knit community and knew each other well. Answers were to take the form of one of four alternatives rated as follows:

4   Very keen
3   Keen
2   Quite keen
1   Not keen

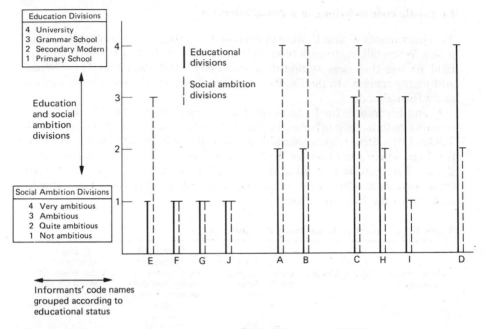

Figure 3. Informant's Ambitions plotted beside their Educational Achievements.

There was a striking amount of agreement among informants in their classification of the other participants' aspirations. Figure 3 illustrates the disparity that often exists between informants' ambition and attainment by plotting their aspirations beside their educational achievements.

Detailed information on individual informants further highlights the interesting disparity between informants' social ambitions and their social status in other terms. Informants A and B, both shop-assistants—though B is now a housewife only—and both educated to the age of 15 at primary and secondary-modern schools, have the same social ambition as C, a secretary with grammar-school education. A often talks of attending night classes in Coleraine Technical College. Some informants rated A as 'extremely' rather than 'very socially ambitious'. The reason for B's social ambition is perhaps more obvious, since she married a local teacher, now headmaster, and presumably sees herself not as the daughter of a council-worker and an eleven-plus failure, but as the wife of the local headmaster. (The headmaster is not a native of the area.)

E is also an interesting case. She is a canteen assistant in the local school and left school at the age of 14. Her husband is a storeman in a factory in Coleraine. One of her good friends is C, the secretary with grammar-school education. Her home, inside and outside, is one of the best kept in the village. As the graph shows, she has much higher social ambition than one might expect from a consideration of her educational and occupational status.

H and I provide more interesting information on the factor of social ambition. These informants are two brothers with grammar-school education.

They are the sons of a local farmer. Informant I now owns the farm, and his brother H works as a work-study officer in a Coleraine factory. H's social aspirations are somewhat higher than those of his brother. Possibly the fact that I works at home 'wi' muck an' beasts an' things' (see p. 46) causes him to have fewer aspirations than his brother. It is worth noting that three informants stated on their answer sheets in Experiment S that informant I was not just 'not keen to get on in the world' but 'not at all keen'. Perhaps the social ambition scale should have had five or six rather than four points (see also comment on A above).

Informant D is a grammar-school teacher, now teaching in Coleraine, though at the time the experiments were conducted she taught in another neighbouring town. Her social ambition falls short of that of informants A, B or C. Possibly the fact that she has high social status through her educational achievements makes her less ambitious than people who are less socially secure in terms of education or occupation. Maybe she is an anomalous case, as she was the only suitable person for selection in her educational and occupational group.

F, G and J are informants with both low social ambition and low social status in other terms. F is a domestic help, G a car mechanic and J a despatch worker in a bakery. Though A, B and E, their approximate educational and occupational equivalents, show considerable social ambition, it would seem that there are also people in Articlave such as F, G and J whose social aspirations correspond closely to their social status in traditional terms.

Figures 4 and 5 show the relation between informants' social ambitions and their treatment in Experiment Two (Code 2) of two of the major linguistic variables in Articlave. The other major variables show similar relations.

By comparing the linguistic indices for the lowest and highest social ambition divisions (divisions 1 and 4 respectively) in Figures 4 and 5, one can see clearly that division 1 has much higher indices and thus less standard linguistic behaviour than division 4. Division 1, the lowest social ambition division, consists of informants F, G and J who have low educational and occupational status, but also of farmer informant I who belongs to high educational division 3 (grammar-school education). Division 4, the highest social ambition division, consists of informant C who has high educational and fairly high occupational status, but also of informants A and B who are shop assistants with only primary and secondary-modern school education. It is therefore clear that the linguistic behaviour of informants A, B and I is related to their respective degrees of social ambition rather than their social status in terms of educational and occupational attainment.

The linguistic behaviour of informants in ambition divisions 2 and 3 is often clearly related to their social ambition rather than their social status in traditional terms. Informant E (high ambition division 3) has much more standard linguistic behaviour than her educational or occupational equivalents J, F and G in low ambition division 1. Informant H, though grammar-school educated, always has much less standard speech forms in Experiment 2 than informants A, B and E who are less well educated but much more socially ambitious (H ambition division 2, E division 3, A and B division 4). H's linguistic behaviour, except in the case of the variables (ng) (see

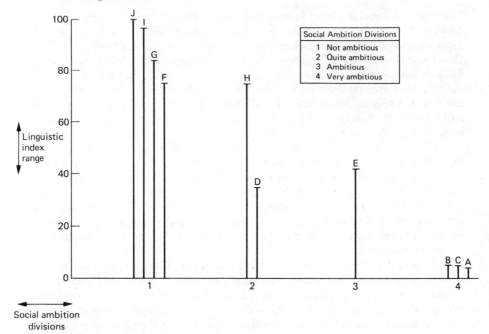

Figure 4. Social Ambition and the variable (ng) in Experiment Two.

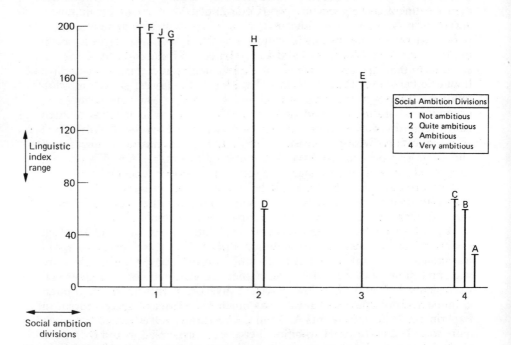

Figure 5. Social Ambition and the variable (aɪ) in Experiment Two.

Figure 4), (ɪ) and (yes, aye), is always more standard than that of people in lower ambition division 1. Division 1 contains his brother I who has had exactly the same degree of education. The linguistic behaviour of H and E is therefore more closely related to social ambition than to educational or occupational attainment.

The linguistic indices of informant D (ambition division 2), however, are not always clearly linked to D's degree of social ambition. As can be seen from Figures 4 and 5, D's linguistic behaviour is more standard than that of informant E who has greater social ambition. Tables 1 to 6 (see also Figure 5) show that D's indices, particularly in Experiment Two, are either lower than or similar to those of informants in highest ambition division 4. An explanation for this is provided by the fact that D is university educated: fairly high levels of education may well leave a mark on linguistic behaviour in spite of a lack of social ambition.

On the other hand, D's indices in Experiment One can be much higher and thus less standard than those of people in higher ambition divisions 3 or 4. It is an important fact, that is, that D is sometimes far short of the indices of other much less well educated but more socially ambitious informants.

Conclusions

The literature on stylistic variation in language (e.g. Crystal & Davy, 1969) generally includes references to the *interlocutor* and to the *topic* of conversation as important factors in determining the linguistic variety to be employed in a given situation. In this study of a rural community, it has been possible to give a quantitative illustration of the importance of these factors (and to suggest that there are practical implications here for dialectologists working in present-day rural communities). It has also been possible to show that differences in the linguistic behaviour of individuals (which may often be obscured in larger scale studies dealing in grouped scores) may be accounted for by socio-psychological factors (cf. Labov, forthcoming) such as the degree of an individual's social ambition.

4

Present tense verbs in Reading English

Jenny Cheshire

This paper describes some patterns in the use of one variable morphological feature in Reading English, and shows how variation in the use of the feature reflects the interaction of linguistic and social constraints. The linguistic constraints governing the use of the feature are syntactic and lexical, and the social constraints are aspects of the vernacular culture to which the speakers belong. The patterns of variation also give some insight into linguistic changes that may have taken place in the dialect.

The feature whose use is described here is the present tense verb stem. Whereas in standard English the verb stem has an –s suffix with third person singular subjects only (cf. I walk, you walk, he walks, we walk, they walk), in Reading English the –s suffix is variably used with other subjects also, as in the examples[1] below:

> I knows how to handle teddy boys
> You knows my sister, the one who's small
> They calls me all the names under the sun, don't they?

The verbs *say, have* and *do* are usually considered as irregular because the third person singular form involves a vowel change as well as the addition of the –s suffix. These verbs also occur in a variable –s form in Reading English, with subjects that are not third person singular:—

> We has a little fire, keeps us warm
> We does things at school with tape-recorders
> And so I says, can I have my satchel back?

Present tense *be* has the same forms in Reading English as it has in standard English.

The Data

This description of present tense verbs is part of a larger-scale study of morphological and grammatical variation in the speech of adolescents in

[1]All examples used in this paper are taken from recordings made in adventure playgrounds in Reading.

Reading, which is based on recordings of 'vernacular' speech. The term 'vernacular' is used by Labov to refer to speech that is at the informal end of the stylistic spectrum, where minimum attention is paid by the speaker to the speech forms he uses (see Labov, 1970).

In this vernacular style, patterns in the use of dialect features tend to be regular and consistent, since speech is governed by the norms of the vernacular culture. Other styles, in which varying degrees of attention are paid to speech, may give a confused picture of dialect forms, since the speech forms used will tend to shift in an apparently erratic manner towards the prestige forms of the speech community. In the case of adolescents, the norms of the vernacular culture are usually transmitted and perpetuated by the peer group.

Three groups of adolescents were recorded in two different adventure playgrounds in Reading. The playgrounds were seen as 'trouble spots' by local residents, because of the fights and fires that often took place there. They were used during school hours, as well as after school, since most of the children did not attend school regularly.

The groups were recorded over a period of eight months, which allowed time for me to become friendly with the children and for them to become used to the presence of the tape recorder. Speakers were recorded with one or more friends in whatever groups occurred naturally, and they were left to interact without interruption. There did not appear to be any visible differences in the interaction that took place between speakers when they were recorded, compared to when they were not. Swearing, laughter, jokes and obscenities occurred frequently, and fights and scuffles often developed.

Thirteen boys and twelve girls were recorded, and for the purposes of analysis they are divided into three groups, corresponding to three groups of friends: the Orts Road group, which is all male; the Shinfield boys group, consisting of three boys only, and the Shinfield girls group. The age of the speakers ranges from nine to seventeen, though most speakers are aged between 11 and 15.

Overall variation in use of the non-standard suffix

Preliminary figures showing the total variation in use of the nonstandard verb forms by the three groups of speakers are given in Table 1. The verbs *have* and *do* are analysed separately from other verbs because in addition to having irregular present tense verb forms in standard English, they also have different syntactic functions, since they appear in sentences both as main verbs and as auxiliaries. The verb *say*, on the other hand, is included in the analysis of regular present tense verbs, since its syntactic behaviour is the same, and since the frequency of use of the non-standard form of *say* is approximately the same as the frequency of use of the non-standard forms of other verbs.

The figures in the table represent the percentage use of the non-standard form by each group of speakers, i.e. the number of occurrences of the non-standard form expressed as a percentage of the potential number of occurrences of the form. The bracketed figures indicate that the number of occurrences of the verb with non-third person singular subjects is small and that the figures do not necessarily, therefore, give an accurate picture of the

Table 1: Frequency of use of the -*s* suffix with non-third-singular subjects

Group %	regular verbs	have	do
Orts Road	50.13	39.29	13.64
Shinfield boys	65.96	[66.67]	25.00
Shinfield girls	52.04	36.00 ..	12.50

extent of the variation. (Following Labov, 1972a, less than five occurrences of a feature is considered to be small.) In general, however, occurrences of present tense verbs are much greater than five. The total number of occurrences of present tense verbs with non-third singular subjects are: regular verbs: 1027; *have*: 66; *do*: 62.

In spite of the gap in the table caused by insufficient data for use of the feature with *have*, it can be seen that the frequency of use of non-standard verb forms tends to form a regular pattern, with regular verbs occurring in the non-standard form most frequently, and *do* occurring in the non-standard form least frequently.

More detailed analysis of the use of non-standard forms of these verbs reveals patterns of variation that give some insight into the factors controlling variation.

Linguistic change and variation in non-standard forms of *have* and *do*

Table 1 shows the frequency of use of non-standard forms of *have* and *do*. Non-standard forms of *have* occur only with non-third person singular subjects, as do non-standard forms of regular verbs; when the subject is third person singular, the form used is the same as the standard English form. The verb *do*, however, has three separate non-standard forms, all of which are used variably.

Do with non-third-singular subjects occurs in a variable suffixed form, analogous to the non-standard forms of *have* and of regular verbs with non-third-singular subjects.
Examples:

> Everytime we does anything wrong, he sticks you.
> That's what I does, anyway, I just ignores them.

In addition, *do* with a third person singular subject occurs in a non-standard form, without the −*s* suffix.
Examples:

> But it hurts my dad more than it do her.
> She cadges, she do.
> Mary, Mary, quite contrary, how do your garden grow?

A third non-standard form, spelt here *dos* (pronounced [duːz], occurs variably with all subjects, though mostly with third person singular subjects.

Examples:

> All the headmaster dos now is makes you stand in a corner
> We dos some fishing
> One bloke stays at home and dos the house cleaning and all that.

The situation is further complicated by the fact that when *do* is used as an auxiliary in a negative sentence, the non-standard form *don't* is used almost invariably with third person subjects:
Example:

> He don't want to look at your ugly face

Table 2 shows the percentage frequency of all three forms of *do*, in positive sentences, by all speakers.

Table 2: Frequency of use of different forms of *do*

%	does	do	dos
3rd singular	37.70	52.46	9.84
other subjects	14.52	83.87	1.61

Use of the three forms can be seen to fluctuate in an erratic manner: the form *do* predominates in use with all subjects, yet with third singular subjects this is a non-standard form, and with other subjects this is the standard form.

If we look at the way in which nonstandard forms of *have* and *do* are used in the recordings, however, some regular patterns of variation emerge that show that use of the forms is not random, but is governed by the syntactic behaviour of these verbs in sentences.

Have and *do* both occur in sentences as main verbs and as auxiliaries. In addition, *have* occurs with a following infinitive, to express obligation.
Examples:

have: main verb	We has a muck around in there.
	I have a good time with the missis
have: auxiliary	Well, I have got a boyfriend.
	He said, why have you been away?
have: infinitive	You just has to do what these teachers tell you.
	Sometimes on Saturdays I has to stop in.
do: main verb	We does things at school with tape recorders.
	And all they does is get the shit out.
do: auxiliary	Well, how much do he want for it?
	Your dad do play cricket, though, don't he?

Table 3 shows the frequency of use of the non-standard form of *have* with non-third-singular subjects, in each of the syntactic constructions in which it occurs. Total use of the non-standard form by all speakers is included in the table, since data for the Shinfield boys group is small.

Table 3: Frequency of use of non-standard *has* with non-third-singular subjects

Group %	*have*: main verb	*have*: infinitive	*have*: auxiliary
Orts Road	50.00	71.43	0.00
Shinfield boys	[100.00]	—	0.00
Shinfield girls	51.61	37.93	0.00
All speakers	51.06	39.02	0.00

It can be seen from the table that when *have* is an auxiliary verb in the sentence, it never occurs in the non-standard form. In other words, auxiliary *have* in Reading English behaves in the same way as auxiliary *have* in standard English. It is only when *have* is a main verb or when it is followed by an infinitive that variation occurs.

One possible explanation for this might be that the forms of auxiliary *have* used by the speakers represent forms resulting from a linguistic change that has been completed, whereas forms of main verb *have* (including *have* followed by an infinitive) result from a linguistic change that is still in progress.

Little is known about the morphological and grammatical history of regional dialects in Britain. But observations of southwestern dialects of British English farther removed from London than Reading English suggest that at an earlier stage these dialects had separate forms for auxiliaries and for main verbs. According to this view, auxiliary *have* would have been used in the form *have* with all subjects of the verb, including third person singular subjects, and main verb *have* would have been used in the form *has* with all subjects of the verb, as shown in stage 1 of figure 1.

Figure 1. Linguistic change in the verb *have*

Stage 1			Stage 2
AUXILIARY	have ⎫	all subjects ⟶	⎧ 3rd singular *has*
MAIN VERB	has ⎭	⟶	⎩ 1, 2, 3rd plural *have*

Only one member of the paradigm undergoes change in the case of the auxiliary verb—third person singular verb forms. The Reading data suggest that this relatively simple change is already completed, since third person singular forms of auxiliary *have* all have the standard, suffixed form.

In the case of the main verb, however, all members of the paradigm except one undergo change: it is only third person singular forms of the verb that are not required to change. This more complicated change appears to be still in progress in the Reading dialect: the earlier, suffixed form of the verb occurs approximately 51 per cent of the time with non-third-singular subjects when it is a main verb, and approximately 39 per cent of the time when it is followed by an infinitive. This data, incidentally, supports the view that when *have* is used with a following infinitive to express obligation, it should be treated as a main verb and not as an auxiliary.

A study of the use of non-standard forms of *have* in apparent time would be necessary to confirm that the variation in these data does reflect an on-going linguistic change. It seems likely that it does, however, since non-standard forms of *do*, in Reading English, behave in a similar, though more complicated way.

Like *have*, *do* is used in sentences both as a main verb and as an auxiliary. We can suggest that earlier forms of these two uses of *do* were like earlier forms of *have*, with an invariant suffixless form for the auxiliary and an invariant suffixed form for the main verb. Past tense forms of *do* in this earlier stage would have been *done* (main verb) and *did* (auxiliary), a distinction which tends to be preserved in most non-standard dialects today, as in the sentence below:

Well, he never done it, did he?

The earlier present tense forms would then change in the direction of standard English, as shown in Figure 2.

Figure 2. Linguistic change of *do*

Stage 1			Stage 2
AUXILIARY	*do*	all subjects ⟶	3rd singular *does*
MAIN VERB	*does*	⟶	1, 2, 3 plural *do*

The frequency of use of the non-standard forms *do* (with a third singular subject) and *does* (with a non-third singular subject) in the recordings confirm that these linguistic changes may be in progress, although neither change appears to have been completed—unlike those undergone by earlier forms of *have*. Table 3 shows the frequency of use of the different forms of *do* when it is a main verb and when it is an auxiliary. The negative form *don't* is excluded for the time being. The figures in the table represent the total forms used by all speakers.

Table 4: Frequency of use of non-standard forms of *do*

%	*do*: Main Verb			*do*: Auxiliary		
	do	dos	does	do	dos	does
3rd singular	12.5	37.5	50.0	66.7	0.0	33.3
Other subjects	35.7	7.1	56.8	97.9	0.0	2.1

It can be seen from the table that the earlier auxiliary form (*do*) is still used almost all the time with non-third person singular subjects, as would be expected, since these forms are not affected by the change (the one exception which causes the frequency to be less than 100 per cent must be a hypercorrect form). This earlier form is also used approximately 67 per cent of the time with a third singular subject, a high figure which suggests that the change is far from completion.

The frequency of use of the negative auxiliary *don't* with third singular subjects, given in Table 5, shows that in a negative linguistic environment the change has scarcely begun. It may be that the use of the negative acts as a constraint on the verb form, inhibiting the use of the newer standard English form in this environment.

Forms of *do* when used as a main verb present a more complicated picture.

Table 5: Frequency of use of forms of negative
auxiliary *do*

all speakers %	*don't*	*doesn't*
3rd singular	95.2	4.8
Other subjects	100.0	0.0

The assumed earlier form *does* is still used approximately 57 per cent of the time with non-third person singular subjects, and only 50 per cent of the time with third person singular subjects. This latter form would not be expected to change at all, since earlier forms correspond to the standard English form. The form *dos*, however, is also used with third person singular subjects approximately 38 per cent of the time, and with other subjects approximately 7 per cent of the time. This suggests that *dos* may represent a still earlier form of the main verb, again used with all subjects. This earliest stage, then, is still used 38 per cent of the time with third singular subjects, and the next (and final) stage, *does*, 50 per cent of the time. With other subjects, the intermediate stage is used 51 per cent of the time, about the same frequency as with third singular subjects, and the earlier stage is used only rarely (approximately 7 per cent). The final, standard English, stage is used approximately 36 per cent of the time, which indicates that this change is far from completion, as is the change in forms of auxiliary *do*. Figure 3 shows the three stages of the change.

Figure 3. Linguistic change of *do*

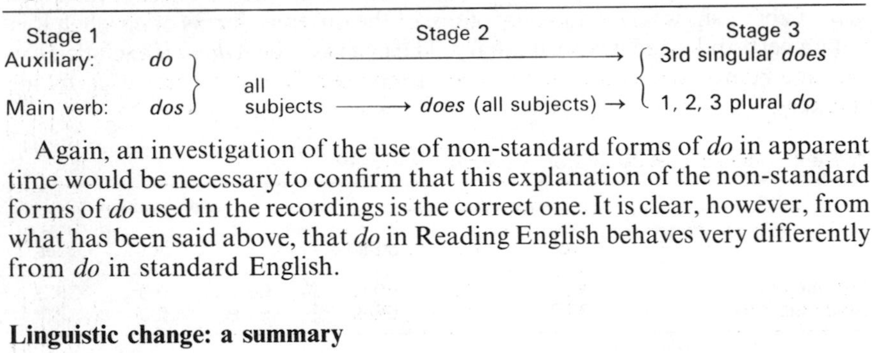

Again, an investigation of the use of non-standard forms of *do* in apparent time would be necessary to confirm that this explanation of the non-standard forms of *do* used in the recordings is the correct one. It is clear, however, from what has been said above, that *do* in Reading English behaves very differently from *do* in standard English.

Linguistic change: a summary

Patterns of variation in the forms of present tense *have* and *do* show that variation in the use of these forms may reflect on-going linguistic changes in the morphology of the verbs. In the case of auxiliary *have*, the change appears to be already completed, but in the case of auxiliary *do* and main verb *do*, the change appears to be far from completion.

It is generally accepted that an earlier form of regular present tense verbs was one that was suffixed throughout the paradigm (see Wakelin, 1972). Variation in the use of the non-standard suffix with non-third singular subjects in regular verbs in Reading English today may also reflect an on-going linguistic change in the morphology of the verb. But an examination of the patterns of use of the non-standard feature in different linguistic environments shows that, if there is a change in progress, it is controlled by linguistic constraints on the form of the verb.

Linguistic constraints and variation in the form of regular verbs.

Regular verbs are used in a wider range of syntactic constructions than *have* and *do*. Their behaviour in all the linguistic environments in which they appear in the recordings was analysed, together with the effect of the time reference of the verb, and of lexical features of the verb. Two linguistic constraints appear to affect the form of the verb: a syntactic constraint, which favours the use of the standard verb form, and a lexical constraint, which favours the use of the non-standard verb form.

The syntactic constraint on the form of regular verbs

Those verbs that are immediately followed by a complement are affected by the nature of the complement in an interesting way. The term 'complement' is used here to describe an embedded sentence which is directly dominated by a regular present tense verb. Complements used in the recordings are of the following syntactic types:

		examples
1	V + –ing	I fancies going over Caversham.
2	infinitive	I wants to kill animals.
3	NP + V	I just lets her beat me.
4	how + infinitive	I knows how to stick in the boot.
5	wh − +S	Oh, I forget what the place is called.
6	if + S	You know if anything breaks on that pushchair.
7	that + S	I believe that there is, you know, life after death.
8	+ S	If you're wearing scruffy clothes they think you're a bloody hippy.

Complements of types 1–4 differ from the other complements in that the subject and tense of the verb are not marked in the surface structure. The tense of the embedded verb in complements of types 1–4 is coextensive with the tense of the verb in the matrix sentence, but the tense of the verb in complements of types 5–8 is independent of, and may be different from, the tense of the matrix verb, as in the sentences below:

> I suppose they went to court.
> I reckon they should pull our troops out.
> I reckon he always will be the king of rock and roll.

Many of the verbs that precede complements in which tense is marked occur in the non-standard form in other syntactic environments, which indicates that it is tense marking that is the significant feature here, rather than, for instance, some semantic property of the matrix verb.

Table 6 shows the frequency of use of the non-standard –s suffix when regular verbs are followed by these two different types of complements.

It can be seen that when a verb is followed by a complement in which subject and tense are marked, the non-standard form of the verb is rarely or never

C

Table 6: Frequency of use of non-standard -*s* form with a following complement

Group %	all verbs	+complement tense unmarked	+complement tense marked
Orts Road	50.13	47.73	2.63
Shinfield boys	65.96	57.14	0.00
Shinfield girls	52.04	50.00	2.13

used. What is not clear is whether the constraint operates only at this superficial level of whether or not tense is marked in the surface structure of the complement, or whether it operates at a deeper level of abstraction, reflecting deep structure differences between the different types of complements. The effect of different complement types has been found to be significant in other areas of syntax (see, for example, the formulation of the conditions on the NEGATTRAC rule in Labov, 1972c). The frequency of use of non-standard verb forms with those types of complement that occur most frequently in the recordings (the $V+-ing$ complement, the $+infinitive$ complement, and the $+S$ complement) suggest that these complements may all be involved in the following complement constraint on the form of regular present-tense verbs, since use of non-standard verb forms in each of these environments appears to form a regular and consistent pattern. Table 7 shows the frequency of use of non-standard forms in each of these environments, for the Orts Road group and for the Shinfield girls group. (There are insufficient data for the Shinfield boys group).

Table 7: Frequency of use of non-standard verb forms with following complements

Group %	V+-ing	+infinitive	+S
Orts Road	61.54	33.33	0.00
Shinfield girls	64.71	46.67	2.70

However, since an attempt to describe the ways in which these complements might differ from each other at a deep structure level is beyond the scope of this paper[2], the syntactic constraint on the form of regular present tense verbs will be described here in terms of its directly observable, surface structure effect as follows:

Constraint 1: regular present tense verbs in Reading English occur with a variable –*s* suffix with subjects other than third person singular, except when they are immediately followed by a complement in which the person and tense of the verb are marked.

The lexical constraint on the form of regular verbs

Some of the verbs used in the recordings are verbs that have a special 'vernacular' meaning. Either they are not normally used in standard English, or they are used but with a different meaning. Verbs of this type are listed in Table 8, with examples of their use.

[2]See Kiparsky and Kiparsky (1968) for an attempt to correlate different types of complements with different semantic base structures.

Table 8: 'Vernacular' verbs in Reading English

'Vernacular' verb	Meaning	Example
go	say	so I goes, oh clear off
chin	hit on the chin	we fucking chins them with bottles
boot	kick	you boot them, don't you
kill	beat in a fight	we chins them, we kills them
leg it	run away	I grabs hold of him and legs it up Blagdon Hill
poke (nose)	be 'nosey'	everyone says I pokes my nose, but I don't
bunk	play truant	we bunks it over here a lot
learn	teach	I just learn myself
bus	go by bus	we buses it down the town

Use of the non-standard −s suffix with non-third person singular subjects is significantly higher with these 'vernacular' verbs than with other verbs. Table 9 shows the frequency of use of the non-standard suffix by the three groups of speakers with 'vernacular verbs', and with all verbs.

Table 9: Frequency of use of the non-standard suffix with 'vernacular' verbs

Group	-s suffix: all verbs	-s suffix: 'vernacular' verbs
Orts Road	50.13	94.29
Shinfield boys	65.96	90.00
Shinfield girls	52.04	95.56

Use of a 'vernacular' verb, then, appears to act as a lexical constraint on the form of the verb, favouring the production of the non-standard suffix. The constraint may be formulated as follows:

Constraint 2: regular present-tense verbs in Reading English occur with a variable −s suffix with subjects that are not third person singular subjects, except when the verb is a 'vernacular' verb, when use of the −s suffix is quasi-categorical.

Rules for the formulation of regular present-tense verbs in Reading English

A concise description of the ways in which present-tense regular verbs in Reading English differ from present-tense regular verbs in standard English may be given by a variable rule (see Wolfram and Fasold, 1974). The following rule would account for the form of regular present tense verbs in standard English:

$$V \longrightarrow V + \quad -s / \underline{\hspace{3cm}} \quad [+3s]$$

The rule states that the verb stem has an −s suffix when the subject of the verb is third person singular.

Let us assume that in Reading English, verbs which have a special vernacular meaning are classified in the lexicon with a sub-categorization feature such as [+VERNACULAR]. The rule above can now be expanded in order to account for the present tense form of regular verbs in Reading English:

$$V \longrightarrow V+ \quad (-s)/ \quad \left\{ \begin{array}{ll} \underline{\quad\quad} & [+3s]^* \\ \sim \underline{\quad\quad} & V\,[+\text{TENSE}]^* \\ \underline{\quad\quad} & [+\text{VERNACULAR}] \end{array} \right.$$

This rule states that the verb stem has a variable $-s$ suffix, which is categorical with third person singular subjects, is favoured when the verb has the sub-categorization feature [+VERNACULAR], but is not used when the verb is followed by a complement containing a verb which is marked for tense. The order of importance of the constraints is shown by their vertical ordering in the presentation of the rule.

Linguistic constraints: a summary

An examination of the behaviour of regular verbs in a wide range of different linguistic environments enabled two constraints on the form of the verb to be isolated, working in opposite directions: a syntactic constraint, favouring use of the standard, suffixless form of the verb, and a lexical constraint, favouring use of the non-standard, suffixed form of the verb.

Table 10 shows the frequency of use of non-standard verb forms when forms that are governed by linguistic constraints are excluded from the total.

Table 10: Adjusted frequency of non-standard verb forms

Group %	Preliminary frequency of regular verbs	Adjusted frequency of regular verbs
Orts Road	50.13	51.20
Shinfield boys	65.96	63.77
Shinfield girls	52.04	51.57

It can be seen that, although two strong constraints were found to control the form of the verb, the variation in the verb form when the effect of these constraints is removed is almost the same as when the constraints are in operation, because the two constraints have opposite effects.

Patterns of variation in the use of non-standard forms of regular verbs, then, reveal some of the linguistic processes that control variation. But the frequency of variation does not diminish when the effect of these linguistic constraints is excluded, which suggests that other processes that are as yet unspecified must govern variation also, and indeed when individual variation in the use of the $-s$ suffix is examined, some of the social factors that control variation can be isolated.

Social factors and variation

Individual variation in the use of the $-s$ suffix is very high, ranging from 11.11 to 81.00 in the case of regular verbs. Individual frequencies for the use of non-standard forms of *have* and *do* also varies widely, but are less reliable since these verbs do not occur so regularly in the speech of individual speakers.

Table 11: Individual frequencies of non-standard regular verb forms

Orts Road

Speaker %	Noddy	Mick	Roger	Kitty	Jed
Frequency	81.00	68.18	58.33	45.71	45.00

Speaker %	Colin	Alf	Puvvy	Barney	Kevin
Frequency	38.46	36.96	33.33	31.58	14.29

Shinfield boys

Speaker %	Perry	Ricky	Gammy
Frequency	71.43	70.83	57.14

Shinfield girls

Speaker %	Cathy	Diane	Kim	Jacky	Marie	Patsy
Frequency	75.00	70.00	60.87	60.00	58.62	52.63

Speaker %	Wendy	Teresa	Dawn	Margaret	Karen	Linda
Frequency	52.38	48.28	30.51	25.00	22.22	11.11

Individual frequencies of non-standard forms of regular verbs for all speakers are shown in Table 11.

The effect of social factors on the speech of the boys will be considered separately from their effect on the speech of the girls, since the interests, activities and peer-group structure of the two sexes is different.

Neither the age nor the sex of the speaker has any significant effect on the form of the verb stem. This was expected, in view of the assumption that vernacular speech in adolescents is controlled by the norms of the vernacular culture, as embodied in the behaviour of the peer group.

Vernacular culture and variation in the boys' speech

An 'index of vernacular culture' was constructed, which separates boys into groups of speakers on the basis of their degree of adherence to the peer group and to some of the norms of the vernacular culture, and which shows to what extent variation in the form of present tense verbs is affected by the degree of adherence of the speaker to the norms of the vernacular culture.

Peer-group status and variation in the use of non-standard forms
Speakers were first scored according to their status in the peer group. The Shinfield boys form a closely knit group, and are given a score of 2. The structure of the Orts Road group is more complicated. The boys did not

consider themselves to be a gang, and they had no name and no leader, although there had in the past been fights between themselves and what they called the 'Shinfield gang'—which included the Shinfield boys group. The group consisted of a central core of three boys (Noddy, Kitty and Jed), who spent most of their time together, and a good deal of time at the playground. These three speakers are given a score of 2. Mick, Roger, Colin and Barney are each given a score of 1—they are 'peripheral' members of the group, who for various reasons did not spend so much time at the playground. Mick, for example, had recently started work, and Roger, who was older than the other boys, spent more time with girls. The other three boys are given a zero score— Alf had at one time been a core member, together with Mick and Roger, but he had now started work, had a steady girl friend, and social aspirations (he wanted to become manager of the shop where he worked), and no longer spent much time at the playground. Puvvy and Kevin were often at the playground but they did not take part in fights and were often jeered at and excluded from group activities by the other boys. Kevin lived in the pub next door to the playground and seemed to have decided that to allow himself to be the butt of the group's jokes was the best way of getting along with his neighbours.

Table 12 shows that when the Orts Road speakers are grouped according to their peer group status, the frequency of use of the non-standard form of regular verbs forms a regular pattern, with a high frequency used by central members of the peer group, and a low frequency used by boys who did not belong to the peer group. The frequency of use of the non-standard form of the main verb *have* follows the same pattern. *Do* is excluded here, because of insufficient data.

Table 12: Peer-group status and frequency of use of non-standard verb forms (Orts Road Group)

%	central members	peripheral members	non-members
regular verbs	68.39	42.33	30.38
main verb *have*	55.55	36.36	33.33

'Toughness' and variation in the use of non-standard forms

'Toughness' was an important aspect of the boys' culture: those boys who were good fighters, who carried impressive weapons (usually chains), who stole, and performed well in confrontations with police were admired and respected, whereas boys who were cowards or poor fighters were ridiculed. Stories that recounted fights or violent films were very popular and were told over and over again.

Each boy is given a score which is designed to reflect his degree of toughness. A score of 2 indicates that the speaker figured in stories about past fights, that he was reputed to be a good fighter, carried a weapon, took part in shoplifting or in setting fire to buildings, and did not lose his nerve when confronted by the police (four speakers). A score of 1 is given to boys who failed on one of these counts: who either did not carry a weapon, or could not fight well, or, as was the case with one boy, had once burst into tears when stopped by a policeman. This last event was often joked about by the other boys, and had cost the boy his reputation. Boys who failed on more than one count are given a zero score (three speakers).

Table 13: 'Toughness' and frequency of use of non-standard verb forms

%	'toughness' score 2	'toughness' score 1	'toughness' score 0
regular verbs	70.72	43.33	26.76
main verb *have*	66.67	43.75	33.33

Table 13 shows that group frequencies for the use of non-standard forms of regular verbs and of main verb *have* form a regular pattern which reflects the degree of 'toughness' of the speakers. Main verb *do* appears to follow the pattern, but it occurs too infrequently in the recordings for the figures to be reliable.

Ambition and variation in the use of non-standard forms

The central nature of 'toughness' in the boys' vernacular culture is reflected in the kinds of work that were considered acceptable by the boys. Their ideas about jobs, however, are considered as a separate aspect of the culture because boys who are given a high 'toughness' score did not necessarily want to do a 'tough' job, and were scorned by the other boys for that reason. Acceptable jobs carry connotations of masculinity or force: it was acceptable, therefore, to want to be a slaughterer, a jockey, a motor mechanic, or to enter the armed forces, but not to want to be a student, a teacher, or to work in a shop or an office. None of the boys attended school regularly, but it seemed to be unacceptable to stay away from school completely, or to be out of work.

Boys who wanted to do a 'tough' job or who had a 'tough' job already—Mick, for example, had just started work as a forklift truck operator—are given a score of 1 (Noddy, Mick, Kitty, Jed, Colin, Perry, Gammy and Ricky), and boys who did or who wanted to do a white-collar job, or who were out of work (Roger) or never went to school (Barney) are given a zero score (Roger, Barney, Alf and Kevin).

Table 14 shows that these scores are reflected in the frequency of use of non-standard forms of regular verbs and of main verb *have*.

Table 14: Ambition and frequency of use of non-standard verb forms

%	'ambition' score 1	'ambition' score 0
regular verbs	38.12	33.33
main verb *have*	52.94	33.33

Vernacular culture index and variation in the use of non-standard forms

The scores allotted to each speaker on the basis of their ambition, their degree of 'toughness', and their peer-group status were combined into what may be termed an index of the degree of adherence of the speaker to the vernacular culture. Other aspects of vernacular culture could of course have been included in the index, but these three aspects were central issues: 'toughness' and the related 'ambition' were frequent topics in group conversations, and peer-group status is obviously also a matter of considerable importance.

The speakers are divided into four groups, on the basis of their total score, as follows:

Group 1:   Noddy, Perry, Ricky
Group 2:   Jed, Kitty, Mick, Roger, Gammy
Group 3:   Barney, Colin, Alf
Group 4:   Kevin, Puvvy

Frequency indices for the use of the non-standard verb form by the four groups are shown in Table 15.

Table 15: Frequency of use of non-standard verb forms and vernacular culture index

%	Group 1	Group 2	Group 3	Group 4
regular verbs	77.36	54.03	36.57	21.21
main verb *have*	66.67	50.00	41.67	25.00

Table 15 shows that the frequency of use of the non-standard verb form follows a regular pattern, in which high frequencies are used by speakers with a high vernacular culture index, and low frequencies are used by speakers with a low vernacular culture index.

Vernacular culture and variation in girls' speech

Although patterns of variation in boys' speech were found to be closely linked with central aspects of the vernacular culture, girls' speech does not appear to be affected by the norms of the vernacular culture in quite the same way.

To begin with, those area of vernacular culture that were considered important by the girls were not easy to define. The norm of 'toughness' did not apply to the girls—some did steal, either from shops or from their mothers, but they did not boast about it in the way that the boys did, and they were not respected for it by their friends, as the boys were. The girls fought, too, but only as an extension of an argument, not as a sport. Their principal interests were pop music and singers, and boys. They disliked school and their teachers, stayed away often, and were anxious to leave at the earliest opportunity, in order to become hairdressers, shop assistants, telephonists or secretaries, but principally to become wives and mothers.

In addition, the girls did not belong to a cohesive peer group in the way that the boys did. Their friendships were more intimate, but they fluctuated rapidly: one of the speakers changed her 'best friend' four times during the time that the recordings were made, and her cast off best friends then became her worst enemies.

Less time was spent at the playground by the girls. Their friends visited them at home, and they were expected to stay at home to help with their younger brothers and sisters, and with the chores. When they went out, they often set off in twos to walk around the town looking for boys.

Four girls, however, stand out as different from the other girls. They were interested in pop singers and boyfriends, like the other girls, but they attended school regularly, did not swear or steal, and said that the other girls were 'rough' or 'common'. The frequency of use of non-standard verb forms in the speech of these 'good' girls is lower than in the speech of the other girls in the case of regular verbs, but slightly higher with main verb *have*, as shown in Table 16. Figures for the use of main verb *do* are again too low to be included.

Table 16: Frequency of use of non-standard verb forms by 'good' girls

%	'good' girls	'other' girls
regular verbs	25.51	57.99
main verb *have*	47.06	44.19

It seems, then, that use of non-standard verb forms by the girls is not consistently governed by the norms of the vernacular culture, as was found to be the case with the boys. Doubtless this is because for girls the vernacular culture is less important. What is more, there is no cohesive peer group to perpetuate vernacular norms for the girls.

It is surprising, in view of this, that the girls use non-standard verb forms with approximately the same frequency as the boys, whose speech appears to be much more rigidly controlled by vernacular norms. Other studies of the use of non-standard speech forms have found that female speakers tend to use non-standard forms less often than male speakers (see, for example, Wolfram, 1969; Trudgill, 1972).

In recordings that were made of the same speakers in a more formal situation, however, the girls adjust their speech more sharply towards standard English usage than the boys do, probably as a result of the fact that their speech is less rigidly controlled by the norms of the vernacular culture.

Style shifting and variation in the use of non-standard verb forms

In addition to the recordings made in adventure playgrounds in Reading, a set of recordings was made in the schools that the children attended. Teachers were asked to record the children with a few friends and the teacher present. Not all of the speakers were able to be recorded at school. Some had left school, and most of them did not attend often, and were not popular with their teachers. The Shinfield boys were all recorded at school, and five members of the Orts Road group and five members of the Shinfield girls were also recorded. The frequency of use of non-standard forms of regular verbs and of main verb *have* are shown in Table 17.

It can be seen from the table that all groups use fewer non-standard verb forms in the more formal speech style, but the girls' use of non-standard forms tends to decrease more sharply. This suggests that girls may be more aware of the pressures exerted on speech by the overt norms of the speech community,

Table 17: Frequency of use of non-standard verb forms in vernacular style and in formal style

regular verbs %	vernacular	formal style
Orts Road	53.87	27.16
Shinfield boys	65.96	35.00
Shinfield girls	49.46	13.16

main verb *have* %		
Orts Road	47.37	42.86
Shinfield boys	[100.00]	33.33
Shinfield girls	37.14	11.11

and confirms that the covert norms that govern the vernacular have less effect on their speech than they have on the boys' speech. (cf. Trudgill, 1972).

Conclusion

Patterns of variation in the use of non-standard verb forms in Reading English show that variation is controlled by both social and lingustic factors. In boys' speech, variation is governed by norms that are central to the vernacular culture, and are transmitted through the peer group. Variation in the girls' speech appears to be a more personal process, and less rigidly controlled by vernacular norms. In a more formal situation, when more attention is paid to speech, the girls adjusted their use of non-standard verb forms more sharply in the direction of standard English than the boys did.

All speakers are subject to two linguistic constraints on the form of regular present tense verbs, of which one favours the use of the non-standard verb form, and the other favours the use of the standard form. In addition, variation in the forms of the verbs *have* and *do* appears to be due to linguistic changes in progress in the morphology of the verb stem.

5

On the sociolinguistics of vocalic mergers: transfer and approximation in East Anglia

Peter Trudgill and Tina Foxcroft

The loss of phonological contrasts through linguistic change is known to be rather common, and there are in particular many well attested cases from many languages of losses of contrast through the merger of vowels that were formerly distinct.[1] In many of these cases, we have evidence from an earlier stage in the language when the vowels in question were distinguished, and we also have information on the later stage when the merger has been completed and what was formerly two (or more) vowels has now beome one. Most often, however, we are not very well informed as to what went on in between, during the intervening period when the merger was being carried through. How exactly did the merger take place, and what exactly did speakers do while the merger was being completed? We are still, that is, rather ignorant about the actual mechanisms involved in vocalic mergers.

The same thing is also true of certain aspects of sound change in general. There has, for example, been a certain amount of controversy in recent years (see Postal, 1968; King, 1969, amongst others) as to whether sound change is best regarded as a gradual or a sudden process. The prevailing view today (see Labov *et al.*, 1972; King, 1975) would appear to be that sound change is essentially gradual. But it is legitimate to ask: if this is the case, what exactly is meant, in this context, by the term *gradual*? If speakers modify their language *gradually*, what exactly does this involve, and how exactly do they do it? In this paper we shall attempt to begin to answer this question with reference to the problem of vocalic mergers using data from empirical sociolinguistic research of various types.

The East Anglian merger

If we examine the development of the English language, we can note (see Kurath, 1964) that the modern English vowel /ou/, as in *go*, *home*, has been involved in a vocalic merger and is the result of two different (main) sources in Middle English. The first is the monophthong ō [ɔ:], as in *road*, *go*, while the

[1]We are very grateful to J. K. Chambers for comments on an earlier draft of this paper.

second is the dipthong ou [ɔu], as in *flow, know*. (The distinction is still, of course, in most cases reflected in the orthography.) Now if we are interested in what exactly happened while the merger that resulted in these two Middle English vowels becoming one was taking place, it is useful to note that there are some varieties of modern British English where the vowels are still distinct. For instance, in a study of the English spoken in Norwich (Trudgill, 1974a) it was shown that speakers of this variety have a high back rounded vowel in items descended from the Middle English monophthongal forms: *road* /ruud/; *go* /guu/, while items that had Middle English diphthongs have a wide diphthong of the type: *flow* /flʌu/; *know* /nʌu/. This means that there are minimal pairs such as the following:

/uu/	/ʌu/
moan	mown
rose	rows
sole	soul

(See also Wells, 1970.)

Further investigations have shown, however, that in many other parts of East Anglia, this vocalic contrast is now being lost; the two vowels are becoming merged. In this paper we shall examine the mechanisms involved in this on-going vowel merger, and examine to what extent the description 'gradual' is an accurate one in this case. In doing this we shall draw on empirical studies of rural dialects carried out in Eastern England by Lowman (cf. Lowman and Kurath, 1973) in the 1930s;[2] by the Survey of English Dialects, in the 1950s (see Orton and Tilling, 1969); and a study of urban varieties carried out by ourselves since 1974.[3]

The progress of the merger

Most of the evidence we have suggests that this East Anglian merger has indeed so far taken place gradually. It has certainly, for instance, been gradual geographically. Figure 1 suggests that the geographical progress of the vowel merger northwards and eastwards from the London region is a genuinely gradual process. South of line 1 on the map is an area where there is no trace at all of the older distinction between *moan* and *mown*. Between line 1 and line 2 is an area where, in conservative rural dialects of the 1930s, the only trace of the distinction was the relic pronunciation of one word, *go*, as /guu/. (Even today, some older speakers in places as far south as Watford have /guu/.[4]) Between line 2 and line 3 is a region where /uu/ occurred in several words of this type in rural dialects in the 1930s but where by the 1950s it survived only in *go*. Between lines 3 and 4, /uu/ appears in the 1950s rural dialect records, as a relic pronunciation, in a number of words in addition to *go*. (Even today /uu/ appears in *go* in a number of urban centres in this area,

[2]Lowman's records were made available by R. I. McDavid Jr., to whom we are very grateful.
[3]This research was financed by a grant from the SSRC.
[4]Recordings made by David Sutcliffe.

Figure 1. The East Anglian merger

such as Northampton.) And between line 4 and line 5 the distinction survives, in the Survey of English Dialects records, throughout the lexicon, but not consistently (see below). Between lines 4 and 6, in the west, and lines 5 and 6 in the east, the distinction is currently consistently preserved in rural areas, but has suffered a marked loss in urban areas. And in the region north of line 6, including Norwich, the distinction survives today, even in urban areas, more or less consistently.

The change is also gradual socially. As Table 1 shows, in the East Anglian towns where the merger is not yet completed, middle-class speakers are adopting the merger before working-class speakers. The merger, we can say, is spreading from the middle class downwards.

Table 1: Degree of merger of /uu/ and /ʌu/

		Merger Consistent	*Merger Variable*	*No Merger*
	% informants			
Lowestoft:	middle class	30	40	30
(1975)	working class	0	23	77
G. Yarmouth:	middle class	33	17	50
(1975)	working class	0	40	60
King's Lynn:	middle class	33	20	47
(1975)	working class	0	0	100
Norwich:	middle class	4	46	50
(1968)	working class	0	0	100

It is also probable that the change is gradual stylistically, in that speakers adopt the merger in some stylistic contexts, and that it later spreads to others. In Norwich, as we have seen, the distinction is preserved more or less intact. But Figure 2 (from Trudgill, 1974a) shows that, even here, some speakers use, on average, a smaller amount of phonetic distinction between the two lexical sets in more formal styles than in less formal styles.

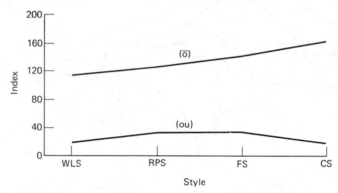

Figure 2. *moan* (ō) and *mown* (ou) in Norwich: Lower Middle Class speakers (200 = [uː]; 0 = [ʌu]; WLS = word list style; RPS = reading passage style; FS = formal speech; CS = casual speech)

Strategies for vowel mergers

If we accept that this merger is taking place in a way that is in some sense gradual, we can then ask: how exactly does this happen? Two possibilities suggest themselves. First, speakers could employ what we might perhaps call the strategy of *transfer*. They could variably, and one by one, transfer lexical items from one lexical set to another. That is, they could begin, on occasions, to pronounce words such as *road* as /rʌud/ rather than /ruud/, and gradually do this more and more often, and with more words.

Alternatively, speakers could employ a second tactic which we can call *approximation*. That is, they could gradually approximate the two vowels by bringing them closer together phonetically until, finally, they become identical. In the present case, this might involve the gradual lowering of the first element of the diphthong in words of the *go* type, and/or the raising and rounding of the first element of the diphthong in words of the *low* type (see Table 2).

Table 2: Transfer and Approximation

Transfer:	road	/ruud/ >	/rʌud/
Approximation: road		[ruud] >	[rəud]
rowed		[rʌud] >	[rəud]

Transfer

If we examine the evidence, we see that quite a lot of it suggests that speakers actually adopt the first strategy. They transfer words from one lexical set to another, with different words being affected at different times. This process involves, that is to say, a form of lexical diffusion.

Even in Norwich, which is in the centre of the geographical area which does not have the merger, at least one word has undergone this process. In the rural districts surrounding Norwich, the word *no* is pronounced /nuu/ by many older speakers, especially when it is said emphatically. Norwich speakers, however, consistently pronounce *no* as /nʌu/—except where it functions as an adverbial, in which case the /uu/ is retained. Thus we have:

/nʌu ðæs nuu gud/
No, that's no good.

We can also note that throughout Norfolk all items which had Middle English ō in the context ___/1/C as in *old*, *bolt*, *cold* now have /ʌu/ rather than /uu/. In some cases, that is, diffusion of the innovation may not be genuinely lexical but rather influenced by phonological conditioning. In other words, the change may also be *linguistically* gradual, in that it affects some environments before others (cf. Bickerton, 1975a; Bailey, 1973a). However, this change may well be of some antiquity (see Kurath, 1964) and cannot be relied upon as evidence here.

Table 3: Transfer

	toad	smoke	coal	oak	poker	own	grow
Grimston	ʉː	ʉ·	ǫu	ou	ou	uu	uu
Tuddenham	üː	üː	ʌu	ʌu	ʌu	ʌu	ʌu
Bentley	ɔu	ɔu	uu	ɔu	ʉu:	ɔu	ɔu
Tillingham	ʌu	ʌu	ʌu	ʌu	ʌu	ʌu	ʌu
(after the Survey of English Dialects)							

More convincing is the material provided by the Survey of English Dialects. Table 3 shows that, while Norfolk informants (Grimston—see Figure 1) have a clear contrast between the two lexical sets, and informants from southern Essex (Tillingham) have none, informants from geographically intermediate areas (Tuddenham and Bentley) have transferred some but not all of the /uu/ words to the /ʌu/ set.

Further illustrations of the strategy of transfer are provided by Milroy and Milroy (this volume) for Belfast. They show that items such as *pull* and *took* alternate between /ʌ/ and /ʉ/, and that the lexical set involved in this alternation has diminished since the nineteenth century, certain words having been stabilized in the /ʉ/ set.

Transfer and diffusion

The strategy of transfer is a phenomenon which is well-known to dialectologists. They observed early on that isoglosses for a particular phonological variant could be located at different points depending upon which lexical item was considered (see Bach, 1950). Thus, for example, the German /ɔks/—/ɔs/ *Ochs* 'ox' isogloss does not follow the same line as that for /zɛks/—/zɛs/ *sechs* 'six' or those for other similar items. Some dialects, that is, have transferred some lexical items but not others, and geographical differentiation of this type is simply the spatial reflection of lexical diffusion.

However, we also have to acknowledge that the probability is that speakers transfer items from one set to another spasmodically and irregularly. If this is so, then we can suppose that a dialect field-worker in Tuddenham or Bentley might, on some other occasion, have obtained examples of transfer in different or additional words. (This suggestion is supported by the occurrence, in the region currently under consideration, of the SED entries for Mendlesham, which has the word *toad* with both [ʌʊ] and [ü:].) This also suggests that the bundling of isoglosses such as those for German *Ochs* and *sechs* may in some cases be an artifact of traditional dialect methodology. A more accurate picture might be of a consistent [-ks-] area and a consistent [-s-] area divided by a zone of variability within which speakers alternate between one pronunciation and the other.

Examples of supposed lexical diffusion must also, for the same reason, be treated with caution. If one were, for example, to attempt to draw an isogloss across England for northern /æ/ as opposed to southern /ɑ:/ in items such as *after, past*, on the basis of SED material, then the location of this isogloss would depend very much on which word was examined. Lexical diffusion *may* be a factor here, but the variability may also simply be due to the pronunciation which the field-worker happened to elicit on the day. Indeed, observations of a relevant area of Lincolnshire[5] show that some speakers, at least, alternate between /æ/ and /ɑ:/ in items of this sort, just as New York City speakers (Labov, 1966) alternate between /r/ and zero in the set of *cart*, and Norwich speakers (Trudgill, 1974a) alternate between /ʉʉ/ and /uu/ in the set of *boot*.

In any case, it is clear that transfer, no less than approximation, can be a gradual process.

Approximation

We have also to note that there is some evidence to suggest that the strategy of phonetic *approximation* is also often adopted. First, there are a few transcriptions in the rural dialect records which *may* represent intermediate articulations. One example is the notation used for the *low, know, snow* set in the SED locality Kedington, which alternates between [ʌʊ] and [ǫʊ].

[5]Observations made by Trudgill and J. K. Chambers.

Perhaps more significant than this, however, are the more detailed recordings made in Norwich. Here, 13 of the 60 informants recorded in 1968 produced some variability in their realizations of these two vowels. (These informants constitute the 46 per cent of middle-class informants shown in Table 4.) One problem in dealing with realizations of this type is that the analyst is faced with what is in fact a phonetic continuum. The solution that was adopted in this case was to transcribe each instance as either definitely an example of East Anglian /ʌu/, definitely an example of East Anglian /ʊu/, or as something intermediate. Most often these intermediate vowels have as a first element a rounded vowel in the mid-central region resembling that of RP /əu/.

Table 4 shows exactly what happened in the case of this group of speakers. (The other speakers, it can be seen, have either the RP no-contrast system, or the consistent East Anglian system.) The variable speakers have *no* transfer of /ʌu/ items to the /ʊu/ class. There is minimal (1 per cent) transfer of /ʊu/ items to the /ʌu/ class. The major strategy is that of approximation: a minority—28 per cent—of /ʌu/ items have an intermediate vowel; and a majority of the /ʊu/ items (52 per cent) have an intermediate vowel.

Table 4: Vowel approximation in Norwich

		% vowels /ʌu/	*Intermediate*	/ʊu/
4% MC informants:	*low* class	0	100	0
	go class	0	100	0
46% MC informants:	*low* class	72	28	0
	go class	1	52	47
50% MC informants	*low* class	100	0	0
+100% WC informants:	*go* class	0	0	100

Merger and approximation

If we accept that approximation, as in the case of these middle-class Norwich informants, can take place, we have also to consider the possibility that 'intermediate' does not necessarily mean *merged*: vowels may approach each other without actually becoming identical. In fact, some recent work of Labov and his associates (Labov, 1975; Nunberg, 1975) deals with a number of cases where precisely this has taken place—where, during the course of linguistic change, distinct vowels have become phonetically closer without actually merging. However, the most interesting point to emerge from this work is that it seems that, if the approximation is close enough, speakers will themselves perceive the vowels as identical *even when they are not*. This at first somewhat startling discovery has important implications for historical linguistics (see Labov, 1975). It may, for instance, provide an explanation of how lexical sets such as those of *meat* and *mate*, in earlier forms of English, appear on the basis of all the available evidence to have merged and then, at a later stage, to have split again. The suggestion is that they may have actually never merged at all. What happened was perhaps simply that the approximation became so close that speakers perceived—and therefore reported—the vowels as being identical. Since, however, they were *not* actually identical, the lexical sets remained distinct and were therefore able, later on, to diverge again.

We do not as yet have any data of this type for East Anglia /uu/ and /ʌu/, but a case of exactly the same type is provided by the apparent merger in Norwich of the vowels of the sets of *beer* and *bear*. All except the very oldest of Norwich informants report that these two vowels are identical (see Trudgill, 1974a). Local dialect poetry also uses the two vowels as rhymes:

> Bor, ha' yew sin that marrer layin' by the pulpit stair?
> They reckon tha's the biggest we'a had in forta year!

and Ah, more'n once I'a stopped there jus' to hear
>   Their lovely songs what fill the evenin' air.

and The Plough, o'course, stood out right clear;
>   The Saven Sisters tew, were there;
>   I see the Hunter artra Hare,
>   An plenty more
>   Ole friends I'a know'd fer many a year,
>   An looked out for.

(Kett, 1975.)

However, as Table 5 shows, it is only younger informants who have genuinely identical pronunciations.

Table 5: /ɪə/ and /ɛə/ in Norwich

		beer	*bear*
Informant:	1 (age 92)	[bɪiə]	[bɛiə]
	2 (age 67)	[be·ə]	[bɛ·ə]
	3 (age 45)	[be̞:]	[bɛ:]
	4 (age 26)	[bɛ̞:]	[bɛ̞:]

There is also a further development which, on the face of it, is very surprising. This is that many, particularly teenage informants actually have vowels in the set of *beer* which are more open than those of *bear*. That is, the two vowels appear to have passed each other in phonetic space. (Figure 3, from Trudgill (1964a), also suggests the same development, but this is based on grouped and averaged index scores; 0 = [ɪə], 200 = [ɛ:].) It is not entirely clear how this development should be possible. It may be that, as in the cases reported by Labov, there are small phonetic differences between the two lexical sets which remain unnoticed not only by the native speakers who make them but also, in this case, by the analysing linguist. If this is so, then these differences (as the transcriptions given in Table 5 suggest) must involve features other than tongue-height, such as secondary articulations or articulatory setting (see also Knowles, this volume, on the inadequacy of some phonetic transcriptions for sociolinguistic work). Alternatively, it might be that speakers have been able to keep these vowels phonologically or psychologically distinct through 'knowledge' of pronunciations used by older speakers in the speech community or through stylistic alternations. Whatever

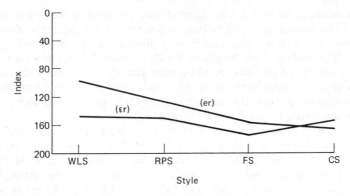

Figure 3. *beer* (er) and *bear* (ɛr) in Norwich: Upper Working Class speakers

the explanation, it is clear that approximation may be a complex kind of process, and that reports of mergers should be treated with caution.

Explanations

In the case of East Anglia /ʌu/ and /uu/ we appear to have established that the two merger strategies—transfer and approximation—can both be adopted. In the northern part of East Anglia we find *approximation*, centering around an RP-like vowel [əu]. This results, in the case of some middle-class Norwich informants and some rural Suffolk speakers, in an indeterminate situation which, as we have just noted, must be treated with caution. The urban speech of Ipswich, however, appears (see Table 6) to have achieved a more advanced, more stabilized situation than that of the more northerly city of Norwich. In Ipswich, an intermediate [əu]-type vowel is consistent in all items, except that phonological conditioning has led to [ʌu] occurring as an allophonic variant before /l/. The process of merger through approximation is here, that is, genuinely complete, suggesting that this is also a possible future development for Norwich.

In the southern part of East Anglia, on the other hand, items from the original /uu/ class are *transferred* to the /ʌu/ class, in some cases leaving behind a number of relic forms with /uu/. This gives /ʌu/ in most of the rural Essex dialects and in the urban dialect of Colchester.

Two final questions therefore remain to be answered. First: why, under

Table 6: Working class informants, 1975 survey

	road	*rowed*	*roll*
Norwich	[uu] = /uu/	[ʌu] = /ʌu/	[ʌu] = /ʌu/
Lowestoft	[əu] = /uu/	[ʌu] = /ʌu/	[ʌu] = /ʌu/
Ipswich	[əu] = /ou/	[əu] = /ou/	[ʌu] = /ou/
Colchester	[ʌu] = /ou/	[ʌu] = /ou/	[ʌu] = /ou/

approximation, is the vowel /uu/ affected much more than the vowel /ʌu/ (see Table 4)? The answer may well be that, in southern England, the vowel [uu] is *conspicuous* in that it is phonetically very different from the vowels used by other speakers outside East Anglia in words of this set. The contrast between Norwich *boat* [buu²] and advanced London [bæʉ²] is very marked and often noted by speakers from both areas. Attention, conscious or subconscious, is therefore directed more to this lexical set than to the other. (Norwich /ʌu/ is of course much closer to the London form.)

Secondly: why do some speakers adopt the strategy of transfer, and others approximation? One clue is provided by the fact that it is *middle*-class speakers from the *north* of the region who use approximation, and *working*-class speakers from the *south* who use transfer. This suggests rather strongly that the difference is the result of different targets. Speakers in the north of East Anglia are not directly exposed to or influenced by London speech a great deal, but middle-class speakers in this area *are* influenced by the prestige accent RP—which happens to use a vowel intermediate between the two East Anglian vowels. Speakers in the southern area, on the other hand, are exposed, through geographical proximity, to London speech, which in its less advanced forms has a vowel very like the /ʌu/ already found in East Anglia. Hence the strategy of transfer. This hypothesis is strengthened by data from King's Lynn. This town is on the periphery of linguistic East Anglia and also, crucially, has a large London overspill population. Table 7 shows that some speakers here adopt one strategy and some the other. Some speakers, we can assume, are taking RP as their model, while others are responding to the London model which, because of the overspill policy, they are also directly exposed to.

Table 7: King's Lynn

Informant:		1	2	3	4	5
nose		[uu]	[ɵu]	[ɵu]	[uu]	[ʌu]
knows		[ʌu]	[ɵu]	[ʌu]	[ɵu]	[ʌu]

The suggestion is, then, that although the consequences of transfer and approximation may be phonological, the initial impetus, and the choice between the two strategies, may well often be phonetic in origin. What is involved, initially, is simply the imitation of particular pronunciations in individual words. Imitation, however, is not a helpful explanation for what takes place where mergers are not the result of external influence. What, for example, occurred in the first variety of English to merge the vowels of *go* and *low*? The Norwich merger of *beer* and *bear* (see Table 5) cannot be ascribed to any external influence and, like similar developments described by Labov *et al.* (1972), is clearly taking place through approximation. It may be, then, that transfer takes place only where influence from external varieties is involved.

But even the merger of *beer* and *bear* raises a further difficulty. Why does the approximation that is occurring in this case involve principally the lowering of the vowel of *beer* rather than the raising of that in *bear*? Labov's work suggests that there may be wide-spread or even universal tendencies of sound change, possibly articulatory or acoustic in origin, at work in developments of this kind. One of the strongest of his findings, however, is that tense vowels tend to become closer, lax vowels more open—which does not fit the present case. There may, alternatively, be explanations concerned with phonological space, phonological patterning, or articulatory setting. However, we have to concede that, in our present state of knowledge, when it comes to establishing exactly what factors are involved in changes of this type, we remain rather ignorant. (Or, as they may continue to say in parts of East Anglia for some time yet, we simply /dʊunt nʌu/.)

6

The Nature of Phonological Variables in Scouse

Gerry Knowles

1 Introduction

Scouse is the dialect which developed in Liverpool in the nineteenth century, and has since spread to the surrounding districts of Lancashire and Cheshire. Until the middle of the last century, Liverpool drew its population from the counties of the Northwest of England; but after the potato famines of the 1840s, hundreds of thousands of Irishmen passed through the port, and many of them settled there. At the time of the 1861 census, 25 per cent of the city population were Irish immigrants. The resulting dialect is an interesting hybrid: on the phonological level, it remains similar to the dialects of neighbouring Northern towns, but phonetically it has been heavily influenced by Anglo-Irish. In the present century, Scouse has taken part in general developments in British English, and has been extensively standardized in phonology, grammar and vocabulary.

As a result of standardization, Scouse has a number of phonological variables which are not restricted to Liverpool, and most of which are widespread over the North of England. For instance, word-pairs such as *mud/good*; *pass/gas*; *scarce/curse*; *book/Luke* and *singer/finger* make perfect traditional rhymes, but the first member of each pair is subject to modification in middle class speech, under the influence of the standard forms. Such variables are—superficially at least—easy to identify and analyse. However, an analysis which concentrated on this kind of variable alone would systematically miss the Anglo-Irish influence, the 'Scouse element', which so sharply marks Liverpool speech off from the rest of the Northwest. It is important to note that the sort of Liverpool speaker who had *mud*/mʌd/ and *pass* /pɑːs/ is also almost certain to exhibit a number of phonetic features which are less easily identifiable, but which give a general impression of a 'middle-class voice'. Such a person will consequently sound less 'Scouse' and less 'Irish' than one who has *mud*/mʊd/ and *pass*/pas/. It would therefore be naive to single out the vowels [ʌ ~ ʊ] and [a ~ ɑː], extract from them vowel height, length, degree of retraction and rounding, and to assume that this alone is what conveys sociolinguistic information and reflects social stratification. What we have to do is to find some way of identifying the many and elusive continuous variables and low level rules which affect a person's speech as a whole, and mark his social status.

Sociolinguistics has grown out of general linguistics, and as a result, the sort of variables we naturally look for are those involving linguistic units. I would suggest, however, that we should be looking for sociolinguistic information direct, whether linguistic units are involved or not. To do this will call for a special kind of phonetic theory. Phoneticians have, for good reason, concentrated on linguistic phonetics, and set up a number of categories which are used to bring about phonological contrasts in the languages of the world. There is no reason to suppose *a priori* that these are also the categories which convey sociolinguistic information: indeed, it would be surprising if it were so. There are a number of popular labels—'back-street twang', 'talking far back', 'sing-song', 'talking down your nose' etc.—which refer to sociolinguistic information which is not at present amenable to analysis. In this paper, I shall show how the familiar kinds of variable are not always as simple as they at first appear, and that this initial simplicity results from inadequate phonetic techniques; I shall also suggest ways of tackling more subtle kinds of information in intonation and articulatory setting, which are essential for a full understanding of sociolinguistic variation.

2 Variation and Transcription

Phonetic transcription is so familiar in any linguistic work that it is easy to overlook how complex a process it is. It does not simply convert sounds into symbols: it extracts information. In a phonemic transcription, we extract linguistic information, and we cannot do this without first establishing the phonemic system. Similarly, if we wish to study variables, we have first to find out how the sociolinguistic information is conveyed, and then extract it. An impressionistic transcription may be a necessary first stage, but it is essentially a hit-and-miss affair, and must be replaced as soon as possible by some kind of systematic transcription.

The shortcomings of impressionistic transcription can be illustrated in the astonishing virtuosity sometimes found in dialect surveys, giving details far beyond what any phonetician could give with any confidence, accuracy or consistency. Even so, the detail still does not suggest the original form, unless one happens to be familiar with the dialect in question. One has to imagine a 'Yorkshire voice' in order to read a transcription of Yorkshire dialect, or a 'Texas voice' to read a Texan transcription, and so on. The fieldworker will certainly be responding to sociolinguistic information, but he has no way of representing it, and leaves the reader to reconstruct it for himself.

In a systematic transcription, what we need to mark will not necessarily be 'states' of the traditional kind. For linguistic purposes, it is a convenient and useful fiction to treat utterances as sequences of phonetic 'states', because at some level sentences really are linear sequences of vowels and consonants. In the case of sociolinguistic rules, on the other hand, 'states' will sometimes only confuse matters. Take for example the realization of Scouse /t/. As for other Scouse stops, complete closure for /t/ is obligatory only in certain environments, such as initially in a word or stressed syllable, or next to another homorganic closure; in such cases the release of the closure may be very slow, thus *ten* [t^ɛn], *want* [wʊnt^s]. In other cases the control mechanism is more like that for a tap than a plosive, and it is immaterial whether contact is made or not, thus *water* [wɔː^ɛ], *cat* [ka^s]. If we try to transcribe /t/, it seems to vary from 'stop' to 'affricate' to 'fricative'. However, it is quite arbitrary at what point the burst of noise following the release is considered long enough to be called 'affrication'. Secondly, a tapped fricative sounds like a 'stop' or a 'fricative' according to whether the listener responds to the consonant itself or to the duration of preceding segments; it can be heard as both at the same time, or even mistaken for an 'affricate'.

This last point illustrates a further problem, namely that the listener may well identify segments from information in the environment. In the phonemic analysis of *send* for instance, we might identify the final consonant as 'voiced' on account of the duration of the nasal, even though /d/ itself may be devoiced. Consider now the problem of /ð/, for which Scouse has the Anglo-Irish dental stop in addition to the standard fricative. In a word like *breathe*, we will hear much sociolinguistic information long before we get to /ð/: if that information is 'middle class', it is difficult to hear /ð/ as anything but the standard fricative, and if it is 'Scouse', then /ð/ is almost bound to sound like the Anglo-Irish stop.

Suppose we were unaware of the difficulties, and went ahead with an impressionistic transcription. No matter how poor and inaccurate it might be, we could not very well avoid finding a greater frequency of 'affricated' and 'fricative' /t/ in working-class than in middle-class speech, and a corresponding high frequency of the Anglo-Irish /ð/. A statistical analysis would then apparently give the authority of mathematical precision to our method. In fact the statistics would not be valid, because until we have identified the variables properly, we have no computible units on which to base our calculations.

3 Variation and Scales

Naivety in transcription can lead to naivety in interpreting variables. If we try to identify a variable by examining an impressionistic transcription, then quite naturally it appears as a set of competing phonetic states as represented by the symbols: for any variable, the speaker has to make a choice from several variants. These variants can sometimes be plotted on a linear scale, following Labov (1966); they can then be given code numbers, and the variation analysed statistically.

Let us start instead with the speaker himself. We can assume he has a message consisting of a string of vowels and consonants, and a number of speech production rules which convert the string into a continuously varying acoustic signal. Both what he puts in the string and his production rules are subject to social pressures, and he will vary them accordingly. Any variation can have a number of different phonetic results, depending on where it takes place in relation to the rules. For example, in *sure*, a speaker may decide not to carry out the rule changing /uə/ to /ɔː/; what he actually says then depends on the rules he chooses for the production of /u/ and /ə/. The variation is multi-dimensional, and the notion of a linear scale inappropriate. Some variables look at first as though they can be effectively handled by the linear scale model; closer examination proves that they have to be dealt with by variable rules of speech production.

3.1 (ʌ)

The simplest example is probably (ʌ). In Liverpool, as in other Northern towns, *mud* rhymes with *good* in popular speech, but varies to [mʌd] in educated middle-class usage under the influence of the standard form. There are a number of intermediate forms that can be transcribed collectively with shwa. Thus, (ʌ) seems to vary on a very simple scale:

$$(ʌ - 1): [ʊ] \qquad (ʌ - 2): [ə] \qquad (ʌ - 3): [ʌ]$$

Higher scores for this variable will be found in middle-class than in working-class speech, and in formal than in informal style.

However, there are problems with [ə,ʌ]. For most vowels it is possible to find some kind of norm or 'target quality', especially if they exist as words in isolation, e.g. /u/ 'who', /ɪ/ 'it', /ɔː/ 'or'. Intrinsic allophones, varying in duration and quality, can be explained by reference to the phonetic environment. Forms of [ə,ʌ], on the other hand, vary in height, retraction and rounding, but not according to any definable rules, and without any apparent target. Secondly, it is not clear at what point [ʊ] becomes [ə], or [ə] becomes [ʌ]. The borderlines are arbitrary, and probably depend on the ear and the sociolinguistic background of the hearer. Suppose a Liverpudlian makes the vowel of *mud* very slightly more open and less rounded than the vowel of *good*. This minute difference might be enough for another Liverpudlian to realize that he is 'speaking nicely' and using [ə]; a Southerner is likely to hear this vowel as the Northern [ʊ].

These problems only arise, however, if we present the variable on a linear scale. What is happening, surely, is that speakers know to modify their [ʊ] without being quite sure what to modify it to. At some arbitrary degree of modification, a sufficient phonetic difference is made for the listener to mark it in his transcription.

3.2 (ɑː)

A word like *aunt* has the vowel [a] in Scouse, making it like *ant*; RP has [ɑː], making it like *aren't*. A few middle-class speakers adopt the RP vowel, but more commonly a compromise is found, intermediate in quality or duration between [a] and [ɑː]. We can represent the compromise forms *ad hoc* with the symbol [A]. The variants of (ɑː) seem to lie on a linear scale:

$$(ɑː–1): [a] \qquad (ɑː–2): [A] \qquad (ɑː–3): [ɑː]$$

Higher scores will again be found in middle-class speech and in more formal styles.

However, this variable cannot be taken in isolation, because [a] does not occur at all in RP. Where [a] does not correspond to RP [ɑ:], it corresponds to RP [æ]. In other words, Scouse [a] is always subject to modification. There are two rules involved:

Rule A: a → æ   as in *bad* [bæd], *jam* [dʒæm]
Rule B: a → ɑ: as in *fast* [fAst, fɑ:st], *dance* [dAns, dɑ:ns]

There is considerable resistance to rule B, and occasionally rule A will be applied instead, giving the hypercorrect [fæst, dæns]. If we are using a scale rather than a rule, this [æ] has to be plotted before (ɑ: − 1). Thus:

$$(ɑ: − 0) : [æ]$$

Unfortunately the linear scale puts the variants in the wrong order for computing variable scores. Although (ɑ: − 0) is essentially a middle-class feature, its use would lower the score instead of raising it.

3.3 (ɛə)

In Liverpool and neighbouring parts of the Northwest, no distinction is made in popular speech between /ɛə/ and /ɜ: /, so that *fair* sounds exactly like *fur*. Some middle-class speakers adopt the RP vowel where appropriate, but more commonly a compromise is found in [ɛ:], without the centring off-glide. Once again, this looks like a linear scale of variants:

(ɛə − 1) : [ɜ:]   (ɛə − 2) : [ɛ:]   (ɛə − 3) : [ɛə]

But again, the choice is not among states or forms, but whether or not to apply a modification rule. If the speaker does not apply it, he still has to choose rules to produce the central monophthong: (a) rounded, (b) fronted, or (c) plain; if he chooses the fronted type, this can in turn vary from a closer to a more open variety. If we force this variation into a scale analysis, the points on the scale turn out to be themselves scales on the next level. Thus:

(ɛə − 1) : (a) [ɵ:]   (ɛə − 2) : [ɛ:]   (ɛə − 3) : [ɛə]
(b) (i) [ë:], (ii)[ɛ̈:]
(c) [ɜ:]

The characteristic Scouse vowels are [ë, ɛ̈], the latter being the more conservative. Together they seem to be replacing the traditional and widespread Northwestern vowel [ɵ:]. Middle-class people who retain (ɛə − 1) tend to use the plain RP-type [ɜ:], and this shades off with slight rounding into [ɵ:], and with slight fronting into [ë:].

3.4 (uə) and (oə)

As in urban speech in England generally, the phonemic merger of /oə/ and /ɔ:/ is being closely followed by the merger of /uə/ and /ɔ:/. Very, very roughly indeed, the time-scale in Liverpool is something like this:

	born before 1918	*born 1919–1938*	*born since 1938*
sure	ʃuə	ʃuə	ʃɔ:
shore	ʃoə	ʃɔ:	ʃɔ:
Shaw	ʃɔ:	ʃɔ:	ʃɔ:

To pronounce these words, the speaker has first to choose whether to carry out the merger or not, or even to find a compromise vowel. He then has the choice of several ordered but optional low-level rules, which operate not just for these vowels, but more generally in Scouse phonology:

		uə	oə
1	lax [u,o] before an unstressed vowel:	ʊə	ɔə
	or		
2.	(a) diphthongize [u,o]:	ɪúə,íuə	óuə
	or		
	(b) front [u]:	ʉə	
3	modify VVV to V + glide + V:	ɪwə	owə
4	front final [ə]:	uɛ, ?uɛ	oɛ, ?ɔɛ
		ɪúɛ, íuɛ	óuɛ
		ʉɛ, ɪwɛ	owɛ

These rules generate a large number of very slightly differing forms, which it would be quite pointless to attempt to plot on a linear scale. Only the first rule, incidentally, is at all prestigious, and the others operate mainly in working class speech.

3.5 (ng)

In Liverpool, and in other parts of the Northwest as far south as Birmingham, and as far east as Sheffield, [ŋ] is for many speakers an allophone of /n/ occurring before /g,k/. Phonetic [g] is deleted in the middle of consonant clusters, as in *rings* [rɪŋz] or *banged* [baŋd], but it is pronounced word-finally, as in *song* [sɒŋg], *thing* [əɪŋg], and before a vowel, e.g. *singer* [sɪŋgə], *banging* [baŋgən]. This looks like the simplest of all possible variables, with the presence or absence of [g]:

$$(ng - 1): [ŋg] \qquad (ng - 2): [ŋ]$$

However, a final oral stop can arise in Scouse from other sources than phonological /g/, and g-deletion can be carried out at more than one level. The linear scale would here actually obscure the observable variation.

To being with, g-deletion can occur on the phonological level, giving for *sing* the choice of two representations, /sɪŋg/ or /sɪŋ/. A number of low-level rules now operate.

Rule A: a final voiced consonant lengthens the preceding segment, producing [sɪŋ:g] or [sɪ:ŋ].

Rule B: final [g] can be deleted, as it is redundant after lengthened [ŋ:].

Rule C: the release of a final nasal is made audible, and sounds like a weak homorganic stop. There are thus four forms of (ng):

	sing	sɪŋg	sɪŋ
Rule A:	sɪŋ:g	sɪ:ŋ
Rule B:	sɪŋ:	
Rule C:		sɪ:ŋᵍ

A fifth form [sɪŋ:ᵍ] is theoretically possible, if rule C is applied to the output of rule B; but in practice this would be indistinguishable from [sɪŋ:g] resulting from rule A. Of these rules, only C is specifically Scouse, producing stigmatized forms; a stop which realizes phonological /g/ is quite prestigious locally, and is even used by middle-class women.

4 Hypercorrection

Hypercorrection gives an interesting insight into the nature of variables. A linear scale can perhaps indicate the results of hypercorrection, but only modification rules of the kind suggested for (ʌ), (ɑ:) and (ɛə) can explain why it should arise in the first place.

An informal study of my own slips of the tongue suggests that there are two quite different kinds of hypercorrection. The first is simple lexical confusion. I known in general how RP speakers pronounce words, which have /ʊ/ and which /ʌ/, which have /æ/ and which /ɑ:/, and so on. There are just a few words like *putty* and *nasty* which baffle me; I cannot recall whether RP has /pʊtɪ/ or /pʌtɪ/, /næstɪ/ or /nɑːstɪ/, and I have to look them up in a pronouncing dictionary. Where the speaker is confused in this way, he is likely to carry out the modification rule in words where it should not apply. Perhaps the commonest hypercorrections thus produced are *butcher* /bʌtʃə/ and *bush* /bʌʃ/; others include *passage* /pɑːsɪdʒ/ and *curse* /kɛəs/.

The other kind of hypercorrection occurs when a sensitive vowel occurs twice in a tone-unit, producing e.g. *cup-hook* /kʊphʌk/, *gas-mask* /gɑːsmæsk/ and *chairperson* /tʃɜːpɛəsən/. The person who says /kʊphʌk/ is sufficiently concerned about his speech to aim at the standard pronunciation: if he is selecting variants from a linear scale, it is remarkably perverse of him to select (ʌ − 3) in *hook* where it is inappropriate, and choose the non-prestigious (ʌ − 1) for *cup*! A more convincing hypothesis is that the second sensitive vowel interferes with the operation of the modification rule, so that the wrong vowel sometimes gets modified, leaving the appropriate one unmodified. Here are some more extended examples, which I have unintentionally produced myself:

> I've *pulled* /pʌld/ a *button*/bʊtn/ off my jacket.
> *Good luck*! /gʌd lʊk/
> a *book* /bʌk/ being *pu*(blished) /pʊ . . ./
> and the wolf *ran* /rɑːn/ after /æftə/ it.
> the *black* /blɑːk/ *castle* /kæsl/

Now I know perfectly well how RP speakers pronounce these words, and I would get them right in isolation. So these are not cases of lexical confusion. In each case, the first occurrence of the sensitive vowel attracts the modification rule, even though it is the wrong vowel.

The hypercorrection seems to occur within the tone-unit, as in this example:
It's`'not a *jug* /dʒʌg/, but it's as`'*good* /gʌd/ as a *jug* /dʒug/.
I know how *jug* is pronounced in RP, and accordingly modified my /dʒug/ to
/dʒʌg/ in the first tone-unit; in the second tone-unit *good* incorrectly attracted
the rule, and changed to /gʌd/, leaving *jug* unmodified as /dʒug/.

5 Intonation

If linear scales are insufficient to deal with segmental variables, they are of
even less use for suprasegmental features, such as in intonation. It is certain
that variation exists—e.g. Yorkshire intonation differs from RP—but it is
very difficult to pin it down precisely. Nor can we rely on superficial phonetic
features, for after all, pitch can only rise, fall or stay where it is; and rises, falls
and level tones are found in all varieties of English. To deal with variables in
intonation we have first to identify the rules for intonation, and then trace
variables to differences in the rules among varieties.

Scouse and RP at first look very different. The tonetic stress marks
developed by Kingdon (1958) for RP do not fit Scouse properly, simple rises
and falls are scarce, and there are half a dozen distinct tones, all of which are
different types of rise-fall. There are also several distinct fall-rises, and pre-
nuclear tones do not correspond to anything in R.P. However, if we formulate
our rules correctly, these differences are extremely unlikely to prove anything
but superficial.

One important difference is in the way segments fit the pitch contour of a
tone. Now what we call a 'tone' is strictly the pitch movement that follows the
peak of the vowel of the stressed syllable. It so happens in RP that there is no
significant difference in pitch between the beginning of the syllable and the
peak; for this reason the handbooks rarely mention pitch levels before the
peak. In Scouse, on the other hand, there is a significant difference. At the
beginning of an accented syllable, the pitch moves away from its previous
level, and then changes direction at the peak. In other words, a fall is regularly
preceded by a preliminary rise, and a rise by a preliminary fall. Once we
identify the rule, Scouse begins to look a little more related to RP.

A less superficial difference is found in the features employed to distinguish
tones. RP has a two-way distinction of simple and complex tones, that is
between *fall* and *rise-fall*, and between *rise* and *fall-rise*. Scouse has a three-
way distinction of simple, intermediate and complex. The intermediate type
differ from the simple tones in that instead of gliding smoothly up or down
they skip suddenly from one pitch level to another; thus ˙· contrasts with
˙˙˙·.. and .·˙ with ...·˙˙˙. They differ from the complex tones in that they do
not change pitch direction; thus ˙˙˙·... contrasts with ˙·.·˙ and ...·˙˙˙ with
.·˙·.. Phonetically, the intermediate tones are liable to confusion with the
contrasting simple tones, but phonologically they function more like the
contrasting complex tones. A feature of middle-class speech is that the
distinction between intermediate and complex is lost, and the complex tones
replace the intermediate.

Given the intermediate type, we might conclude simply that Scouse has a richer inventory of tones than RP. Alternatively, we can take the analysis further by investigating the rules for the use of tones. Consider the tones used for yes/no questions, and in particular the question *Are you from Liverpool?* According to the handbooks, such as O'Connor and Arnold (1973), the normal RP tone will be a rise, in this case on the word *Liverpool*. Scouse, on the other hand, will have an intermediate tone skipping down from high to low pitch. In more detail, the pitch makes a preliminary rise through /l/ and reaches high pitch on the accented vowel /ɪ/; this high pitch is maintained through the second syllable /və/, and then it suddenly skips down to a low pitch on /puːl/. Superficially, the Scouse and RP tones are completely unconnected.

However, despite the handbooks, it is actually rather common in English to ask a yes/no question with a fall-rise, and this is the link between the Scouse and RP tones:

(i) RP: .·   (ii) 'common': ·.·   (iii) Scouse: ·· ·. . .

What we have called the 'common' tone looks more basic than the others, and could be the source from which they derive: RP has suppressed the initial fall, whereas Scouse has suppressed the final rise. Both suppression rules are sociolinguistically significant. As already mentioned, middle-class Liverpudlians are likely to use the whole complex fall-rise rather than the intermediate type skip-down. In the wider context of English as a whole, the RP simple rise is possibly archaic, as the suppression rule has been dropped. The simple rise is certainly used in linguistically conservative parts of the country, such as in Lancashire and Yorkshire; possibly elsewhere there is a change between generations, older people using the rise, and younger people the fall-rise.

Other apparently alien features of Scouse intonation can be shown to be closely related to English intonation as a whole. What is emerging from a study of Scouse intonation—early stages of which were reported in Knowles (1974)—is a set of ordered rules for the use of tones in English; late rules modify tones slightly and determine details of their realization. Sociolinguistic variation seems to be confined to these later rules.

6 Articulatory Setting

Important as variables in segments and intonation may be, we have yet to tackle what is possibly the most important source of all for sociolinguistic information. This is the 'Scouse voice', the total undifferentiated characteristic sound of a Liverpudlian. Articulations are usually described with reference to the minimum number of organs which are necessarily involved. When describing /b/ for instance, we refer to the lips, the velum and the vocal folds; but we do not specify the width of the pharynx, the position of the hyoid bone or the height of the mandible. Much of this secondary activity facilitates the primary articulation—e.g. the efficient voicing of stops depends on a sufficiently low supra-glottal air-pressure, which in turn depends on the state of the pharynx—but it is also sociolinguistically determined. For any dialect, the organs of the vocal tract have certain preferred positions, which may differ from those they have in the physiological state of rest. The movements away from and back into the preferred positions gives a variety of speech its characteristic 'colour'. The preferred shape of the vocal tract is known as the *articulatory setting*. Settings are in fact a very old idea—see e.g. John Milton's *Of Education* (1644)—which has become respectable again following Honikman's article (1964), and the work of Laver (1968). They are described by traditional dialectologists, e.g. Holmer (1942), as well as by some sociolinguists, such as Trudgill (1974a).

The Scouse setting has been described in detail elsewhere (Knowles, 1974). Of most interest here are the setting of the velo-pharyngeal mechanism, and the setting of the jaw. The velo-pharyngeal mechanism involves a group of organs acting together as a unit, for example in deglutition. In Scouse, the centre of gravity of the tongue is brought backwards and upwards, the pillars of the fauces are narrowed, the pharynx is tightened, and the larynx is displaced upwards. The lower jaw is typically held close to the upper jaw, and this position is maintained even for 'open' vowels. The main auditory effect of this setting is the 'adenoidal' quality of Scouse, which is produced even if the speaker's nasal passages are unobstructed.

The setting of the tongue effectively velarizes all consonants. This is most noticeable in voiceless apical consonants like /t,s,θ/, but certainly affects the quality of others, including /m,v,dʒ/. Velarized /r/ sounds rather like a simultaneously apical and uvular approximant. Scouse /l/ does not vary from 'clear' to 'dark' as in RP, but is velarized in all positions; consequently it sounds 'dark' where RP has the 'clear' allophone, and perversely 'clear' where RP has its 'dark' or pharyngealized /l/.

The effect of the jaw setting is that the tongue has to move in a restricted space; being at the same time pulled to the back it loses much of its natural mobility. Tongue-tip consonants are made instead with the blade; for /r/, the tip is not curled back, but just slightly raised, and in this position it often strikes the roof of the mouth in passing. Scouse /r/ is often perceived as a 'tap' or a 'flap'.

Vowels—other than back ones—are incompatible with the setting, at least as vowel production is usually understood. Vowel quality depends not so much on a particular articulatory position, as on the auditory correlates of the lower formants. Corresponding vowels in Scouse and RP are recognizably similar in quality, but whether they are produced with anything like the same tongue shapes is an open question. Tongue shape must be affected when an 'open' vowel is produced with a close jaw, or a 'rounded' vowel with spread lips.

An interesting question with regard to settings is exactly what it means to exaggerate the setting, and 'put on' a particularly 'thick' accent. To some extent, the features of the setting are gradable; the degree of velarization can be increased or diminished, the jaw can be more or less close, and so on. More interesting is what happens when the setting conflicts with the requirements of the phonology. To produce an [s] for instance, the tongue has to be grooved to direct a narrow jet of air against the cutting edge of the upper front teeth; the setting prefers a velarized laminal articulation. The tongue is sufficiently flexible to combine efficiently any two of these three demands, and the other is overridden. In most cases the grooving has priority, and either the velarization pulls the blade back leaving the tip to make the articulation, or else the velarization is weakened. In a 'thick' accent the setting might be given priority, reducing the efficiency of the grooving, and allowing the air to escape more diffusely, thus making [s] more like [ʃ].

Although the setting is the most important component of the 'Scouse voice', there are others which we can only mention here. One involves the integration of phonology and setting with facial gesture, which sometimes modifies lip-rounding to labio-dental approximation. Another concerns the switch from speech breathing back to physiological breathing at the end of an utterance, which produces in Scouse such phonetic exotica as aspirated fricatives, as in *bush* [buʃh]. A third component is the degree of overlap between segments, or more interestingly, the lack of overlap, which gives rise to such pronunciations as *shrink* [ʃərɪŋk].

7 Conclusion

The conclusions to be drawn from the above examples and discussion depend on the relative importance one attaches to the two sides of sociolinguistics. If one is more concerned with the social side, with the effect on speech of the social situation and the standing of the speakers, then the distortion of the data inherent in Labov's 1966 model is possibly acceptable. Even if we transcribe /t/ inaccurately, and our interpretation of (ʌ) is misconceived, the results we get concerning the social distribution of the variables may not be too far wrong. The problem is that we may have anticipated the results in the way we transcribe and interpret the variables.

If, on the other hand, we are more concerned with the linguistic side, with the phonetics and phonology of variation, or if we wish to describe stratification in a dialect, then Labov's 1966 model is at best inadequate, and at worst misleading. If we were to force the variables discussed above in 3.1–3.5 into linear scales, and then restricted our description of Scouse to a detailed analysis of this small set, we would give a completely false idea of the dialect.

What we need to study variables properly is a theory of sociolinguistic phonetics. Several models of linguistic phonetics have been proposed over recent years (Jakobson and Halle, 1956; Chomsky and Halle, 1968; Ladefoged, 1971) to account for the possibilities of phonological contrast. Sociolinguistic phonetics, on the other hand, is concerned with the options open to the speaker at different stages in speech production, and the way these options can be used to convey sociolinguistic information about the speaker. A theory of sociolinguistic phonetics will also clarify the status of the several different kinds of rule we have described informally here in our discussion of variables in Scouse.

7

Secondary Contractions in West Yorkshire Negatives

K. M. Petyt

The following is a discussion of one feature of the non-standard English of the industrial towns of West Yorkshire, and is largely based on data collected in Bradford, Halifax and Huddersfield.

The lexical set with which we shall be concerned is detailed below: briefly, it is the contracted forms of the negatived copula, auxiliaries and modals. Forms like *wasn't, hadn't, can't* etc. are of course quite common in Standard English; in most cases a contracted form of *not* [nt] has been added to the preceding verb form, e.g. [ɪznt, hævnt] etc. The few exceptions are mostly where the final consonant of the verb has been dropped (perhaps, in some cases, for phonotactic reasons), and the vowel has changed, usually in both length and quality e.g. [ʃæl nɒt]→[ʃɑ:nt], [kæn nɒt]→[kɑ:nt], [wɪl nɒt]→[wɑʊnt], and sometimes [æm nɒt]→[ɑ:nt]. (When used in declarative sentences, e.g. [aɪ ɑ:nt du:ɪŋ ɪt], this form, though not uncommon among working-class speakers in the area, is frequently castigated as substandard, [aɪm nɒt] being regarded as 'correct'; but in interrogatives [ɑ:nt aɪ] is more commonly accepted, probably because [æm aɪ nɒt] seems over-formal). In [du: nɒt]→[dəʊnt] the vowel change is only in quality, and there is of course no loss of consonant.[1]

Though there is surprisingly little trace of such forms in the traditional dialect accounts of the area, in West Yorkshire today non-standard forms produced by a further contraction are common. For the description of this phenomenon it is useful to divide the contracted forms of Standard English into two groups, since (a) these differ in terms of the phonological shape of both the standard and the non-standard forms; (b) while one of these groups is subject to secondary contraction over a wide area of Britain, according to my own informal observations, the other is contracted only in a much smaller region, including West Yorkshire.

1   The first group has the phonological shape /XVCnt/ (where X = C or Ø), and contains the following:

---

[1] [du:nt] would of course be odd phonologically, since /u:nt/ does not occur in English. *Won't* is probably to be explained partly in terms of ME *wol*, an alternative to *wil*, and *don't* may be modelled on this. For further discussion cf. Strang (1970, p. 151).

isn't	doesn't	mustn't
wasn't	didn't	needn't
haven't	couldn't	mightn't
hasn't	wouldn't	oughtn't
hadn't	shouldn't	(usedn't)

The form *usedn't* is bracketed here because observations suggest that it is relatively uncommon in colloquial English today; certainly it is very rarely heard in the area I am concerned with. A form such as 'I didn't use to do that' is much more likely than 'I usedn't to do that'; the former is subject to secondary contraction (affecting *didn't*), the latter, being much more formal, is not.

The form *oughtn't* is sometimes similarly replaced by *didn't ought*, but my observations suggest that this is not so commonly the case: I have noticed many instances of *oughtn't* in the colloquial speech of the area, and this form *is* subject to secondary contraction (as also is *didn't* in *didn't ought*).

2   The second group has the phonological shape /XV̄nt/ (where X = C or Ø), and contains:

aren't	won't	daren't
weren't	shan't	(mayn't)
don't	can't	

The form *mayn't* is bracketed because observations suggest that in the 'permission' sense it is hardly ever heard in the area (even in uncontracted form), *can't* being used instead; in the 'possibility' sense it sometimes occurs in tags e.g. 'it may be so, mayn't it?', in which cases it is probably never contracted. There is evidence that *mayn't* is becoming uncommon in English generally: Palmer (1974, p. 21) says simply 'There is no negative form *mayn't*. We have only *may not*'; and Quirk and Greenbaum (1973, p. 37) say that '*mayn't* is restricted to British English, where it is rare.'

The secondary contraction follows the same basic pattern in both groups: the first member of the final consonant group is dropped. This could be expressed in terms of the following rule:

$$C \to \emptyset / V \_\_ C_1^2$$

where the deleted C may be /n/. (The symbolization C_1^2 indicates that there may be (at most) two or (at least) one consonant following that which is deleted in this secondary contraction.)

This is an example of a variable rule, and applies with different frequency according to a number of linguistic, social, and geographical factors, as we shall see later. It is however not a genuinely phonological rule in that it is lexically restricted to the items specified here (cf. (ii) below).

Because the phonological shapes of the two groups differ, so also do the effects of this rule:

(i)   in the first group it is the final consonant of the verb which is deleted. Thus: /XVCnt/ → /XVnt/

Note that there is no change in the vowel; this is then a difference from the primary

(Standard English) contraction as it affects say [ʃæl nɒt] or [wɪl nɒt], where the final consonant is also lost: there the change is /XV₁Cnt→XV̄₂nt/ i.e. the vowel is lengthened and changes in quality also.

(ii)   in the second group the consonant affected is the /n/ of the negative. Thus: /XV̄nt→XV̄t/

> Note that though the phonological shape /XV̄nt/ also occurs in English words not produced by the primary contraction of 'verb + not' e.g. *count* (this is not the case with the /XVCnt/ shape), the secondary contraction is lexically restricted to words derived by the primary contraction: thus [kaːnt]→[kaːt] but not [kaʊnt]→ *[kaʊt].

The actual forms will now be examined in more detail. Since this is a feature only of non-standard English, non-standard forms will be referred to: using RP forms as examples would be totally artificial since secondary contractions would never apply with say [hædnt] or [dəʊnt]—whereas they are quite likely with [adn²] or [doːn²]. My transcriptions are fairly 'broad' in both the technical sense (they do not attempt to show fine phonetic detail) and the non-technical (by which the term is popularly used to indicate a variety of speech which is markedly 'Yorkshire').

1   /XVCnt/

isn't	[ɪznt]→[ɪnt]		oughtn't	[ɔːtnt]→[ɔːnt]
wasn't	[wɒznt]→[wɒnt]		needn't	[niːdnt]→[niːnt]
doesn't	[dʊznt]→[dʊnt]		mightn't	[maɪtnt]→[maɪnt]
didn't	[dɪdnt]→[dɪnt]		mustn't	[mʊsnt](→[mʊnt])
couldn't	[kʊdnt]→[kʊnt]		hasn't	[aznt]	
shouldn't	[ʃudnt]→[ʃunt]		hadn't	[adnt]	→[ant]
wouldn't	[wʊdnt]→[wʊnt]		haven't	[avnt]→cf. below

The final consonant has been written throughout as [t], though especially in the forms which have undergone secondary contraction [?] is common, though less so in prevocalic than in preconsonantal environments.

Examples

[ɪt ɪnt iːzɪ tə duː ða²]
It isn't easy to do that
[wɒnt ɪt ə pɪtɪ]
Wasn't it a pity?
[ɪ dʊn² laɪk duːɪn ða²]
He doesn't like doing that
[a dɪn² wɒnt tə kʊm]
I didn't want to come
[kʊn² jə duːʷ ɪ²]
Couldn't you do it?
[jə ʃunt ə sed ða²]
You shouldn't have said that
[a wʊn² laɪk tə biː ɜː]
I wouldn't like to be here

[jɔːnt tə seː ða²]
You oughtn't to say that
[jə niːnt ansə, ðen]
You needn't answer, then
[a maɪnt ə biːn eːbl tə stɒp]
I mightn't have been able to stop
(cf. below, on *mustn't*)

[iː an² dʊn ðat, az ɪ]
He hasn't done that, has he?
[iː an² dʊn ðat, ad ɪ]
He hadn't done that had he?
(cf. below, on *haven't*)

While an example such as that given here for *couldn't* is not unusual, the contracted form is sometimes avoided because of homophonic taboo resulting from the fact that the /ʌ/–/ʊ/ contrast is absent from the phonemic inventory of the majority of speakers in this area; schoolboys of a certain age sometimes perform the contraction in the phrase *you couldn't* with obvious delight!

The form [mʊnt] is bracketed because it is uncommon. It can be heard: e.g. [ɪ² mʊs bɪ ðaʔ, mʊnt ɪ²], where it obviously is the contracted negative of *must*. But one must be careful to distinguish such instances from those where it is the negative of the 'dialect' modal *mun* e.g. [ɪ mʊn duːʷɪ², mʊnt ɪ]; *mun* is of Norse origin, and according to the famous grammar of Joseph Wright (1892, p. 151), which refers to his native village on the outskirts of Bradford, it was in traditional dialect used for 'a necessity dependent on the will of a person', as distinct from 'a logical or natural necessity' for which *must* was employed. In the area today *mun* has virtually disappeared, and the majority of speakers simply do not contract *mustn't* any further: it is thus an exception to the rule; whether the fact that it has usually already 'lost' a final consonant (i.e. it is [mʊs] rather than [mʊst] except prevocalically) has anything to do with this is not clear.

Contraction of *hasn't* and *hadn't* produce the homophonous [ant]. One would have expected *haven't* to yield the same result, and this can occasionally be heard in other parts of Britain; but in this area *haven't* is kept distinct from the other two in a way which suggests that the contraction rule may not be quite as simple as that given above. Note that in all the words in this group except *haven't* the C of /XVCnt/ is alveolar and thus homorganic with the following [nt]; but in *haven't* it is labiodental—and here the contracted form is [amt ~ am²] or occasionally [aɱ²]. So perhaps something like the following applies:

1	/XVC nat/→/XVCnt/	'Primary Contraction'
2	/n/ assimilates in place to /C/	(Applies vacuously except with *haven't*)
3	/C/→Ø	'Secondary Contraction'
4	[ɱ]→[m]	(Applies only to *haven't*; caused by loss of conditioning environment through 3)

Finally, note that it is only the nasal which assimilates: final [t] does not change place of articulation—witness prevocalic [amta] 'haven't I', never *[ampa]. (Even 'haven't we' is [am²wɪ] rather than *[ampwɪ] as might have seemed phonetically plausible; cf. also [am²jə] 'haven't you', [am²ðə] 'haven't they' etc.)

Contracted forms other than those listed here can sometimes be heard:

(i)   in interrogatives a 'tertiary contraction' may yield [ɪnɪ²] 'isn't it', [wɒnɪ²] 'wasn't it', [dʊnɪ²] 'doesn't it', [anɪ] 'hasn't he' etc., with the /t/ of the negative now deleted. I have observed such examples from working-class speakers; they are included in the statistical treatment below with the secondary contractions since this process has occurred.

(ii)   higher up the social scale /t/ is also occasionally omitted, in forms like [dʌznɪt], [iznɪt], [wʊdnɪt], which I have heard as high as the Middle Middle Class (as defined below); but since the secondary contraction has not operated, these forms are ignored in the statistics which follow.

I shall now attempt to link the amount of use of the non-standard forms (secondary contractions) with factors such as style, class, sex, age, and town. Figures are based on a survey carried out in the autumn of 1971 and reported in Petyt (1977); the aim of this survey was to investigate the extent to which features of 'dialect' and/or 'accent' still survive among the population of this area. I interviewed a random sample of just over 100 informants, drawn from the three main towns of the 'wool district': Bradford, Halifax and Huddersfield. The sample contained roughly equal numbers of males and females, members of all age-groups from 10 + to 80 +, and of five social classes which may be labelled Middle and Lower Middle Class, Upper, Middle, and Lower Working Class (these classes were established for the purposes of this study only, on the basis of a total 'score' for various objective categories of education, occupation, income, and standard of living).

The percentage of secondary contractions of /XVCnt/ words recorded in my survey from members of the different social classes in the 'styles' distinguished (as in Labov, 1966) as 'casual', 'careful', and 'reading'[2] are shown in Figure 1. The total percentage of such forms in all styles by members of the different age-groups is shown in Figure 2. No clear differences emerged between the sexes or between speakers from the different towns.

The dotted lines in the graphs are to indicate that certain scores are 'suspect'. In Figure 1 that for the Middle Middle Class in casual speech is unexpectedly low, and the reason may well be the small amount of data; there were only three informants in this group (as compared to 13, 28, 43, 19 respectively in LMC, UWC, MWC, LWC) and they produced little casual speech: only eleven instances of this /XVCnt/ 'variable' occurred in their casual speech data, in none of which the contraction occurred.[3] Clearly all scores for this group have to be treated with caution, as being possibly not reliable. In Figure 2 the figure for the 80 + group is also perhaps not reliable, since this small group is 'class biased': there were only three such informants, all in the lowest class.

Figure 1 shows that the frequency of secondary contraction relates to class and style in a way that has been shown to be usual with features considered to be 'substandard': they are heard more commonly towards the lower end of the social scale, but all classes use them more frequently with increasing informality. Figure 2 shows no overall trend such as usually shows up with a variable involved in linguistic change; the highest use of contracted forms is obviously among the two youngest groups, but the general pattern of this graph is normal for variables not involved in linguistic change (see also Trudgill, 1974), and it is possibly a reflection of the fact that 'speech consciousness' is greatest in middle age, when one has wider contacts and is perhaps most keen to 'get on' (see Labov, 1966).

[2] /XVCnt/ and /XV̄nt/ words were never contracted in 'word list' style.
[3] Note that if the next instance *had* been contracted the graph would have looked 'regular'. This illustrates the unreliability of such small amounts of data.

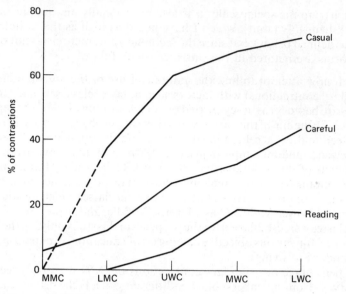

Figure 1 /XVCnt/: style and class

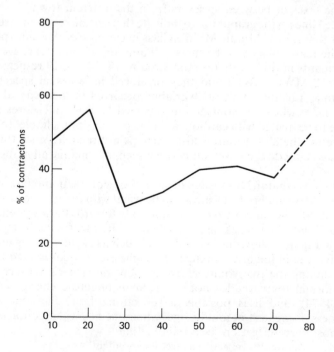

Figure 2. /XVCnt/: age

2/XV̄nt/

aren't	[aːnt]→[aːt]	shan't	[ʃaːnt]→[ʃaːt]
weren't	[wɜːnt]→[wɜːt]	can't	[kaːnt]→[kaːt]
don't	[doːnt]→[doːt]	daren't	[dɛənt]→[dɛət]
won't	[woːnt]→[woːt]		

With this set the glottal stop is very common as a realization of /t/; in fact, [t] is unusual, even prevocalically.

Examples

[aː2 jə kʊmɪn]
Aren't you coming?
[ðɪ wɜː2 redɪ]
They weren't ready
[a doː2 θɪŋk a wɒnt tə]
I don't think I want to
[a kʊd duːʷ ɪ2 bʊr a woː2]
I could do it but I won't

[wɪ ʃaː2 bɪ ðɛə]
We shan't be there
[a kaː2 elp ɪ2]
I can't help it
[ad laɪk tə bʊr a dɛə2]
I'd like to but I daren't

A special contracted form of *don't know* [dʊnoː ~ dəʊnəʊ ~ dʌnəʊ] etc. was observed in all social classes. It was ignored for 'scoring' purposes below.

The forms of *dare not* vary within the area. While [dɛənt] and [dɛət] are heard in most parts, in some parts (I have insufficient data, but I suspect from observation and from remarks of informants that it is mainly in Bradford) there may occur what looks like a very irregular form [dɛədnt]: e.g. [ad laɪk tə duːʷ ɪ2 bʊr a dɛədnt], where a consonant appears to have been added rather than one deleted. Now in fact this [dɛədnt] is homophonous with the contracted form of the past *dared not*. Nelson Francis (1968), discussing the negatived past and present forms of modal *dare* shown up by the Survey of English Dialects, says that there is an 'exceedingly complex and confused situation . . . *dare* is in a very unstable state morphologically, which is perhaps partly a consequence of its position on the periphery of the modal system'. Formerly there was a contrast in English generally between strong *dare—durst* (modal) and weak *dare—dared* (full verb), but (i) the *durst* form has now disappeared from Standard English and also from some dialects, with *dared* taking over, and (ii) many speakers do not distinguish present and past in the modal: Nelson Francis shows that for over 50 per cent of SED informants the past and present forms are homonymous, and in just under half of these it is the past form which has been extended to the present. Now in Yorkshire the levelled form is most commonly the present (and I have observed *daren't* used as past by speakers from the area of my survey e.g. [a dɪdnt duːʷ ɪt—a dɛənt]), but at SED locality Y22, on the outskirts of Bradford, the past form [daːdnt] was recorded in present tense usage; this form, under the phonetic influence of the standard language yields the [dɛədnt] familiar today.

Figure 3 shows the percentage of secondary contractions in /XV̄nt/ words by class and style, and Figure 4 breaks the casual and careful style scores down by sex. The total scores by age-groups are seen in Figure 5, while the Table 1 gives the total scores in each style for informants from the three towns:

Table 1: /X̄nt/

	Casual	Careful	Reading
Bradford	76	46	7
Halifax	47	33	8
Huddersfield	46	31	9

With style the situation is as would be expected with a feature felt to be substandard: secondary contractions are less common as formality increases. But with class the position is not so clear: Figure 3 shows that only in the reading passage scores are the classes more or less in the 'expected' order, with non-standard forms becoming commoner the lower one looks on the social scale; in conversation, both casual and careful, the highest use of contracted forms appears to be among the Upper Working Class, with Middle and Lower Working Classes following in that order. Yet Figure 4 shows that when the

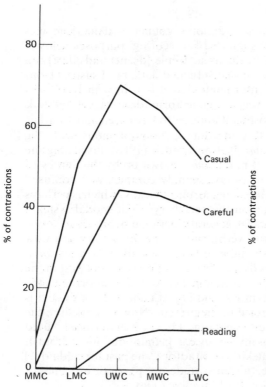

Figure 3. /X̄nt/: style and class

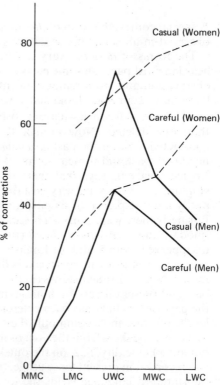

Figure 4. /X̄nt/: sex, style and class

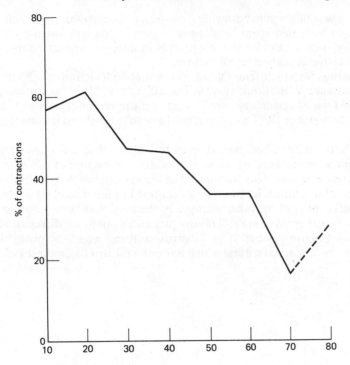

Figure 5. /XṼnt/: age

figures are subdivided by sex it emerges that this order applies only to men, whereas women are stratified regularly in respect of this feature.

The age-group figures are of particular interest, both because:

(i)   they show that (if we ignore the 80 + group, since class has been shown to be an important factor and therefore the score for this class-biased group is probably not reliable) there is an increase in the amount of secondary contraction from the 70 + to the 20 + group (this increase is in fact found with both sexes, but the fairly small amount of data for some of these smaller groups makes the graphs not quite so regular). And also because:

(ii)   they suggest a reason for the above unexpected class order among men: use of the contracted forms is highest among the under-30s and lowest among the over-60s: the percentage of male informants in these age-groups in the three Working Class groups in my sample is as follows:

	UWC	MWC	LWC
Under-30	55	40	15
Over-60	18	27	61

These figures surely go some way towards explaining the relative order of Working Class groups of male informants in my sample, and should perhaps

D*

serve as a warning against drawing over-hasty conclusions, say about 'Upper Working Class men spear-heading a linguistic change', on the basis of a sample of such a size that the informants in any one sub-group may not be representative in respect of all factors.

The scores for the different towns show that contractions of /XV̄nt/ words are commoner in Bradford than in the other two. My observations suggest that this type of secondary contraction is more regionally restricted within Britain than that of /XVCnt/, and it could be that Bradford is quite close to its centre.

The facts outlined here would seem to suggest that a linguistic change is taking place in this area, by which secondary contraction of /XV̄nt/ words is becoming commoner with time, and that the change has progressed further in Bradford than in the other two towns examined. It is particularly interesting in that, unlike most of the other changes in the area that have occurred during the last century or so or are still taking place, it is not in the direction of RP or Standard English: rather it is towards a form which is probably considered to be non-standard and which is more typical of the lower social classes.

8

On intonational variability in Tyneside speech

John Pellowe and Val Jones

1 Introductory

Prosodic systems ought to be of central importance to sociolinguists.[1] One argument in favour of this assertion is that there is an important parallel between two sorts of social information which can be conveyed by these systems. First, we can note that a speaker may use prosodic systems to transmit his affective states and attitudes to a hearer; to specify the role to be attributed to syntactic structures; and to indicate the relative informational importance of different parts of his utterance. Insofar as this information is social, we can refer to it as intrinsic social information ('intrinsic' in the sense that it is part of the on-going interaction and might be agreed upon by participant hearers).

Intrinsic social information is very frequently conveyed by varying not simply various prosodic features, but rather the patterns of co-occurrence and relative distributions of prosodic and paralinguistic features. Very many intonational features, unlike segmental phonological features, have exceedingly variable *domains* of realization. For example, a feature such as *allegro* in a system of *tempo* may have as its domain two syllables or twenty-two syllables; a tone unit may be co-extensive with one word or three complex clauses; and so on. We can refer to such variability as *realizational* variability, and suggest that it is the organization of such realizational variations, with respect to other levels of linguistic structure, which gives rise to much intrinsic social information.

Secondly, prosodic systems are also able to convey *extrinsic* social information. This will frequently be projected through what we can refer to as

[1]We are indebted to Vince McNeany for his initial analyses, and to Ann Pellowe for tedious labour on the raw data. Our thanks also, for comments on various previous versions, to Barbara Strang, David Crystal, Vince McNeany, John Local, Diane Hart-Hay, Graham McGregor, John Frankis, Claire Cannell, none of whom is either responsible for errors and inconsistencies, or necessarily holds these views. We have joint responsibility for the paper but we divided the labour: Val Jones did all of the computing (data input, programming, formatting), John Pellowe did most of the writing (selection of material, graphics), both did the revisions. We are grateful to the Research Fund of the University of Newcastle for a grant to one of us (J.P.) which made the data preparation for this work possible.

varietal variability. It is a matter of widespread naive and professional comment (and see Knowles, this volume) that intonational systems exhibit regional and social differences which are typologically similar to those amongst vowel systems, consonant systems, and syntactic contrasts. This variability permits the hearer to make inferences concerning various extra-linguistic attributes of the speaker, based on what he interprets as characteristic patterns in the speech of the speaker.

What differentiates extrinsic from intrinsic social information, then, is that its acquisition by the hearer is not part of the focused intention of the speaker (as reflected, for example, in the co-occurrence patterns of his realization of syntax and intonation). Indeed, the speaker may be completely unaware of the basis, nature and even the making of such inferences on given occasions.[2] Thus extrinsic social information is 'extrinsic' in the sense that it is 'outside' the interaction and is a more private product of the hearer.

The interaction of intrinsic and extrinsic social information and of realizational and varietal variability makes intonation an important area of study for sociolinguistics. It ought to be emphasized, however, that it is only possible to make the gross distinctions we have made by ignoring the huge range of intentions, and their realization, which is open to both speakers and hearers in any interactive situation. Clearly, for example, it is open to the speaker to make varietal variability a source of *intrinsic* social information. That is, it can be part of the speaker's focused intention that the hearer acquires social knowledge, relevant to an understanding of the current utterance, from varietal differences, rather than from realizational differences, (for jokes, self-deprecation, biographical veracity, evocation of attitudes stereotyped to that variety, etc.). Similarly, certain patterns of realizational variability, from a given speaker at a particular moment, may carry *extrinsic* social information instead of (or as well as) intrinsic social information for his given hearer. Thus, a speaker chiding his hearer, but wishing to be seen to be doing so 'pleasantly' (intrinsic), has co-occurrent realizations of *low* (pitch range), *piano* (prominence), and *glissando (down)* (rhythmicality), but is interpreted as being 'too worn out to tell me off' (extrinsic).

Many kindred examples of functional-formal asymmetry in the use of intonational systems render the above distinctions less clear-cut than they may appear to be, but no less useful for all that.

2 Goal and perspective

To illustrate the motivation for the distinctions made above, consider the following:

[2]Such facts are often revealed in the *post hoc* unravelling of misunderstandings. There is a class of misunderstandings which appears to arise from the hearer's having projected extrinsic social information too strongly upon the semantics of the speaker's utterance. This is revealed by an unravelling statement by the hearer such as 'I thought since you are *x*, that when you said *y*, what you meant was *z*.' Here *x* is information of an extrinsic sort whose derivation by the hearer is often a source of amazement to the speaker ('where on earth did you get that idea from?'). We are indebted to Claire Cannell for this observation.

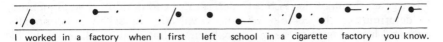

I worked in a factory when I first left school in a cigarette factory you know.

(Speaker: 35, female, housewife/shop asst., (husband: toolmaker), council house, born and continuously resident Tyneside (Byker).)

All the tones in the utterance are level tones. Problems of interpretation for the linguist, in assuring himself that they *are* level tones, let alone assigning them syntactic functions, are barely less than those which a visiting, southern, RP-speaking, hearer might have in discriminating amongst various intrinsic social meanings on the one hand, and between intrinsic and extrinsic social meanings on the other. Do the first two level tones stand in the same (syntactic) functional relationship to each other as the elements of a fall plus rise (compound) tone might in a non-localized RP variety? Would the function of the relationship between 'cigarette' and 'factory', as realized here, (drop, booster, level) be equivalently realized by a fall-rise (complex) tone on 'cigarette' in a non-localized variety? Would the hearer be responding comprehensibly as far as the speaker was concerned, if he responded as to an attitude of boredom on the part of the speaker, or uninterest imputed to *him* by the speaker? (These two attitudes were the dominant ones elicited by the tape in judgements by hearers who themselves spoke a range of varieties other than Tyneside.)

It seems clear to us that these and a host of other questions, of a functional kind, cannot be begun to be answered until we have a detailed understanding of the varietally different systems of forms in terms of their *distributions with respect to each other*. We cannot determine the intrinsic social information which can be conveyed by particular co-occurrent intonational features from the intonational systems of some variety until we know, in some statistical detail, what are the place and the significance of those features in those systems. Thus, it makes no sense to ask what the functions of level tone in Tyneside varieties are, *vis-à-vis* level tone in non-localized varieties, because such a question invests significance in the formal identity of the two. The formal identity of the two is precisely what needs to be established before such questions make sense since if, for instance, we discover that the numerical and syntagmatic distribution of level tone in Tyneside varieties is very different from those distributions in non-localized varieties, we shall have little reason to imagine that they constitute the 'same' tone at all (cf., the problems raised by 'cigarette factory' etc.).

Before we can understand the ways in which intrinsic social information is generated and understood in inter-varietal exchanges, we must have a precise knowledge of the varietal variability which is a backcloth to it. Our aim, then, is to develop and apply methods for comparing varietally different intonation systems, and to do so in ways which are consonant with the wider perspective of the Tyneside Linguistic Survey (TLS), of which this work forms a part. Some features of that perspective are briefly rehearsed in order to introduce what follows. (More information may be had from Pellowe, 1967; Pellowe, 1970; Pellowe *et al.*, 1972a; Pellowe *et al.*, 1972b; Pellowe, 1973; 1976; forthcoming; Pellowe and Jones, forthcoming.)

The general aim of the TLS is to determine (and develop general methods for determining) the ecology of speech varieties in urban environments. 'Ecology' here is used in the biological sense; that is, we wish to know, for some urban environment, what the *number* of varieties is, what the *frequency of occurrence* of each variety is, and what the associations between varieties are (linguistically, socially, spatially, temporally) (cf. Pielou, 1969; Boughey, 1969). We have argued elsewhere that a suitable way of implementing this aim is to model various capabilities of naive hearers (Pellowe, 1976; Pellowe *et al.*, 1972b). A model of these capabilities which proves very apt is the spatial one. A hearer can be thought of (and often thinks of himself) as *locating* a variety in a mental variety *space*, as *placing it closer* to ones to which it is similar, and *further away* from ones from which it is dissimilar. Our implementation of this model involves us in setting up a space with *n* dimensions (Atkin, 1974), in which each dimension is some linguistic feature which varies. The ecology of the speech varieties, for a given environment, is then established by seeing how a representative selection of speakers from that environment is dispersed in that space.

Representativeness of speakers is important, but no more important than the representativeness of the dimensions. If the space is to accommodate the speakers properly, it must have dimensionality and dimensions to suit the variability of the sampled population. If, in the population, there are speakers of *non-localized* varieties having certain intonational systems and realization norms (Crystal, 1966; 1969) and also speakers of *localized* varieties having apparently different intonational systems and realization norms (Pellowe, 1970), then the variety space must reflect such things in its dimensions. Were it not to do so, then co-variation between the intonational systems on the one hand, and varietally characteristic features of, e.g., segmental phonology and syntax on the other, would go undetected. Since it is in the nature of co-variation that change in one variant may lead, at the least, to instability in the other, failure to build such things into the variety space would certainly lose information valuable to a linguistic theory of linguistic change. We must consider varieties as wholes. It is of course possible partially to describe speech varieties in spaces having only one *type* of dimension (say, segmental phonological) or having only five or six dimensions, or both (e.g. Labov, 1966; Le Page *et al.*, 1974; Trudgill, 1974a). Such accounts however, do not give us a detailed understanding of the patterns of association between the variants of different linguistic systems in the same variety, or of the variants of different linguistic systems across different varieties. Hence, such kinds of accounts as these do not provide an adequate base for a social-psychological understanding of speaker-hearer behaviours.

Speakers are 'dispersed' in the variety space on the basis of a proximity measure between every pair of speakers in respect of each of the dimensions. Put from another point of view, one can say that the application of each dimension to the population divides that population up in some specific way. The variety space then represents groups of speakers who are similar in respect of the addition of all these 'successive' divisions. The choice of dimensions is therefore very important. Since dimensions are determined by the system of analysis which one is using, the choice of analytic system is also important. We require systems of analysis which are sufficiently delicate to discriminate between different varieties, but which are also capable of exhibiting those differences by permitting differing profiles of co-occurrent features (*sensu* Quirk, 1965). For instance, Halliday's (1967) system is too highly determined as to the mutual dependencies between intonational systems for it to work for cross-varietal work of the kind here outlined. For prosodic and paralinguistic features, the analytic system which comes closest to satisfying the above criteria is that devised by Crystal (Crystal and Quirk, 1964; Crystal, 1966; 1969).

3 Previous work

We know of no previous research which has been directly concerned to give quantitative, comparable analyses of the prosodic and paralinguistic systems of different varieties of the same language co-occurring in the same speech community. Labov (1964b) establishes four criteria for determining useful quantitative variables, and they are satisfied by intonational features, 'but at present', he writes, 'we lack the large body of theory and practice in codifying intonation which we have for segmental phones' (1964b, p. 176). Crystal notes the dearth of research also: 'There is remarkably little attention paid to . . . an aspect of speech which I would hold was of major importance for the linguistic definition of social categories, namely, the non-segmental phonetic and phonological characteristics of utterance' (1971, p. 185). Crystal also writes that 'there have been few attempts to transcribe utterances in order to indicate the frequency of occurrences and distribution of specific effects' (1975, p. 85).

Crystal's (1966) quantitative studies of the prosodic and paralinguistic systems of educated (southern) British English, and an investigation into the correspondence between prosodic and grammatical features of English by Quirk *et al.* (1964) do not suffer from these shortcomings. Their principles, and some of their findings (Crystal, 1966; Crystal and Quirk, 1964; Quirk *et al.*, 1964) were contrasted, in a pilot project, with a small sample of localized Tyneside speech (Pellowe, 1970). It was assumed in this project that marked differences between the frequency or the co-occurrence distributions of features in Tyneside and 'RP' would form the basis for a satisfactory dimension of the variety space. Twelve such dimensions were originally suggested as a result of differences between that Tyneside corpus (245 tone units (TUs)) and the corpus of Quirk *et al.* (1964) (1880 TUs). The twelve dimensions were: relative and absolute standardized frequencies of tones (2 dimensions), relative and absolute interactions between tones and form classes (6), and relative and absolute interactions between tones and terms from the pitch range system (cf. Crystal and Quirk, 1964, p. 45; and below). (Examples of these dimensions or 'variables' include: mean length, in words, of TUs; percentage of tones which are level tones; percentage tags not carrying tone; percentage drops immediately preceding nuclear tone.) Since the original pilot work, the number of dimensions has been increased without reference to further data, by subdividing categories and by including dimensions which can represent variation in the paralinguistic systems of tension, voice qualifiers, and voice qualifications (Crystal, 1969). (We now in fact reject our former willingness to erect dimensions which are not directly derived from data.)

4 Sample, features, analysis

The data to be considered in the rest of this paper are the frequencies and co-occurrence distributions, for some of the more important elements from three classes of features, for twenty speakers. The data from these speakers were amongst the first to be processed by the computer programs and are from one of the random samples of the original TLS sample design (the phase 3, Gateshead, sample, cf. Pellowe *et al.*, 1972b, p. 21 ff.). Their ages range from 17 to 70, and there are 9 women and 11 men, distributed as follows (letters are mnemonics for informants, bracketed numerals show socio-economic class according to: V unskilled manual, IV skilled manual and routine non-manual, III lower supervisory, II higher supervisory):

Table 1: Details of speakers.

Age	17–20	21–30	31–40	41–50	51–60	61–70	*Total*
Men	—	N(III/II) We(IV) Mc(III/II)	He(V) Cr(IV) Ch(III) An(IV)	Gr(IV)	O(IV)	Ga(V) Wi(IV)	11
Women	D(V)	—	S(IV) Wa(V) F(IV)	T(V) BW(V) Ha(V)	Cl(V) Ar(V)	—	9
Total	1	3	7	4	3	2	20

All informants left school at the legal minimum for their dates of birth except *N* and *Mc*, who had received full-time tertiary education (polytechnic and college of education respectively). All informants had lived continuously on Tyneside, and so had their parents, except *Ch* (born in Ulster of Ulster parents, but moved to Tyneside shortly after birth) and *Gr* (born of rural-living parents in Tyneside's rural hinterland).

The three classes of linguistic features discussed here are tones, selected form classes, and terms in the system of pitch range (see below). It is worth emphasizing that each of these classes of features is considered to be independent of the others (cf. Crystal and Quirk, 1964). Thus, although there will be significant rates of co-occurrence between elements from the system of tone and elements from the system of pitch range in a particular variety, it is also quite clear that those rates of co-occurrence vary between varieties. The only way to cope with this is with independent systems.

The systems here analysed are represented as follows. Tone is represented in a system of eight terms: $\searbackslash$ (fall), $\diagup$ (rise), $\vee$ (fall-rise), $\wedge$ (rise-fall), $\searbackslash + \diagup$ (fall plus rise), $\diagup + \searbackslash$ (rise plus fall), — (level), ø (zero, i.e. no tone). Form class is represented by one of nine terms: n (common noun), N (name), adv (adverb), padj (premodifying adjective), fadj ('adjective' as complement), pron (as subject or object), tag (clause final, includes 'phatic' (*you know*; *I think*) as well as 'syntactic' (he is, *is he*; he is, *isn't he*) types), vb (finite verbs), ø (zero, i.e. some form class other than these). The simple system of pitch range is represented by a system of seven terms: extra high booster, high booster, booster, continuance, drop, low drop, zero (i.e. no marked pitch range feature). (Pitch range has been described in detail elsewhere, cf. Crystal and Quirk, 1964, p. 45 ff; Crystal, 1969, p. 144 ff, but a few remarks may be helpful. Differences of pitch which occur within an utterance may be divided into those which are dynamic (i.e. constitute glides) and those which are static (i.e. comprise contiguous syllables of different pitch).[3] These latter, static, pitch differences are the elements of the pitch range system. Elements are recognized according to the nature and degree of the relationship between the pitch of the syllable under consideration and that of the previous pitch-prominent syllable.)

The co-occurrence of any feature from these three sets with any others can thus be represented by an ordered three element code. There are 504 possible co-occurrence codes for these three systems, derivable from Table 2.

Table 2: Matrix for co-occurrence codes

1 *Tone*		2 *Form class*		3 *Pitch range*	
ø	G	ø	G	ø	G
\	H	n	Q	extra high booster	A
\	J	N	R	high booster	B
V	K	adv	S	booster	C
∧	L	padj	T	continuance	D
\+/	M	fadj	U	drop	E
/+\	N	pron	V	low drop	F
—	P	tag	W		
		vb	X		

Thus, for instance, a rise-fall occurring on an exclamatory word (*well*) would be coded LGG; a name preceded by a booster, GRC; a fall on an intensifier preceded by a continuance, HGD, and so on. Examples of codings together with their ordinary transcriptional equivalents, are as follows:

He's	not	going	to	the	match	tomorrow	is	he	not?

HVG	GXG				PQB	GSE	PWB	GGE

It's	completely	different.	Aye,	I	will	do.	Age,	er	there.

GVG	GXG	HUD	KGG	GVG	PXE	GQC	LSD

Note that occurrences of terms from any of the systems which do *not* co-occur with terms from the other two systems are coded nonetheless (e.g. GXG, GGE, KGG, etc.). Clearly adequate information on *occurrence* is a necessary prerequisite for any satisfactory account of the frequency of *co-occurrence*.

[3]Level tone is not dynamic in this sense, but excellent reasons are adduced for its inclusion as a tone by Crystal (1969, pp. 215–17).

The analysis of prosodic features in several varieties by different analysts is not without problems. We have already alluded (section 2 above) to the fact that different hearers often hear the same utterance in different ways— that is, as being different. The generality of the TLS model is such as to predict that linguists are no more exempt from this effect than other users of language (Pellowe, 1967; Pellowe *et al.*, 1972b); hearers who speak differently will hear differently or, in the case of linguists, hear and transcribe differently. This is not only true of phonetic transcription (Ladefoged, 1960; Pellowe *et al.*, 1972a; Oller and Eilers, 1975). We have evidence that it is also true of syntax, semantics, and intonation. It does not seem to be an effect that can be totally eradicated by training (Pellowe and Jones, forthcoming), which we do not find surprising. Since on the one hand we wish to understand as fully as possible the position of speakers in our computed variety space and, on the other, we wish to make full use of our prosodic analyses (a difficult and time-consuming business) we need to calibrate the different analytic behaviours of prosodic analysts.[4]

Replication by one of us (J.P.) of analyses by David Crystal and of analyses of Vince McNeany shows that analyst differences (in respect of the systems of tone and pitch range) fall into four classes of two types: (a) simple, (b) complex.[5] The two classes of simple differences were:

(i)   one analyst hears a lone pitch range feature the other doesn't (most frequent was booster *vs.* ø, a difference which occurred in both directions for both pairs of analysts (D.C.: J.P.; J.P.: V.M.));

(ii)   one analyst hears a tone, the other doesn't (most frequent were / and — *vs.* ø, a difference which occurred in both directions for both pairs of analysts).

The two classes of complex differences had to do with (i) kinesis, (ii) contrastivity.

(i)   In the first, both analysts hear pitch difference but one of them hears it as static (pitch range) while the other hears it as dynamic (tone). The most common token of this type of difference (for both analyst pairs) was when one heard a *booster* and the other heard a *rise*.

(ii)   In the second kind of complex difference (contrastivity), both analysts hear dynamic pitch changes but they differ as to its precise nature. For D.C.:J.P. the commonest token of this type was rise *vs.* fall-rise; for V.M.:J.P. the commonest token was fall *vs.* level (the difference occurred in both directions).[6]

In considering the structure of prosodic variation discussed below (section 5), it is important to bear in mind that the final representation of speakers in the total computed variety space will take account of such calibrations of analyst differences as these.

The data from the 20 speakers discussed in the next section comprises 4066

[4]It would be a serious misinterpretation of our whole approach to imagine that calibration is a data-cleaning exercise. What we learn from analyst differences (*not* discrepancies) is something about the linguistic systems which are being analysed and the processes by which their realizations are normally apprehended.

[5]We are very grateful to Professors Randolph Quirk and David Crystal and the Survey of English Usage for making available a copy of one of their tapes and its analysis (by D.C.). They are in no way responsible for, and may not be in agreement with, our use of their material.

[6]For details of a theory of prosodic contrastivity see Quirk and Crystal (1966), Crystal (1969; 1975) and for problems arising in cross-varietal cases see Pellowe and Jones (forthcoming).

TUs (mean of 204 TUs per informant; highest number of TUs for one informant 273, lowest 142). Occasionally, comparison is made with the results of Quirk *et al.* (1964). Their sample (of 10 speakers, in two panel discussion groups) yielded 1880 TUs (a mean per speaker of 188 TUs). However, the TLS informants were speaking in a loosely structured interview (by the standards of e.g. Oppenheim, 1966). Results of Crystal and Davy (1969) and of Crystal (1975, p. 96 ff) show that the realization patterns of prosodic and paralinguistic features are likely to change under such changes of interactive purpose. In spite of this, the comparisons prove useful.

5 Structure of variation

Our objective, then, is to develop a methodology for the comparison of the intonation systems of different linguistic varieties. We do this by comparing the distributions of prosodic features in Tyneside and non-localized speech. We determine variation within Tyneside English by establishing the differential co-variation of certain of these features one with another and with other linguistic features. Because of the exploratory nature of this paper and the limitations on space, we represent this co-variation amongst features in pictorial form, and provide commentary on the most significant points in those depictions.

Frequency distribution of tones

We deal first with the frequency distributions of tones. Figure 1 shows the

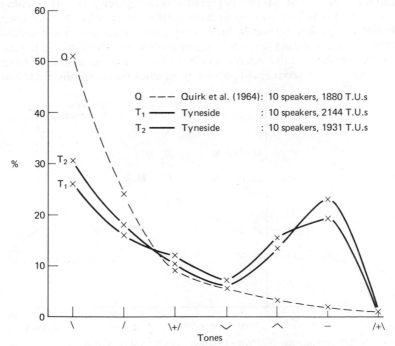

Figure 1. Gross percentage distribution of tones for 3 samples

gross percentage distribution of each tone in each of three samples. Against the trace for Quirk's (1964) sample are given those for *two* Tyneside samples (T$_1$ and T$_2$), each being a random half of the twenty speakers here considered (T$_1$ = *He, Ga, Wi, S, Wa, N, O, Cl, T, Cr*; T$_2$ = the rest). The match between the two random halves is good, certainly in respect of the overall differences from the trace for Quirk's (1964) sample (henceforth abbreviated to Q). There is a sizeable difference between non-localized varieties (Q) and Tyneside-localized varieties (T$_1$, T$_2$) in respect of the relative fractions of falls, rise-falls and levels. Such differences as these may be thought of as *diagnostic* of these two classes of variety. This is certainly true at this level of representation, i.e. gross percentages for whole samples (cf. the important work of Garvey and Dickstein, 1972). We could choose a different level of representation for the percentage distribution of tones by, for instance, choosing individuals rather than whole samples. If we do this (not pictured here), we find that the component members of a distribution like T$_1$ show considerable differences of tone distribution, but that, even with such an unmatched group of ten speakers, these differences are patterned. Such patterning of individual differences of tonic distribution within T$_1$, given the fit between T$_1$ and T$_2$, suggests that the differences may be stable. We examine this possibility in subsequent graphs.

Consider firstly the relative fractions of falls and rises represented for the three samples in Figure 1. Non-localized varieties (Q) appear to have a much larger percentage difference between falls and rises (25 per cent) than do localized (T$_1$, T$_2$) varieties (10 per cent). If we specify this (percentage difference between falls and rises) as a dimension we might expect to find a distribution of speakers in which those with high values were less localized than those with low values. Figure 2 examines this and shows the difference between the number of falls and the number of rises as a percentage of tones, plotted by age, for all speakers (T$_1$ and T$_2$). Four elements of this picture are

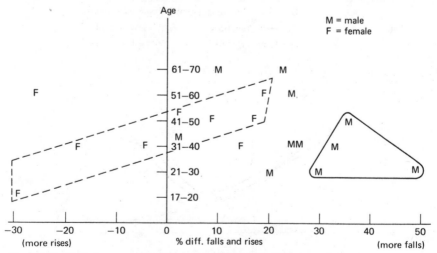

Figure 2. Plot of age against difference between falls % tones and rises % tones for 20 speakers

worth emphasizing here. First, the expectation expressed above that the dimension would discriminate localized from non-localized varieties is not satisfied by this graph. This can be understood by noting that the dimension is, however, sex-differentiated: men have high values on the dimension, women have low ones. All the speakers in Quirk's sample were men, having a mean value on the dimension of +25 per cent.[7] It is therefore fairly clear that, rather than being diagnostic of the localized/non-localized nature of the variety, the dimension seems to be primarily diagnostic of sex. Secondly, however, the four men having the highest values (*Mc, N, Ch, Gr*: 28+ per cent—see enclosed area on Figure 2) are those who differ from the rest of the sample in either education (*Mc, N*) or nuclear family residence pattern (*Ch, Gr*). Thirdly, for the remaining men, there is a strong tendency for their realization patterns to embody about 20 per cent more falls than rises, irrespective of age. And, fourthly, amongst women there is an *age trend* which indicates that younger women are realizing rises in more and more TUs in which their elders would have realized falls (see the dotted area on Figure 2). This is a trend which seems to be socially significant for members of the speech community. It seems, for example, to be a behaviour being emulated by *Ar* (see Figure 3) who in terms of her age should have a value of +15 per cent or so but who in fact has a value of −26 per cent. (We know independently that *Ar* goes dancing, listens to pop music and reads teenage magazines.) But given the complex nature of the dimension (*percentage difference* between falls and rises), what might be involved in the mental processes underlying such social salience is somewhat hair-raising (cf. Bickerton's suitable satire, 1971, pp. 460–61).

In the light of our remarks in section 1 above, it will be clear that we do not imagine that these trends will be without their connections in other parts of the tonic system. In Figure 3 we picture the detailed relationships, for individuals, between the frequencies of rises, falls and levels (the three most frequent tones for the T sample as a whole). There are certain clear *patterns* of frequency distribution here which are represented qualitatively in diagram 1(a). For women speakers (see Diagram 1(a)) there are two types of sub-variety of tone distribution:

1   in which the percentage of rise tones is considerably greater than the percentage of fall tones (4/9 speakers)—cf. Figure 2 and our discussion of it;
2   in which the reverse is the case (5/9 speakers).

Each of these types has two sub-types: (a) in which the number of *rises* and of levels is about equal, (b) in which the number of *falls* and of levels is about equal. Amongst men, variation of frequency pattern of this kind is much less widespread: there is considerable uniformity of the frequency percentage of

---

[7]Notice that the men in the Tyneside sample have a similar mean percentage difference. This similarity is probably spurious for two reasons:
(i)   there is reason to imagine that panel discussion (Q) and informal interviews (T$_1$, T$_2$) would elicit different types of realization pattern (Crystal and Davy, 1969), in which case distributional *sameness* indicates *difference* of underlying system;
(ii)   comparison of the university-educated speakers in Q with the most educated speakers in T (*Mc, N*) shows that the latter have a far *higher* percentage difference (falls/rises) than the mean Q value and are therefore likely to be producing realizations of a different system.

rise and fall tones. There is one tone-frequency pattern in common between men (a) and women (IIa) which, as a pattern, accounts for 13/20 members of this sample. (It is worth noting that the three women having this common pattern are in socio-economic class V.) This shared pattern however, is quantitatively different for men and for women (see Diagram 1b). Firstly, the

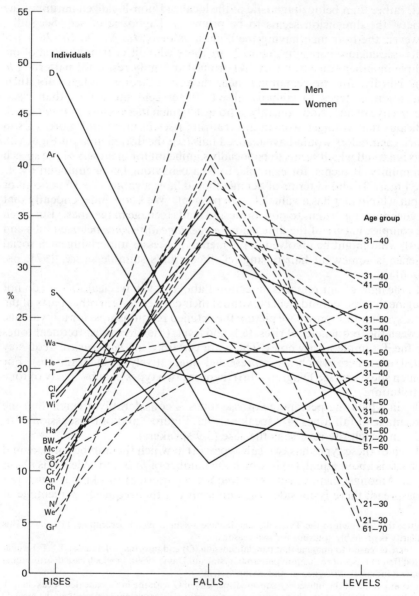

Figure 3. Traces for 20 individuals of numbers of rises, falls and levels, percentage all tones

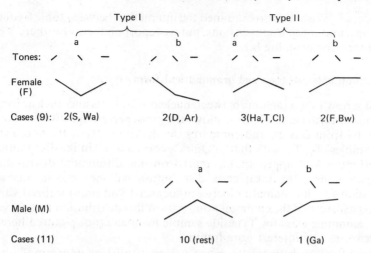

Diagram 1 (a) Tone frequency patterns for women and men (from Figure 3)

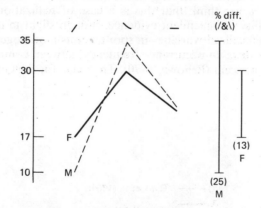

Diagram 1 (b) Distinction between pattern F,II(a) and pattern M(a)

mean percentage difference between rises and falls is *lower* for women (13 per cent) than for men (25 per cent) (in spite of the results of Figure 2). Secondly, the percentage difference for women falls within the range of the percentage difference for men. If we choose to use such tone frequency patterns as a dimension (each pattern being some fraction of a dimension), it will not be a dimension which discriminates men from women according to any simple principle. Where there is a qualitative difference of pattern (F, I(a) against M(a), for example) the discrimination will be all-or-none. But when the patterns are qualitatively the same (F, II(a) against M(a)), the discrimination can only be probabilistic, and the probabilities inherent in the pattern will have to be continuously monitored from the sample of speakers being considered. (We have also examined the interaction between tonic frequencies on simple and complex dimensions, but we report on these elsewhere: Pellowe and Jones, forthcoming b.)

Interaction between tone and grammatical form classes

We turn now to interactions between nuclear selections and nuclear locations in terms of form class. Figure 4 shows the gross percentage distribution of all nuclei by form classes, and compares the distributions of the two Tyneside sub-samples (T_1, T_2) with that of Quirk's corpus (Q). Unlike distributions by tone (Figure 1) it appears that, apart from the differential distribution on common nouns, the form class distribution will not provide us with a dimension for discriminating between localized and non-localized varieties. (We have dissected the common noun part of this distribution by age, sex and socio-economic class for Tyneside sample members (not pictured here), and no trends of any interest were found.

The difference between the mean values of nuclear nouns in T and Q is significant, but it probably has to do with the distinction between panel discussion and informal interview rather than that between groups of sub-varieties. That is, we think that this is a case of realizational rather than varietal variability. Independent evidence, though slight in quantity, of the use of Tyneside localized varieties in spontaneous monologue and informal conversation yields a co-occurrence frequency between common nouns and all nuclei of 44 per cent (Pellowe, 1970). The value for the Quirk corpus was

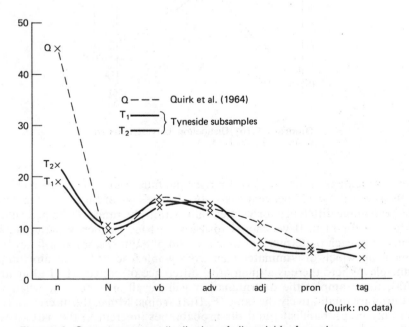

Figure 4. Gross percentage distribution of all nuclei by form class

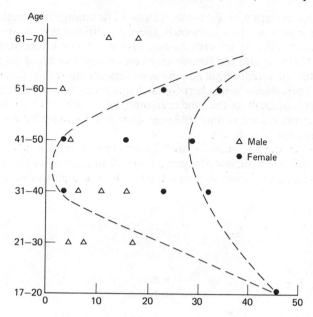

Figure 5. Percentage distribution of nuclear adverbs carrying ╱ and ╲╱, on age

45 per cent. This view is confirmed by plotting the percentage of nuclei on common nouns (x) against the percentage of common nouns not carrying tone (y) (not pictured here). When we did this we found that the whole sample clumped together quite closely with a mean value on x of 23 per cent and on y of 43 per cent. That is, the dependency between the number of non-tonic common nouns and the fraction of tones carried by common nouns does not significantly vary in the sample considered here. Given the complex dependencies we have observed amongst elements of the tonic system, this can only mean that the common noun differences given by Figure 4 are *not* varietal.

Comparison of the results of Quirk *et al.* (1964) and of Pellowe (1970) shows that of all the form classes taken account of by them (considering the distributive effect of form class on tones) *adverbs* are the most likely to distinguish localized from non-localized varieties. Pellowe (1970) found that a significantly higher percentage of rises and fall-rises were realized on adverbs in localized varieties than in non-localized varieties. Figure 5 pictures the sample distributed by age and sex on the percentage of nuclear adverbs realized as rises and fall-rises. No interesting regularities are represented for age in the sample as a whole. For *women* however, though it is an unexpected and complex finding and on this quantity of evidence by no means generalizable, there is a very interesting distribution. The values of the dimension are parabolically distributed. (The two curves represent (a) women from all available age groups with the highest values, (b) women from all available age groups with the lowest values.) The change of direction occurs at around the age of 40. In other words, there is a differentiation, in terms of the percentage of nuclear adverbs having rise and fall-rise, between the sub-varieties of young and old female speakers on the one hand (high), and the sub-varieties of middle-aged female speakers on the other (low). Clearly a larger number of female speakers for each age group is required before we can have any certainty about this, and even then, what such a differentiation might mean will remain unclear until we know, from less complex but related results, what correlates to look for.

Plotting the dimension of Figure 5 (percentage of nuclear adverbs carrying rises and fall-rises) against the percentage of nuclear adverbs carrying falls (not pictured here) shows that men tend to have a high frequency of nuclear

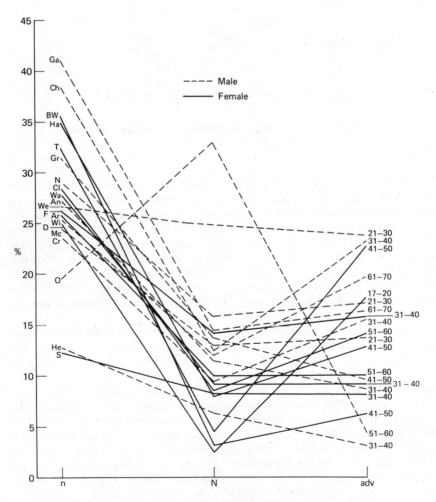

Figure 6. Percentage of falls distribution on n, N, adv., by person

adverbs which are realized as falls and a low frequency which are realized as rises and fall-rises. Women show the converse tendency. Equally interesting, however, is the finding that *amongst* men there is an age trend. Younger men tend to have a high fraction of nuclear adverbs with falls and a lower fraction with rises and fall-rises. Older men tend to have the converse pattern.

So far we have only considered one form class—adverb—in any detail, but it is clear that form class and tone interact with complex dependencies just as do elements within the tone system. Figure 6 pictures the percentage of falls on

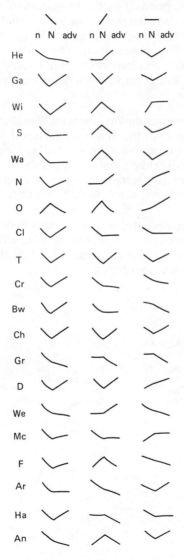

Diagram 2 Pattern summary of frequency distributions of \, ⁄, ‾ tones on n, N, adv, by informant, column 1 from Figure 6

common nouns, names and adverbs for individuals in the sample. Diagram 2 (column 1) lists the qualitative patterns of Figure 6 by informant. It also lists patterns from figures like Figure 6 (but not pictured here) which deal with the distribution on common nouns, names and adverbs of rises and levels. In Diagram 3a we take the patterns of Diagram 2 and list informants who share the same patterns of tonic distribution across these three form classes. Diagram 3b represents these similarity lists in a two dimensional grouping in so far as this is possible. There is much of interest in this material, but we only have space to make a few points. Firstly, the pattern of distribution of falls on common nouns, names and adverbs is much less variable within this sample (12, 7, 1 for the three pattern types (cf. Figure 6, Diagrams 2 and 3a)) than it is for rises (8, 6, 6 for the three pattern types). Secondly, however, the *available* patterns of distribution on common nouns, names and adverbs are the same for both rises and falls. For example, varieties differ as to whether for falling tones

either (i)	the number on common nouns and on adverbs is about the same and *greater* than the number on names;
or (ii)	the number on common nouns and on adverbs is about the same and *fewer* than the number on names;
or (iii)	the number on common nouns is greater than the number on names which is greater than the number on adverbs.

Varieties differ for exactly parallel reasons in respect of rising tones. Thirdly, though the relative commonness of the patterns of distribution of rises (8, 6, 6) is similar to that for those of level tones (9, 5, 6), the actual patterns of distribution for level tones are different.

Tone	\			/			—		
Patterns:	∨	∟	∧	∨	∟	∧	∨	/	＼
Shared by:	Ga	He	O	Ga	S	Bw	Ga	O	Bw
	T	Gr		T	Wa	Cr	T	Wi	Cr
	Ch	We		Ch	O	Ha	Ch	N	Ha
	D	An		D	Wi	Mc	Cl		
	Wi	S		N	An	Gr		D	Gr
	N	Wa		Cl	F	Ar	S	Mc	
	Cl	Ar					Wa		F
	Bw			He			Ar		
	Ha			We			He		We
	Cr						An		
	Mc								
	F								
Totals:	12	7	1	8	6	6	9	5	6

Diagram 3 (a) Lists of informants by shared frequency patterns of \, /, —
on n, N, adv

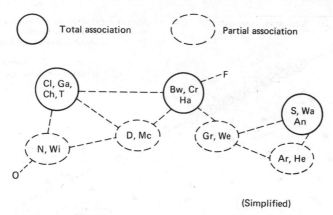

(Simplified)

Diagram 3 (b) Overall groupings of informants on 3 (a) above

Interaction between pitch range and tone

Finally, we introduce interaction between the system of pitch range and that of tone. (For further details and more general remarks about the systematic nature of varietal variability in the prosodic systems of pitch range see Pellowe and Jones (forthcoming)). Figure 7 gives *two* accounts of the relationship between levels and the simple system of pitch range. The first trace is linear by definition. It takes the number of level tones *co-occurring with a pitch range feature* and plots the number co-occurring with a 'generalized booster' against the number occurring with a 'generalized drop'. (Extra-high boosters, high booster, boosters and continuances all count, for this picture, as generalized boosters. Low drops and drops all count, for this picture, as generalized drops.) For levels having a pitch range feature, the sample is quite strongly grouped around a value of 24 per cent drop+level (76 per cent booster+level). There are no marked interdependencies with social macro variables, although values above 45 per cent of drop+level appear to be restricted to male varieties. (More cases need to be considered for this to be more than tentative.)

The second trace in Figure 7 plots generalized boosters and generalized drops with levels (as before), but as a percentage of *all* levels (i.e. levels with and without pitch range features). High values of drop+level (but now above 35 per cent) continue to be interpretable as male. In addition men *and* women of high socio-economic class tend to have fewer levels with generalized booster (regardless of the proportion with drops) than men and women of lower socio-economic class. Finally there is much *less* variation amongst *women* than amongst men in respect of these co-occurring features.

The differential association of a class of pitch range features (generalized booster) with two tones is shown for half of the sample (T_1) in Figure 8. Neither the percentage distribution of boosted falls nor that of boosted levels shows any association with social macro-variables, nor are they associated with each other. This is not a merely negative finding however. It is very

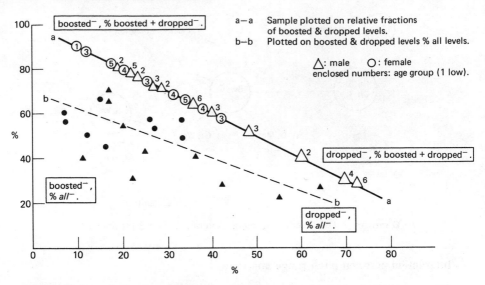

Figure 7. Two distributions of boosters and drops on level tone, by individual

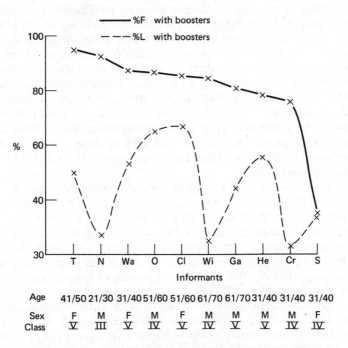

Figure 8 Distribution of boosters on falling and level tones, for T₁ (10 speakers)

important to be able to establish that co-occurrent features have a potential for differential distribution, since if we could not establish such potentials we should be unable to place the confidence we wish to in the patterns of variable dependency amongst intonational subvarieties which we have discussed here.

6 Summary

We have presented a crude conceptual framework which distinguishes two kinds of variability in prosodic systems. We have applied the general sociolinguistic methods developed within the Tyneside Linguistic Survey to a description of a limited number of features from 4,066 tone units. We have shown that within such a framework the application of such methods can elicit structure of sociolinguistic importance from intonational variation.

From a group of twenty speakers who had not been matched at all in any strict sense, trends associating sex, age and socio-economic class with dimensions which represented single tones, interactions among tones, interactions of tones with form classes, and interactions of tones with terms from the system of pitch range, have been displayed. Just as important however, have been the demonstrations of forms of patterning of parts of the sample in respect of various features which had nothing to do with these social macro-variables. In general, we do not at present see any reason to imagine that all, or even most, of the structural variation in such features as we have been discussing will correlate with social macro-variables (such as socioeconomic class). The primary goal must be to find not dimensions which successfully correlate with such things, but dimensions which are stable for changed samples and which are capable, in *combination*, of eliciting the structure of the variation in those samples. Only when we know enough about such stability and structure will we know what level of thing to look for as correlate. Although each successive dimension may project a markedly different ranking or a different degree of association on the sample members, it is important to remember the *additive* nature of the dimensions in the total variety space. The relations among speakers given by tonic distributions alone are different from those given by tonic/form-class distributions, but the space which is defined by the locking together of these, and other, dimensions will finally group speakers in ways which will reflect both the complexity of their behaviour, and that of their hearers.

9

RP-accented female speech: The voice of perceived androgyny?

Olwen Elyan, Philip Smith,
Howard Giles and Richard Bourhis

This paper is concerned with an empirical investigation into the social significance of two British accents when used by women.[1] At the outset, we will review previous work (based mainly on male data) which suggests that the use of the prestige accent in the United Kingdom (Received Pronunciation: RP) confers considerable social advantages on its users in a number of contexts. We will then report a study which is interpreted as showing that when females adopt an RP rather than a regional accent they are perceived not only as more competent, but also as both more male-like on certain personality attributes *and* as more feminine (that is, androgynously). These findings are then discussed in relation to a social psychological theory of sociolinguistic behaviour.

A number of studies in a variety of cultures have shown that dialect and accent are important cues in gaining an immediate impression of another person (see review by Giles and Powesland, 1975). Much of these data have been gathered by use of the 'matched-guise' technique (Lambert, 1967). The procedure involves judges listening to a series of apparently different speakers reading the same emotionally-neutral passage of prose and then being required to evaluate the speakers on various rating scales. The speakers are, in fact, one and the same person using different realistic guises of the particular dialects and accents under study. The main advantage of this technique is that it goes some way towards eliminating the effects of stimulus speakers' idiosyncratic voice characteristics such as rate, loudness, timbre, pitch and so forth. The effects of these individual differences are of course interesting in themselves, yet they would tend to confound the results of studies designed to elicit evaluative reactions to dialect (or accent) differences across groups.[2] According to Lambert (1967), this method reveals more about listeners'

[1]The authors would like to express their gratitude to Messrs Hodkin, O'Sullivan and Otty of Bristol Polytechnic for their cooperation in the execution of this study, Ms M. and J. Swarbrick for their excellent voice recordings, and Ms J. A. Williams and Dr D. M. Taylor for their comments on this manuscript.
[2]Criticisms of this technique have been raised a number of times (Tajfel, 1962; Agheyisi and Fishman, 1970; Lee, 1971; Robinson, 1972) and have been discussed in Giles and Bourhis (1973; 1976b) and Giles and Powesland (1975).

feelings about speakers than can be found in direct attitudes questionnaires.

Work in Britain using this technique has shown that people tend to evaluate accents on a prestige continuum (Giles, 1970; 1971a). Informants from two regions in Britain were asked to rate the status of a variety of speakers with different accents. On the basis of their judgments, it was found that speakers may be placed along a continuum of accent prestige with users of RP possessing the highest status, regional accented speakers next highest, and those with accents of an industrial town (e.g., Liverpool, Birmingham) possessing the least prestige of all. Although there were small differences in the perceived prestige of these accents according to the age, sex, social class, regional origin and personality of the judges, the overall uniformity of people's reactions was surprisingly high. Moreover, in a subsequent study (Giles, 1972a), it was found that the broader the accent spoken in a particular region, the less prestige the speaker had even among members of the speaker's own community.

Other studies have looked at evaluative dimensions other than accent prestige. Contrasting RP-accented speakers with speakers of regional accents such as those found in Yorkshire (Strongman and Woosley, 1967), Scotland (Cheyne, 1970), Somerset (Giles, 1971b; 1972b) and Cardiff (Giles and Bourhis, 1976a), it has been found that speakers of RP are perceived as having more competence (e.g., intelligence, self-confidence) but less integrity and social attractiveness (e.g., sincerity, kindheartedness) than regional accented speakers. Furthermore, Bourhis, Giles and Lambert (1975) showed that speakers in Wales who shift their accents in the direction of an RP-accented interlocutor are perceived as being more intelligent and well-educated, but less trustworthy and kindhearted than those who maintain their regional variety. Thus, RP speakers are upgraded on traits related to socioeconomic status, while regional accented speakers are upgraded on dimensions related to integrity and social attractiveness (cf. Tajfel, 1959).

These findings tie in interestingly with other results that suggest that the RP accent may prove *dis*advantageous in areas where the regional accent serves as a marker of ethnic or national identity. To the extent that it functions as a symbol of in-group loyalty and solidarity in such areas, the regional accent may be preferred to RP (cf. Giles, Bourhis and Taylor, 1977). This was how Bourhis, Giles and Tajfel (1973) explained their finding that Welsh listeners upgraded Welsh-accented and Welsh language speakers on most evaluative traits in a matched-guise study while downgrading those who spoke with an RP accent. Similarly, Bourhis and Giles (1976) in a naturalistic study found that Welsh bilinguals reacted more favourably to a request for help when it was voiced in Welsh-accented English, or the Welsh language itself, than when the request was made with an RP accent. In this study, the audiences attending a Welsh dramatic performance were invited to help the management by cooperating in a short audience survey. This information was transmitted to the audience during the interval via the loudspeaker system using various guises on different occasions—some nights in Welsh, some in RP, and some in Welsh-accented English. It was found that almost three times as many people completed the questionnaire when the plea was voiced in Welsh rather than in

English, and of the reactions to the English pleas, over three times as many people cooperated when it was a Welsh rather than an RP accent.

Despite the obvious complexities that findings such as these introduce into our discussion, there are more results (thus far anyway) supporting an argument that RP speakers are at a distinct social advantage in a variety of formal situations. Giles, Baker and Fielding (1975), in addition to eliciting attitudinal reactions to accented speech, designed a study to investigate behavioural reactions as well. This study involved a stimulus speaker asking two matched groups of high-school students to provide him with written information concerning what they knew about psychology. In this face-to-face situation, the request was made in an RP accent to one group while the other heard the same request by the same speaker in a regional (Birmingham) accent. The speaker was rated as being more intelligent, and more words were written to him, when his request was voiced in the prestige variety. Therefore, even when both verbal and non-verbal cues are made available to listeners, RP speakers are upgraded in perceived competence and helped more than regional speakers.

As a final demonstration of the social significance of accents here, it has been found that listeners upgrade the quality of an argument when it is spoken in RP as opposed to a regional variety. Nevertheless, listeners only tend to be *persuaded* by an argument when it is voiced in an accent with which they can identify (Giles, 1973a; Powesland and Giles, 1975). In other words, RP listeners in these studies changed their attitude on a controversial issue more when the communicator was RP than when he was regional accented, whereas for regional accented listeners, the reverse was the case.

This complex yet systematic array of findings has been largely responsible for the development of a theory to account for why people's speech often changes during the course of an interpersonal interaction. Interpersonal accommodation theory, as it has been called (Giles, 1973b; 1977; Giles, Taylor and Bourhis, 1973; Giles and Powesland, 1975), seeks to describe the strategies that individuals employ in order to either increase or decrease social distance between themselves and their listener(s), and to explain in social psychological terms the motivation behind each strategy. In the context of the present discussion, the theory has been concerned with explaining why individuals tend to modify their accents in the direction of RP in the presence of higher-status others. On the basis of the matched-guise research in Britain, the theory suggests that individuals adopting this strategy (called 'upward accent convergence') will be perceived as more competent and persuasive, and that what they have to say will be perceived as of a better quality and more likely to induce cooperation than if they had maintained their regular accents.[3] These potential rewards in terms of the other's social approval then could arguably be considered sufficient motivation for making one's accent more RP-like in this situation.

However, much of the work on the matched-guise technique outlined above, and hence the theoretical framework deriving from it, is deserving of

[3] The theory is also concerned with 'downward convergence', and strategies of 'speech divergence' (Bourhis and Giles, 1977; Bourhis, Giles, Leyen and Tajfel, in press).

the recent criticism levelled at researchers in sociolinguistics by Kramer (in press). She states that 'as recently as 1972 the assumption within the new discipline [sociolinguistics] has been that the primary subjects it focuses on . . . the "members of the social order" . . . are male.' Only one of the studies discussed here (Cheyne, 1970) assessed people's reactions to *female* speakers' accents. He found that his listeners judged female RP and Scottish accents to be significantly different from each other on far fewer traits than their male counterparts. Considering that most of the studies have used male stimulus voices, the range of evaluative traits provided to the listeners for assessing these speakers were also likely to have been male-biased. Kramer's criticism is also justified when one considers that some studies in North America have already shown that people often react quite differently to male and female speakers of the same dialect community (Lambert, Giles and Picard, 1975; Lambert, Giles and Albert, 1976), and sometimes even in the opposite direction (Lambert, 1967).

In recent years, interest has grown in differences between the sexes with regard to their use of language (Herzler, 1965; Holter, 1970; Barron, 1971; Lakoff, 1973; Kramer, 1974; 1975a; 1975b; Trudgill, 1974a; Thorne and Henley, 1975), and also the ways in which language depicts the sexes (Blakar, 1974; Schulz, 1975; Martyna, in press). Two research areas in this tradition are of particular interest to us in this context. Firstly, work in the United States (e.g., Labov, 1966; Levine and Crockett, 1967; Wolfram, 1968) and Britain (Trudgill, 1972; 1974b) has shown that women tend to produce more prestigious pronunciation patterns than men particularly as the formality of a social situation is increased. Secondly, Kramer (in press) has shown that high-school and college students stereotype the speech of males and females differently. For example, American male speech was characterized as more authoritarian, forceful, deep, aggressive than female speech while the latter was considered to be more clearly enunciated, trivial, gentle and friendly. Moreover, women perceived greater differences between the speech behaviour of males and females than did males. Given that (i) RP speech has been found to be used more frequently by females than males, (ii) members of both sexes seem to have definite expectations concerning each other's speech behaviour, and (iii) conscious of Kramer's criticism of the lack of female representation in present sociolinguistic speech data, it was thought necessary that a preliminary study should be conducted to investigate people's reactions to female accented speech in Britain.

The following study, then, was conducted using the matched-guise technique to determine evaluative reactions to RP versus Lancashire (Northern) accented female speech. The investigation was designed so as to elicit males' and females' perceptions of these speakers and to include not only scales used in the traditional (male) studies but also to adopt measures used in current stereotype research related to masculine and feminine sex traits. This research was conducted to determine whether (i) the previous findings on impression formation of male RP versus regional accented speakers are applicable to the same extent for *female* voices, (ii) the same evaluative trends emerge for both male and female listeners, and (iii) traits relating to masculinity and femininity are perceived to interact with accented speech.

Method

Listener-judges

Thirty-eight males and 38 females attending a polytechnic in Bristol served as judges for the experiment. It was impossible to secure exactly matched samples of listeners. The male judges were recruited from an engineering course while the females were obtained from modern language and business courses. The mean age of the listening sample was 22 years and they derived from all parts of the United Kingdom. In other words, although they were resident in Southern England they were heterogeneous in their regional origins (cf. Giles, 1972a, p. 267)

Stimulus voices

The stimulus voices were prepared by two bidialectal, middle-class female speakers from Manchester who were able to read realistically the same passage of prose in RP and Lancashire accents. The stimulus passage was one adopted by some of the present authors in a previous study (Giles and Bourhis, 1976a). The two speakers read the passage in both guises attempting to maintain the same speech rate, paralinguistic features and impression of personality throughout their recordings. Moreover, an independent sample of 120 college students validated the authenticity of the RP and Northern accented guises.[4] Two other speakers were recorded in order to provide two filler voices to disguise the fact that some of the speakers were recorded twice. The order of speaker presentation on the stimulus tape was as follows:

1   Filler voice (South Welsh accent)
2   Speaker A (RP)
3   Speaker B (Northern)
4   Filler voice (RP)
5   Speaker A (Northern)
6   Speaker B (RP)

Materials

Questionnaire booklets were prepared which required listeners to judge each of the six speakers heard on 25 rating scales. On the basis of previous rating instruments using the matched-guise procedure (see Giles and Powesland, 1975), eight traits were chosen representing four different dimensions. These were: intelligence and self-confidence (*competence* traits); fluency and clarity (*communicative* traits); likeability and sociability (*social attractiveness* traits); reliability and sincerity (*personal integrity* traits). On the basis of work by Williams and Best (1977) on sex stereotyping among college students in the United States, and that of Williams *et al.* (in press) in England, an additional

[4]These students were asked to listen to the stimulus voices very carefully and describe their characteristics. They were described in a manner consistent with our own social and geographical categorizations, and no person attributed a voice as a mimicked guise.

eight traits were adopted representing favourable and unfavourable, male and female sex stereotypes. These were: adventurousness and independence (*positive male* traits); aggressiveness and egotism (*negative male* traits); gentleness and sensitivity (*positive female* traits); weakness and complainingness (*negative female* traits). The work of Spence, Helmreich and Stapp (1974) and Bem (1975) suggested three other scales: self esteem, masculinity and femininity. The above traits (except for masculinity and femininity)[5] appeared on the questionnaire in a random order for each voice and listeners were instructed to rate the extent to which each adjective definitely did, or definitly did not suit each speaker on nine-point rating scales.

A final six exploratory nine-point scales relating to some aspects of female sex-role ideology were included. These scales questioned the extent to which the speakers were at that time (or sometime in the future) likely to be: married; have children; share household responsibilities with spouse; have a job at all; have a prestiguous job; have a well-paid job.

Procedure

A female investigator in her early twenties with an RP accent conducted the study in group administered sessions. The task was introduced in what has become a standard fashion: listeners were led to believe that they were being tested on their ability to infer personality characteristics of speakers using speech cues alone. No reference was made to the investigator's interest in reactions to regional accents or to women. It was presumed however that listeners would not be able to overlook accent variations on the stimulus tape and that these could have varying degrees of influence on their evaluative judgments. When the task had been introduced to the listeners, they were then instructed on the use of the rating scales. Each voice was listened to and rated separately, and after this procedure the investigator debriefed the informants on the purpose of the study and invited their comments in a general discussion.

Results

A series of two-way analyses of variance, with repeated measures on one factor, were performed on the responses to each of the 25 rating scales. The raw data for these analyses consisted of the average rating of the two Northern, and of the two RP speakers for each listener on each of the rating scales. The independent variables were accent of the speaker and sex of the listener. The statistically significant findings for each of the scales appear in Table 1, with F values and associated significance levels indicated.

From Table 1, it can be seen that a significant main effect for accent of the speaker was obtained on 18 of the 25 rating scales, indicating that listeners ascribed most of the traits to the speakers differentially, depending on the speaker's accent. It was found that listeners considered the RP speakers to be higher in self-esteem, clearer, more fluent, intelligent, self-confident, adventurous, independent, feminine and less weak than the regional accented speakers. In addition, the former were more likely to have a job which was

[5]The masculinity and femininity scales appeared after the randomized list on the questionnaire in order to avoid response contamination.

Table 1: Significant F values for the 25 scales

Scales	Accent of speaker effects (df=1,74)	Sex of listener effects (df=1,74)	Accent X Sex, interaction effects (df=1,74)
Intelligence	187.99**		14.36*
Self-confidence	70.13*		
Fluency	244.34**	10.15*	
Clarity	152.57**		
Likeability	12.90*		
Sociability			
Reliability			
Sincerity	11.24*		
Adventurousness	11.70*		
Independence	57.07*		11.04*
Aggressiveness	17.34*		
Egotism	50.13*		7.84*
Gentleness			
Sensitivity			
Weakness	14.05*		
Complainingness			
Self-esteem	63.00*		
Masculinity			
Femininity	16.06*		
Married			
Have children	38.32*		
Share household duties	7.56*		
Own job	32.51*		13.31*
Occupational status	227.31**		18.46*
Occupational salary	206.45**		19.57*

$^*p<.01$ $^{**}p<.001$

well-paid and prestigious and an egalitarian relationship with their spouse in the home, but less likely to have children than Northern accented speakers. At the same time, regional speakers were perceived to be more sincere and likeable, and less aggressive and egotistic than their RP counterparts.

Significant interaction effects emerged on six scales indicating that the way that these items were ascribed to speakers with different accents depended on the sex of the listener. On these six scales (independence, egotism, having a job,

Table 2: Mean ratings for the six significant Accent X Sex interaction*

Scales	Accent of stimulus speakers			
	RP		Northern	
	Male listeners	Female listeners	Male listeners	Female listeners
Intelligence	12.76	14.45	9.42	8.55
Independence	12.66	14.10	10.81	9.37
Egotism	11.81	12.97	9.68	8.05
Own job	12.32	14.68	11.37	10.37
Occupational status	12.00	14.71	7.18	6.89
Occupational salary	10.92	13.68	7.10	6.47

* The higher the rating, the more independent, egotistic, etc. the speakers are seen to be.

occupational status, occupational salary), female listeners polarized their ratings of the speakers indicated by the main effects above. For example, female listeners rated the RP speakers as more independent (egotistic, etc.) and Northern speakers as less independent (egotistic, etc.) than did male listeners. Only one main effect emerged for sex of listener, in that female listeners perceived all the speakers (irrespective of accent) to be more fluent than did male listeners.

Discussion

These findings can be most parsimoniously interpreted as follows. RP-accented females in Britain are upgraded in terms of competence and communicative skills but downgraded in terms of social attractiveness and personal integrity relative to regional accented females. Such data corroborates of course the stereotypes associated with British male speakers outlined earlier. In addition, we find that RP accented women are perceived more favourably on a number of occupational dimensions than Northern accented women. Perhaps more interestingly, however, RP women are expected to bear fewer children, to create a more egalitarian relationship with their husbands and are seen to be more masculine in their sex traits (positive and negative) while at the same time being rated higher on the femininity trait than Northern accented females. Thus, we have a stereotyped picture of RP-accented women as highly competent, articulate, lacking in warmth, masculine in certain ways and yet feminine and espousing egalitarian ideals between the sexes. Interestingly, this profile of the RP accented female is highlighted more by women than by men (cf. Kramer, in press).

At first sight, these results may seem contradictory in the sense that RP women are seen as both highly masculine on certain traits and yet definitely high on the femininity trait as well. Recent research, however, would suggest that these data are amenable to an interesting interpretation. Constantinople (1973) and Block (1973) have highlighted the problem involved in conceptualizing people in terms of a simple masculine-feminine dichotomy. A number of workers (e.g., Spence, Helmreich and Stapp, 1974; Bem, 1975) have measured masculinity and femininity as two *independent* dimensions allowing the expression of both characteristics in individuals of either sex. These studies have found that between 30 and 45 per cent of some American female college populations score high on both masculinity and femininity scales. These individuals, displaying what has been termed *psychological androgyny*, represent themselves as being strongly masculine in certain respects and strongly feminine in others. It has been suggested that androgynous women have a wide behavioural repertoire from which to choose enabling them to cope with the demands of a wide variety of social (and often stressful) situations. This flexibility in behaviour (undoubtedly verbal as well) is of course very adaptive and facilitates self-esteem and psychological health. Indeed, Williams (1977) has demonstrated that androgynous women are less susceptible to psychopathological disorders than other women. Given these notions, it is perhaps not surprising that people may be able to *perceive both* masculine and feminine traits in the behaviour of others. Speculatively, one could label the female RP accent as the voice of perceived androgyny.

Why is it then that the RP female may be stereotyped in an androgynous fashion? Is it that RP accented women are more likely to be androgynous than their regional accented counterparts? This would seem a possibility given that preliminary data exploring the demographic correlates of androgyny suggest that androgynous females have parents of a higher socioeconomic status, and are themselves more educated when compared to sex-typed females (Allgeier, 1975; Williams, 1977). In this sense, the former are more likely to possess prestigious-sounding voices than the latter. Another approach may arguably lie in the fact that the RP accent is seen as the voice of sophistication and social power, and the voice of those who are in a position to exert some control or influence over their social environments. In the case of women then, such attributes may be seen to allow them a considerable opportunity both of accentuating their femininity by use of expensive fineries while at the same time succeeding in male-dominated pursuits. Future work on the causal agents of androgyny, perceived or actual, may well help elucidate this issue. In addition, determining what listeners construed to be the dimensions of the scale 'femininity' in the present study might also be illuminating. It would be interesting to determine whether prestige-sounding females (and males) in other Western societies are also perceived androgynously, and to determine the linguistic characteristics of actual androgynous and non-androgynous males and females.

We stated above that females in the United States and the United Kingdom tend to use more prestige speech forms than men, and Trudgill (1974b) has claimed that this may be due to two factors. First, he states that because women are generally found to be more status conscious than men, they will experience greater pressures to adopt the prestige speech forms. Second, and perhaps more importantly according to Trudgill, is the notion that non-prestige speech (and particularly working-class varieties) is associated with masculinity and toughness and hence finds greater attraction for male speakers (cf. Labov *et al.*, 1968; d'Anglejan and Tucker, 1973). Although our present study has not investigated working-class speech *per se*, it has been concerned with reactions to a non-prestige variety, the Lancashire accent (Giles, 1970). It will be recalled that regional speakers in this study were not rated highly on masculine traits, not even on the scale of 'masculinity' itself; admittedly, they did receive a lower score on the 'femininity' scale. These data would suggest (despite the fact that the trait of toughness was not included[6]) that non-prestige-sounding female speech may not be associated with a general masculine stereotype, and therefore tends to cast some doubt on the weight of Trudgill's second factor above.

This leaves us with the first factor; that is, women adopt more prestigious speech because they are more status conscious than men. The results of the present study allow us to take this a little further theoretically. In line with accommodation theory outlined previously, it is suggested that people tend to use more RP accented speech with high-status others (upwardly converge)

[6]Note however that the trait of *weakness* was included, and listeners afforded the regional speakers a higher rating on this scale than the RP speakers.

because they may be perceived more favourably in terms of status, competence, persuasiveness and the quality of what they have to say. These notions were based primarily on male data. On the basis of our present findings, it may well be that we can propose additional social rewards which women may reap by adopting prestigious speech in this situation. For instance, they will be perceived as more male-like in qualities of independence and adventurousness, less weak, and also be rated higher on the femininity scale. It is true that they may be simultaneously perceived as possessing other less favourable traits, such as aggressiveness and egotism, yet in many of our achievement-oriented (male) contexts these are unlikely to detract much from the hypothesized rewards. Thus, we can suggest that females are more likely to adopt prestige speech patterns since they tend to be perceived favourably on a greater variety of evaluative dimensions than males who adopt a similar speech strategy.[7] In addition, it could be suggested that women have an interest in adopting prestige speech forms since doing so may increase their chance of marrying into a social class that is above their own. Indeed, given the discrimination against women in employment, it has been argued that women are better able to achieve upward social mobility through marriage than through achievement in the work world (Smelser and Lipset, 1966; Chase, 1975).

If women are also *expected* to be generally more status conscious and norm-oriented, this provides another clue as to why RP accented female speech was rated higher on the femininity scale in this study. Presumably, the most feminine females would be the most status conscious ones. If the possession of an RP accent is taken by listener-judges as an index of status consciousness, then it is not surprising that such speakers should also be rated higher on femininity.

Obviously, our study has raised more questions than it has answered, particularly with regard to androgyny and language behaviour. Further research needs to be conducted to determine whether the same evaluative trends would emerge when RP accented females were contrasted with other regional accented female speakers, and to determine the interactive effects of age of speaker, topic discussed, purpose of conversation and the nature of the social context in such studies. It seems important also to tap a greater range of traits related to masculinity and femininity with female and male stimulus speakers and to adopt the stereotyped characteristics of female and male speech found by Kramer (in press) as future dependent measures. Moreover, it may be beneficial to ask independent samples of males and females to suggest the traits and attributes they themselves consider to be important in impression formation (cf. Bourhis, Giles and Tajfel, 1973; Giles and Bourhis, 1976b). Nevertheless, this study again draws attention to the fact that on certain important dimensions non-RP accented speakers are perceived *more* favourably than RP speakers. In the present case, Northern accented females were perceived as less aggressive and egotistic, and more likeable and sincere than RP speakers. At the very least, this chapter has shown that accented speech is just as socially significant for female as it is for male speakers in Britain.

[7]Pilot data collected by us suggest that RP accented males are not perceived androgynously although this obviously requires large-scale empirical verification.

10

Variation and consistency in Glaswegian English

Ronald K. S. Macaulay

> Behaviour does not yield data by parthenogenesis. . . . Behaviour never acts or speaks for itself in creating data; it only speaks when spoken to, when asked a question.
>
> Coombs (1964, p. 29)
>
> The way a question is asked limits and disposes the ways in which any answer—right or wrong—may be given . . .
>
> Langer (1942, p. 1)

During the past twenty years there have been several changes in the kinds of questions that linguists have asked.[1] These changes have come about as a consequence of different views of the aims of linguistic investigation. One view is stated very clearly by Martinet:

> There was a time when the progress of research required that each community should be considered linguistically self-contained and homogeneous. Whether this autarchic situation was believed to be a fact or was conceived of as a working hypothesis need not detain us here. It certainly was a useful assumption. By making investigators blind to a large number of actual complexities, it has enabled scholars, from the founding fathers of our science down to the functionalists and structuralists of today, to abstract a number of fundamental problems, to present for them solutions perfectly valid in the frame of the hypothesis, and generally to achieve, perhaps for the first time, some rigour in a research involving man's psychic activity.
>
> (Martinet, 1963, p. vii)

This approach is seen, for example, in Bloomfield's (1926) Postulates, Bloch's (1948) *idiolect*, and Chomsky's (1965) 'ideal speaker-listener, in a completely homogeneous speech community'. Martinet, however, goes on 'to

[1]The research described in this paper was supported by the Social Science Research Council, The Scottish Council for Research in Education, and the research and development committee of Pitzer College. I am very grateful to Bob Berdan for his invaluable assistance and advice in further analysing the Glasgow data though he might not agree with the position taken here.

stress the fact that a linguistic community is *never* homogeneous and hardly ever self-contained' (*ibid*) and Weinreich, Labov and Herzog (1968, p. 101) argue that this fact must not be ignored in linguistic description:

> . . . nativelike command of heterogeneous structures is not a matter of multidialectalism or 'mere' performance, but is part of unilingual linguistic competence. One of the corollaries of our approach is that in a language serving a complex (i.e. real) community, it is *absence* of structured heterogeneity that would be dysfunctional.

The work of Labov (1963; 1966; 1969; 1972a; 1972b) exemplifies the investigation of 'structured heterogeneity' in the speech community, and his example has been followed by others (e.g. Cook, 1969; Trudgill, 1974a; Wolfram, 1969).

Berdan, however, observes that the homogeneity myth has affected not only most of the work in generative grammar, where it is to be expected because of the extreme position adopted by Chomsky (1965, pp. 3–4), but also much of the work in traditional dialectology and, more surprisingly perhaps, some recent sociolinguistic studies. Berdan complains that the method of presenting the results of sociolinguistic investigations has often made it impossible to determine the extent to which the linguistic variation recorded is within speakers or among speakers:

> Acceptance of the myth has led to a system of data tabulation and reporting that makes it impossible to verify or reject the notion of linguistic homogeneity in sociologically determined groups. Studies report only group means, or in most cases, the results of aggregating data across individuals. . . . There is virtually no reporting of individual data, or even of any statistic such as standard deviations which would indicate some characteristics of the variation within the group. The result of the sociolinguist's myth has been to confound variation within individual speakers with variation among speakers.

> (Berdan, 1975, p. 10)

Dissatisfaction with Labov's approach to linguistic variation on this and other grounds, has led scholars such as Bailey (1973a; 1973b) and Bickerton (1971; 1973a; 1973b) to propose alternative methods of investigation. In the present paper I shall first describe a study carried out in Glasgow using a Labovian approach, and then return to some of the criticisms that have been made of this approach.

The Glasgow study

The Glasgow sample consisted of 16 adults, 16 fifteen-year-olds, and 16 ten-year-olds, with an equal number of males and females in each age-group. The respondents were selected to give equal representation in four social-class groups according to the occupation of the principal wage-earner in the family:

Class I —Professional and managerial
(Registrar General's categories (RG) 1, 2, 3, 4, 13)
Class II —White-collar, intermediate non-manual
(RG 5, 6)
Class III—Skilled manual
(RG 8, 9, 12, 14)
Class IV—Semi-skilled and unskilled manual
(RG 7, 10, 11)

During the months of March and April 1973, I conducted tape-recorded interviews with all the respondents, using a slightly different questionnaire for each age-group. (Details of the study and the actual questionnaires are given in Macaulay and Trevelyan, 1973; and Macaulay, forthcoming.) The tapes of the interviews were searched for variables which might correlate with social class and certain other extralinguistic factors. Five phonological variables turned out to correlate closely with the four social class groupings:

1   (i)   the vowel in *hit, kill, risk*, etc.
2   (u)   the vowel in *school, book, fool, full*, etc.[2]
3   (a)   the vowel in *cap, bag, hand*, etc.
4   (au)   the diphthong in *now, down, house*, etc.
5   (gs)   the use of a glottal stop instead of [t] in *butter, get*, etc.

For each of these variables a scale was developed in which numerical values were assigned to variants following the method introduced by Labov (1963) in his study of the centralization of diphthongs on Martha's Vineyard. For the variable (i) the scale was as follows:

(i–1)   [ɪ]
(i–2)   [ɛˆ] and [ɪᵥ]
(i–3)   [ɛ >] and [ïᵥ]
(i–4)   [əˆ]
(i–5)   [ʌˆ]

Group scores

For each respondent 40 tokens of (i) from the first half of the tape and 40 tokens from the second half of the tape were extracted and assigned the appropriate value from one to five. (Only instances of (i) in fully stressed syllables were extracted and instances of (i) before /r/ were reserved for

[2]A. J. Aitken (personal communication) has pointed out that there is a confusion with regard to the lexical set here. Although Glasgow speakers, like most Scots, do not distinguish *fool* from *full*, for some speakers the word class is subdivided because some lexical items may occur with a front unrounded vowel, e.g. [skɪᵛl] for *school*, and others with a low back unrounded vowel, e.g. [pʌl], for *pull* but *[skʌl] and *[pɪˈl] are not found. The situation is complicated by the fact that the variable (i)) can occur with [ʌ] as a variant. The figures for (u) were calculated by treating the variation as a continuum with fronting as the sole dimension and this may have distorted the actual situation. However, a recalculation of the indices for a random sample of the speakers suggests that the same pattern of social stratification would be maintained even if the word class had been more clearly defined.

separate investigation.) The values of (i) for each respondent were then averaged and multiplied by 100, giving an index figure of between 100 and 500. Table 1 shows the mean (i) index for males and females in each social class.

Table 1

	Class I	Class II	Class III	Class IV
All respondents	202	247	284	294
Males	224	279	287	300
Females	180	215	280	288

It can be seen from Table 1 that there is clear social stratification in the use of the variable (i) since the mean indices increase from the highest social class to the lowest. In articulatory terms, this indicates that the respondents from the lower social-class groups are more likely to use a vowel which is more retracted and lowered than are those from the higher social-class groups. There is also a clear indication of sex differences; in each social-class group, females have lower indices than males. There is also an interesting interaction between social class and sex in that the greatest difference between the classes comes between Class I and Class II for males, whereas for females it comes between Class II and Class III. In other words, Class II females are similar to Class I females in their use of (i) but Class II males are similar to Class III males. The difference between the social-class groups is smallest between Class III and Class IV. Since a similar pattern is found in the other variables and since the comments of the respondents suggest a tripartite social structure, probably Classes III and IV should be grouped together into a single class. This does not mean that there are no systematic differences within this class but they are much smaller than those between the three major social-class groups. Since social classes are relatively crude categories it would be unwise to attach great significance to small differences in linguistic behaviour.[3] If the figures for Classes III and IV are combined as in Table 2, a very clear picture of social stratification is revealed.

Table 2

	Class I	Class II	Class III/IV
All respondents	202	247	289
Males	224	279	294
Females	180	215	284

Table 2 thus presents an example of variation and consistency ('structured heterogeneity'); there is considerable variation in the use of the variable (i) and yet within social class groups defined on the basis of occupation there is similar use of the variable.

An interesting effect of age can be seen in Table 3. In Table 3 the fifteen-year-olds generally have higher indices than the adults in the same social class

[3]See Macaulay (1976) for a more detailed discussion of social class in Glasgow.

Table 3

	Adults	15-yr olds	10-yr olds	Men	15-yr old boys	10-yr old boys	Women	15-yr old girls	10-yr old girls
Class I	174	199	235	189	234	250	158	163	220
Class II	238	249	261	269	279	290	206	219	231
Class III/IV	285	301	281	303	302	275	267	299	286

group and the ten-year-olds generally have higher indices than the fifteen-year-olds. This tendency is least obvious among the Class III/IV respondents and clearest among the Class I respondents. The Class I ten-year-olds are closer to their peers in the other social-class groups than are the adults or the fifteen-year-olds. In other words, the distance between the social class groups increases with age. There is also an interesting sex difference in that Class I fifteen-year-old girls are much closer to Class I women in their use of this variable than Class I fifteen-year-old boys are to Class I men. This may either reflect a greater awareness of the social significance of the variable among the girls or indicate that for the boys working-class speech holds the kind of favourable connotations Trudgill (1972) found among male speakers in Norwich.

Tables 2 and 3 reveal certain aspects of systematic linguistic variation in Glasgow: the use of the variable (i) is related to membership in groups determined by social class, sex, and age. It is the intersection of these three factors which accounts for a considerable amount of the variety of speech to be heard in the city. There is nothing very surprising in this. Since the way we speak is one way of identifying ourselves, it is only natural that, for example, a fifteen-year-old middle-class girl should sound like one.

More revealing, in some ways, is the absence of a correlation. Another extralinguistic factor which was investigated in the Glasgow study is religion. Since approximately 40 per cent of the population is Roman Catholic, it seemed plausible that religious affiliation might have an influence on speech. For none of the five variables examined, however, was there a systematic difference between Catholics and non-Catholics. This is not to say that there may not be other variables which reflect religious affiliation but in terms of these five variables, it appears that Glaswegians do not go out of their way to identify their religion in their speech.

Lexical and phonological constraints

Bearing in mind the criticism of Bailey (1973a) and Bickerton (1971), we can note that it is possible in work of this type (cf. Labov 1969) to investigate linguistic variables in greater detail. Since, for example, no attempt was made in this study to control vocabulary or to elicit particular items, there was a risk of bias through the predominance of certain lexical items in the speech of a respondent. Some attempt to avoid this danger was made in the extraction of items for analysis; no more than three tokens of any item were extracted. The importance of this precaution was confirmed in a detailed examination of the instances of (i) used by the twelve speakers who showed the greatest variation in the use of this variable. It was found that for a given speaker any two tokens of the same lexical item are much more likely to have the same value than any two token of different lexical items.

To some extent this is because of the effect of phonetic context; this was investigated in detail with respect of the (i) variable. Higher values of (i), that is, a lower and more retracted vowel, were found in the environment of voiced consonants than in the environment of voiceless consonants, and a following voiced consonant produced slightly higher values of (i) than a preceding voiced consonant. Lateral consonants and preceding nasal consonants also led to higher values of (i). However, what is most impressive about the effect of phonetic context is that it is consistent across age, sex, and social-class groups. The figures for the three social-class groups are shown in Table 4 (for the other figures see Macaulay and Trevelyan, 1973 or Macaulay, forthcoming).

Table 4

	Preceding consonant			Following consonant		
	I	II	III/IV	I	II	III/IV
Voiceless	189	232	273	191	229	271
Voiced	220	259	311	233	288	325
Nasal	208	275	297	172	221	254
Lateral	247	296	367	222	350	366
All consonants	185	245	296	172	227	283

Table 4 shows that the phonetic factors affecting the quality of the vowel are common to all members of the speech community and that the differences in the use of the variable must be the result of non-phonetic factors.

Individual scores

Bearing in mind, too, the criticisms of Berdan (1975) (see above), we can also note that because of the small number of speakers involved—and because similar patterns were found for all four vowel variables—it is possible to look beyond the *group* means to the rank ordering of *individuals* on the basis of their use of the four variables. Since similar indices showing the average value of the tokens used by each speaker were calculated for each variable,[4] it is possible to

[4]The variable (u) ranges from a slightly fronted high back rounded vowel [ᶜu] to a high front unrounded vowel [ɪᵥ] with intermediate pronunciations also heard. The coding produces indices ranging from 100 for a speaker who consistently uses [ᶜu] to 400 for a speaker who consistently uses [ɪᵥ]. The variable (a) is basically a low central lax vowel which may be advanced or retracted. The coding produces indices ranging from 100 for speakers who consistently use a fronted vowel to 300 for those who consistently use a retracted vowel. The variable (au) ranges from a fairly open diphthong [au] to a high back rounded vowel [ᶜu]. The coding produces indices ranging from 100 for speakers who consistently use [au] to 400 for those speakers who consistently use [ᶜu]. The mean indices for all four social class groups are given below.

	I	II	II	IV
(u)	178	234	295	312
(a)	158	190	242	253
(au)	212	268	335	348

Table 5

Men		Women		15-yr-old boys		15-yr-old girls	
50–13	670	43–13	505	04–12	870	31–12	676
15–13	678	30–13	553	49–12	931	37–12	706
10–23	969	19–23	710	11–22	979	20–22	722
28–23	1012	36–23	884	29–22	1115	51–22	1060
40–33	1169	23–33	1110	26–32	1127	52–32	1105
32–33	1238	47–33	1139	01–42	1139	25–32	1176
27–43	1238	54–43	1200	41–42	1267	02–42	1215
48–43	1248	44–43	1205	24–32	1281	42–42	1278

10-yr-old boys		10-yr-old girls	
09–11	843	46–11	761
21–11	873	12–21	896
13–21	975	22–11	937
14–21	989	08–21	962
35–31	1058	33–41	1129
18–31	1121	16–31	1151
07–41	1193	06–41	1151
04–41	1211	53–31	1185

sum these indices to produce a composite score for the use of the four variables. For example, speaker 50–13[5] has an index of 185 for (i), 163 for (u), 143 for (a) and 179 for (au), which gives him a composite score of 670 for the four variables. By the use of this relatively crude measure it is possible to rank-order the speakers as shown in Table 5.

Consistency

The almost exact correspondence of this rank ordering by composite vowel variable score with that based on social class determined by occupation can be seen in Table 4. With exception of some fluctuation among the Class III and Class IV speakers, which is to be expected if this is actually one class, there is only one speaker out of rank and that is a ten-year-old girl, (22–11). There is a continuum of linguistic variation which corresponds to the continuum of social class found within the city. At the same time, the range of scores and the distances between individuals support the view that the major social-class divisions in Glasgow make up a tripartite system rather than the four-tiered situation which had been predicted and which provided the basis on which the sample was chosen.

   Thus both the linguistic data and the comments of the respondents suggest that it would not be completely arbitrary to claim that there are three major social dialects in Glasgow. Of course, the evidence from a study of this scope cannot be expected to establish the claim on a solid basis or to set the boundaries of the dialects precisely; a much more extensive and intensive

[5]The first two digits identify the particular speaker; the third digit shows the social class group of the speaker (1 = I, 2 = II, etc.); and the fourth digit indicates age (1 = ten-year-old; 2 = fifteen-year-old; 3 = adult).

investigation will be necessary before this can be done. Nevertheless, the consistency of the results from the Glasgow study is very impressive, particularly when it is recalled that the analysis is based on relatively small samples of unrehearsed speech from a single interview which in most cases did not last more than half an hour.

On the whole, indeed, the most remarkable aspect of the Glasgow survey is the great consistency of the results and the impression they give of a relatively stable, socially stratified speech community. There are a number of factors which suggest that this may be an accurate reflection of the actual situation. The first is the general stagnation of the economy since the end of World War I, with the result that the upwardly mobile are likely to emigrate rather than try to improve their lot at home. Secondly, there has been only a relatively small influx of newcomers from other parts of the country in recent years; instead, the population of Glasgow has steadily declined. Thirdly, it is probably accurate to say that there is no significant stratum of the speech community which presents a model of prestige speech qualitatively different from that of the majority. In other words, there is no variety of speech in Glasgow which plays the role that Received Pronunciation does in England and some other parts of Scotland. There are, of course, a few RP speakers in Glasgow but they do not provide a model for any significant proportion of the population. All the Class I speakers interviewed were clearly identifiable as Glaswegians by their speech which in no case could be considered an example of RP. Whatever the reasons, the speech community seems relatively stable and it is highly likely that a more thorough investigation would confirm the general picture of three major social dialects that emerges from the 1973 Glasgow survey.

Variation

On the other hand, the results also reveal considerable variation within each of the social class groups. This can be seen in the percentage of variants of a particular variable used by each speaker. Table 6 illustrates this from the figures for adults in the use of the variable (i). It can be seen from Table 6 that in many cases the standard deviations (SD) are quite high, showing considerable variation within the group. Yet the groups remain distinct except for Classes III and IV where, with one exception, the differences between the means are less than the standard deviation within the group. The individual figures on the use of the specific variants thus confirm the overall picture of three social dialects while at the same time revealing the extent of variation within each dialect. The figures for the other variables reveal a similar pattern.

Table 6 also shows that there is one speaker 19–23 whose use of the variants deviates somewhat from the pattern of other speakers in her social-class group. For each of the other four variables 19–23 displays the same behaviour in using more of the prestige variants and fewer of stigmatized variants than the other speakers in Class II. This speaker was the most formal and constrained of the whole sample during the interview (with the possible exception of her fifteen-year-old daughter whose use of the variables

Table 6: Individual variation among adults: Percentage of variants of (i) for each informant

	Total No.	(i–1) No.	%	(i–2) No.	%	(i–3) No.	%	(i–4) No.	%	(i–5) No.	%
Class I											
15	80	24	30.0	40	50.0	13	16.3	3	3.8	0	0.0
50	80	22	27.5	48	60.0	10	12.5	0	0.0	0	0.0
30	80	28	35.0	45	56.3	7	8.8	0	0.0	0	0.0
45	79	47	59.5	30	37.9	2	2.5	0	0.0	0	0.0
Mean			38.0		51.1		10.0		0.9		0.0
S.D.			12.7		8.4		5.1		1.6		0.0
Class II											
10	42	0	0.0	16	38.1	24	57.1	2	4.8	0	0.0
28	80	0	0.0	32	40.0	37	46.3	11	13.8	0	0.0
19	48	10	20.8	36	75.0	2	4.2	0	0.0	0	0.0
36	50	1	2.0	38	76.0	9	18.0	2	4.0	0	0.0
Mean			5.7		57.3		31.4		5.6		0.0
S.D.			8.8		18.2		21.2		5.0		0.0
Class III											
32	74	0	0.0	12	16.2	36	48.7	19	25.7	7	9.5
40	80	1	1.3	28	35.0	37	46.3	13	16.3	1	1.3
23	62	0	0.0	22	35.5	32	51.6	8	12.9	0	0.0
47	80	2	2.5	33	41.3	38	47.5	7	8.8	0	0.0
Mean			0.9		32.0		48.5		15.9		2.7
S.D.			1.0		9.4		2.0		6.2		3.9
Class IV											
27	80	0	0.0	15	18.8	38	47.5	22	27.5	5	6.3
48	80	0	0.0	34	42.5	30	37.5	13	16.3	3	3.8
44	44	1	2.3	19	43.2	21	47.7	2	4.6	1	2.3
55	40	1	2.5	18	45.0	15	37.5	5	12.5	1	2.5
Mean			1.2		37.4		42.6		15.2		3.7
S.D.			1.2		10.8		5.1		8.3		1.6

(In each class the first two speakers are male and the second two female)

paralleled her mother's). It is perhaps significant that 19–23 was the only speaker who used no glottal stops before a pause or a vowel. It is probably also not a coincidence that 19–23 was deviant in her extreme fundamentalist beliefs and in her severe condemnation of many aspects of contemporary life. Yet despite the extreme formality of her speech 19–23 belongs with the Class II group in her overall use of the variables. Any characterization of social dialects should be broad enough to permit the kind deviation which 19–23 displays.

There are also differences in the extent to which speakers make use of the range of variants heard in the city. For example, speaker 45–13 uses 59.5 per cent (i—1), 38 per cent (i—2), and 2.5 per cent (i—3) whereas speaker 33–41 uses 7 per cent (i—1), 52 per cent (i—2), 34 per cent (i—3), 5 per cent (i—4) and 2 per cent (i—5). It is clear that 33–41's speech is more variable than 45–13's in this respect, though it should be emphasized that both speakers mostly use one of two variants. Since 45–13 is a Class I woman and 33–41 a ten-year-old Class IV girl, it is perhaps not surprising that there should be differences in the variability of their speech. However, there is an interesting interaction between social class and age. Among the adults it is the Class I speakers who use the smallest number of variants. In Classes II, III, and IV there is very little difference among the three age-groups in their range of variants but in Class I the ten-year-olds and particularly the fifteen-year-olds use a much higher proportion of variants than the adults. In fact, the Class I fifteen-year-olds use the highest number of variants and the Class I adults the lowest. In other words, the greatest change in variability occurs in Class I between adolescence and adulthood. In the other social class groups there is relatively little change between generations.

Variation and consistency

The above brief discussion of linguistic variation in Glasgow comes nowhere close to defining the boundaries of the social dialects in that city. Other factors such as syntactic complexity and lexical diversity, as well as intonation and voice quality remain to be analysed for significant variation. Moreover, the subjective reactions of speakers to different varieties of speech need to be investigated more effectively than was possible in the 1973 survey. Nevertheless, when all the pieces are fitted together it should be possible to give a fairly precise description of the distinctive dialect features which enable one member of the speech community not only to recognize another speaker as belonging to the same speech community but also to identify the sector of that community to which he belongs. This kind of identification is carried out every day by ordinary members of the community. It should not be too difficult for linguists to explain how it is done, but only if they look in the right places and ask the right questions.

This is where I find myself in disagreement with scholars such as Bailey and Bickerton who have proposed a 'dynamic' paradigm to account for all linguistic variation. One of the features of their approach is the replacement of the term *dialect* (whether referring to regional or social differentiation) by the more neutral term *lect* 'for any combination of linguistic differences' (Bailey, 1973b, p. 162). Bickerton (1973a, p. 643) puts the point in fairly strong terms when he claims

> to speak of 'dialect' or even perhaps 'languages' may be misleading; these terms merely seek to freeze at an arbitrary moment, and to coalesce into an arbitrary whole, phenomena which in nature are on-going and heterogeneous.[6]

Thus the pendulum seems to have swung in a few years from the extreme of Chomsky's (1965) complete homogeneity to the other extreme of Bickerton's total heterogeneity. As with all extreme polarities, one may wonder whether the truth may not lie somewhere between. Chomsky was clearly and openly

[6]It seems to me that Bickerton is on firmer ground in pointing out the arbitrary nature of 'languages' than of 'dialects'. Given the wide range of phenomena which it is held to encompass it is hard to imagine a precise characterization of 'the English language' and certainly such a language has no native speakers, but the problems of describing, say, 'the dialect of Aberdeen', though immense, are of a different order of magnitude, and I believe that it is correct to claim that there are native speakers of this dialect.

idealizing the situation in postulating 'a completely homogeneous speech-community' (1965, p. 3) but is Bickerton not erring on the other side by claiming that *all* dialectal groupings are arbitrary? If this were the case it would be hard to understand why, for example, there should be a greater bundling of isoglosses at the border between England and Scotland (Speitel, 1969b; Glauser, 1974) than for a considerable distance on either side of the border. It does not seem arbitrary that this division should coincide with a difference in national identification based on cultural differences which are few and slight compared with the overwhelming number of similarities between the two populations. On the contrary, it is much more likely that the speech differences reflect a desire on the part of each population to assert its separate identity distinct from that of its neighbour. The existence of differences among individuals in each population should not be allowed to obscure the extent to which this cultural identification, including its linguistic manifestations, is a group phenomenon.

Similarly, individual differences in the use of socially stratified variables, such as were found in the Glasgow study, should not be taken to imply that there are *no* consistent linguistic differences which can be identified with social class groups. The absence of 'pure types' is a normal situation in science. For example, Hempel (1965, p. 152) cites Kretschmer (1925) on this point:

> We never, even in the most definite cases, come across a pure example in the strictest sense of the word, but always the peculiar individual instances of a type, that is the type itself mixed with slight accretions out of a heterogeneous inheritance.

The central problem in linguistics, after all, is the classification of two tokens, whether whole utterances or only segments, as 'the same' or 'different'. The presence of certain similarities or differences *per se* does not determine the classification as 'the same' or 'different'; that depends on whether the similarities or differences are significant. Exactly the same problem exists in the determination of linguistically significant groups. The mere possibility of grouping several speakers into a 'lect' does not prove that this is a linguistically significant group.

A simple thought-experiment will illustrate the point. Take a group of people in a room and ask them to write down one word. It will now be possible to establish a large number of totally uninteresting linguistic groups: for example, those whose word begins with an obstruent *vs* those whose word begins with a sonorant; those whose word contains only one syllable *vs* those whose word contains more than one syllable; those whose word contains only low vowels *vs* those whose word contains at least one high vowel; those whose word contains either a velar or a labial consonant *vs* those whose word does not contain a consonant of either of those types; and so on, and so on. These would certainly be linguistically determined groups but that fact alone would not make them linguistically significant groups. It might even be possible to find statistically significant correlations between membership in one of these groups and extralinguistic features such as age, sex, education, marital status, colour of hair, astrological sign, and so on. The existence of any such correlations would not make the groups more linguistically interesting because of the arbitrary basis on which membership in the group was determined.

This is the weak point in Bickerton's criticism of Sankoff's 'attempt to define categories which are socially meaningful for the people whose linguistic behaviour is being investigated' (Sankoff, 1974, p. 45). Bickerton (1973b, p. 40) comments: 'Either the relevant social and linguistic categories will exactly coincide (a happy, if unlikely event, which would render Sankoff's statement tautological) or they will not.' However, the exact coincidence of social and linguistic categories is neither a necessary nor a sufficient condition for significance. Given the small number of speakers whose speech is sampled in most surveys and the limited sample of speech which is collected, the possibility of a number of exact correspondences of the kind mentioned in the above thought-experiment must be large. The fact that so few show up in published results is presumably because most linguists do not spend their time in irrelevant and meaningless comparisons.[7] Instead of waiting for happy coincidences, the linguist who is interested in determining socially meaningful linguistic groups must look for the distinctive features which characterize such groups. This is no easy task and it would be foolish to claim that much progress has been made in developing either a theoretical basis or a methodology for this purpose. Nevertheless, the aim of establishing the criteria for membership in a linguistically significant group is an important one, and, in my opinion, a more urgent one than the pursuit of purely abstract panlectal grids, no matter how elegant the latter may appear to be. There is no more reason to believe that linguistically significant groups will be symmetrically distributed across such grids than there is to expect phonological segments to correspond exactly to acoustic segments.

[7] It is possible that some of the contradictory findings on sex differences in the language of children have arisen through chance correlations of this kind. See Macaulay (forthcoming) for a more detailed discussion of this point.

11

Postvocalic /r/ in Scottish English: Sound change in progress?

Suzanne Romaine

1 Introduction

The history of modern English is characterized by fluctuation in the pronunciation of postvocalic /r/. Today in Britain accents which have lost postvocalic /r/ generally have more social status than those which preserve it. In many parts of the United States the reverse is true, but this has not always been the case. Studies by Labov (1966) in New York City and Levine and Crockett (1966) in North Carolina present evidence of change in the prestige norm.

An examination of the literature on Scottish English would not lead us to suspect that a sociolinguistic investigation of postvocalic /r/[1] in Scotland would reveal new results of much interest. While previous studies and other recorded observations admit variation in the pronunciation of postvocalic /r/, they have in general supported Grant's (1914, pp. 35–7) claim that:

> The consonantal effect, in any case, is never lost in genuine Scottish speech and the trill may be said to be the characteristic Scottish sound corresponding to the letter *r*.[2]

We shall present here the results of a recent sociolinguistic investigation[3] which challenge this long and widely held notion that Scots speakers form a monolithic r-pronouncing speech community.

1.1 Previous studies of /r/ in Scotland

Grant (1914) and Williams (1912) provide detailed descriptions of the pronunciation of /r/ in Scotland at the turn of the century. They both agree

[1] The term postvocalic /r/ will be used hereafter in a restricted sense to refer only to word final postvocalic /r/, e.g. *car*.
[2] Grant does however note that there are some Scots dialects in the Northeast where /r/ is regularly dropped before /s/, e.g. /pʌs/—'purse'.
[3] The data for this paper are drawn from my 1975 M.Litt. thesis at Edinburgh University. I would like to thank David Abercrombie and A. J. Aitken for their valuable assistance during the preparation of this thesis. Thanks are also due to Nancy Dorian for helpful comments on an earlier version of this article.

that /r/ is generally pronounced either as a trilled point consonant, [r], which may be reduced to a single tap, [ɾ], or as a voiced frictionless continuant, [ɹ]. While both sources acknowledge that the trilled consonant is the most common as well as socially preferred form, Williams claims that the untrilled [ɹ] occurs much more frequently than is generally imagined. During this time, however, it seems that [ɹ] was associated largely with Highland English speakers. Grant and Dixon (1921) in fact say that [ɹ] is not a 'Scottish sound'.

Grant and Williams also mention the sporadic occurrence of the uvular *r*, [ʁ], which Grant says is not peculiar to any single district in Scotland. It is clear from these early records that [ʁ] was a stigmatized form and that [r] or [ɾ] was the norm for 'polite speech'. Grant considered the use of [ʁ] an idiosyncratic speech defect and both he and Williams recommended the use of [r] for teaching purposes. A much stronger statement of the social values which attached to these variant pronunciations can be obtained from Mutschmann's (1909, p. 17) work in the Northeast:

> The usual and only correct pronunciation of /r/ in all positions (also when final in an unstressed syllable) is a strongly trilled point consonant. The back or gutteral *r* is rather frequently met with in the North East of Scotland; it appears however only sporadically with individual features.

Later MacAllister (1963) speaks in favour of the use of the continuant [ɹ] in postvocalic position, although she says that the Scottish articulation of the /r/, i.e. the trill, is quite compatible with a pronunciation free of local dialect characteristics. Her motivation for advocating this variant is stated in terms of the claimed accompanying modification of the vowels preceding /r/ plus consonant[4] in the desired direction. She argues that (1963, pp. 76–7):

> The student of good speech should study the modifications of ɪ ɛ ʌ to ɜ, the central half-open vowel, before [ɹ] and should remember, as a practical step towards achieving the modifications that the articulation of the fricative [ɹ] results in the enunciation of ɜ before it.

In Buchan, Wölck (1965, p. 29) reports free variation among [r], [ɾ] and [ɹ] postvocalically, both word finally and before a final consonant. Speitel's (1969a) recent investigation of Midlothian dialect also mentions both [ɾ] and [ɹ] in common use. He reports (1969, p. 53) that /r/ is generally realized as a voiced roll with partial devoicing in all positions. In Scottish Standard English (SSE) the voiced frictionless continuant [ɹ] is more frequently found. In more recent studies of Edinburgh schoolchildren by Speitel (personal communication) the use of [ɹ] has been associated with girls of fee-paying schools as a marker of 'polite' Edinburgh speech. This use of [ɹ] has also been mentioned by Mather (1975), MacAllister's endorsement of this variant for teaching purposes would also lend reinforcement to its alleged prestige.

[4]MacAllister is referring to a common Scots three-way distinction of vowels before /r/ plus consonant as in the following examples: *bird-* /I/; *heard-* /ɛ/; and *word-* /ʌ/. A more anglicized system will collapse all these distinctions to /ɜ/. There are also dialects which may have a five vowel distinction before /r/.

2 Sociolinguistic investigation of /r/ in Edinburgh

The basic methodology for this sociolinguistic survey was taken from what might now be called a standard paradigm which was developed by Labov (1966) in New York City. After consideration of the findings of Labov's study and those of a number of sociolinguists in other communities (cf. especially Trudgill, 1974a; and Macaulay and Trevelyan, 1973) four factors were selected from among those likely to be correlated with linguistic variables in Edinburgh. These factors, both linguistic and extra-linguistic, are: age, sex, style and phonetic environment.

For this investigation a corpus of tape-recorded interviews with 24 Edinburgh schoolchildren was collected from one primary school. The speakers were born in Edinburgh of working-class families and were chosen non-randomly on the basis of father's occupation.[5] Four males and four females were chosen from three different age groups, six, eight and ten-year-olds, and were recorded in a face-to-face single interview with the investigator; the ten-year-olds were recorded in an additional more formal style, reading a passage which was specially constructed to contain a high concentration of the variables under investigation.

It was decided to include the variable (r) in this investigation since it was thought that there might be a possibility of a sound change in progress and data collected in the early stages of such a change would be useful to other investigators as a case study in sound change. This suspicion of a possible sound change in progress was not based on any previously recorded observation but on personal recent observations in Edinburgh made by David Abercrombie and this investigator. Abercrombie (personal communication) first noted the loss of postvocalic /r/ in a particular area of Edinburgh where this study was conducted. as we have seen, this possible r-lessness had not been recorded or discussed previously in the literature on Scots. Initial recordings in a secondary school in this area confirmed Abercrombie's impressionistic observations. It was then decided to collect more data which would illustrate the distribution of this phenomenon.

2.1 The variants of (r) in Edinburgh

The three variants of (r) which were observed included:

$$(r-1) \quad [\textrm{r}], \; [\textrm{ɾ}]$$
$$(r-2) \quad [\textrm{ɹ}]$$
$$(r-3) \quad \varnothing^{6}$$

The following three phonetic environments were examined for possible effects of phonetic conditioning on the values of (r):[7]

---

[5]Cf. the 1975 study for details on the selection of informants, socioeconomic character of the school catchment area and the use of father's occupation as an index of social class.
[6]This symbol is used here to indicate absence of word final /r/.
[7]No account was taken of the type of following consonant or place of articulation although this may have some influence. Certainly when the following consonant is a dental or alveolar there is difficulty in distinguishing reliably the different (r) variants. Only word final /r/s were included.

1 (r) $\begin{Bmatrix} \# \\ \#\# \end{Bmatrix}$ -word final /r/ followed by a pause or in utterance final position.

2 (r) ## V-word final /r/ followed by a word beginning with a vowel.

3 (r) ## C-word final /r/ followed by a word beginning with a consonant.

It was decided to score the values of (r) as three discrete variables rather than as one continuous variable as is generally done in the case of variables with more than two variants. The (r) index therefore consists of 3 indices which were calculated by taking the total number of tokens of each (r) variant, i.e. [ɾ], [ɹ], and Ø, over the total number of tokens of the variable multiplied by 100 to yield a percentage score. This was done for several reasons:

1 Although the variants are a class belonging to (r), the move or choice among these different variants does not have the same gradient character as in the case of a vocalic variable, e.g. (i), which represents the vowel of the word class, *bit*, *little* etc., where index values can be seen to go up or down on a scale ranging from 100 to 300 (in this example 100 represents a vowel of [ɪ] quality and 300 represents a vowel of [ʌ] quality) in relation to movement along the phonetic dimensions of height as well as fronting or backing. The (r) variants, on the other hand, are not ordered on a similar continuum with respect to a given common phonetic dimension (cf. Knowles, this volume). For example, a hypothetical (r) index of 220 does not indicate the same thing as an (i) index of 220 because in the latter case there are intermediate values between the realizations which have arbitrarily assigned numerical values while in the case of (r), there is nothing 'in-between' an [ɾ], [ɹ] and lack of /r/. Percentage scores seem to be a more accurate reflection of the individual's behaviour with regard to /r/ pronunciation.[8]

2 Another reason for deciding against a gradient index was to avoid the possibility of ascribing social meaning to the variants of (r) by assigning them numerical values on a scale from 100–300 since it is not certain at this stage what social values may be attached to the different variants.[9]

[8]Although it would be possible to conceive of a phonetic dimension along which these /r/ types could be ordered, I think it preferable at this stage to express the results in percentages for each variant since a variable scale would conceal the locus of the variation. One conceivable alternative to this type of index which employs a gradient scale might be the following:

$$(r–1)\ \text{Ø}$$
$$(r–2)\ [ɾ]$$
$$(r–3)\ [ɹ]$$

If we used a scale where these values were assigned to the different /r/ variants, then scores above and below 200 would indicate that a speaker/group was introducing innovation in his/their use of (r) from an 'assumed norm' of [ɾ]. However, this scale does not avoid the problem referred to above, namely, that this type of index score is misleading. For example, if a speaker has a score of 200, this score might be the result of equal use of (r–1) and (r–3) rather than consistent use of (r–2). Individual speakers could display a wide range of variability and still obtain the same score.

[9]Despite claims of arbitrariness for index scale values, some consideration must be given to the social meaning implicit in the notion of such a scale. Consistent with the practise of describing non-standard varieties in terms of their divergence from the standard, the variable scale is usually constructed to give this same sort of information about individual/group realizations of a variable, so that index scores indicate the extent to which each informant deviates from an idealized standard.

2.2 Results

The first observation which the following results allow us to make is that the pronunciation of word final /r/ is indeed fluctuating in the way indicated by both earlier reports, e.g. Grant (1914) and Williams (1912) as well as more recent studies, e.g. Speitel (1969a). The most striking discovery which emerges however, is the quantitative confirmation of the r-lessness phenomenon observed by Abercrombie.

2.2.1 Phonetic differentiation of (r)

Table 1 gives the percentage scores for each (r) variant in the three phonetic environments. We can see that [ɾ] occurs most frequently of all three variants. Word final /r/ is most likely to be realized as [ɾ] when followed by:

(i)   a word beginning with a vowel;
(ii)   a word beginning with a consonant; and
(iii)   a pause or in utterance final position.

The second most frequent realization is [ɹ] which is most likely to occur before:

(i)   a word beginning with a consonant;
(ii)   a pause or in utterance final position; and
(iii)   a word beginning with a vowel.

R-lessness is the least favoured option of the three. When it does occur, it is most likely to appear before:

(i)   a pause or in utterance final position;[10]
(ii)   a word beginning with a consonant; and
(iii)   a word beginning with a vowel.

Although /r/ pronunciation is clearly variable for this group of speakers, it is not at all completely random. Instead we find a *structured variability* which is correlated with phonetic environment as well as the age and sex of the speaker and style as we shall see in the following sections.

2.2.2 The general structure of (r) variation

Table 2 gives the total indices for each (r) variant for the males and females of each age group. The variation is quite regularly structured when we look at the total scores within each age group. We observe in these figures a neat pattern of sex differentiation which operates without exception. Clear cut differences in the use of (r) exist between the males and females in each age group. The males make consistently greater use of [ɾ] than the females within each age group and greater use of Ø, With the exception of the eight-year-old boys, the scores for [ɹ] are lower than those of Ø. The females on the other hand, consistently prefer the use of [ɹ] more often than [ɾ] and Ø, and they are

---

[10]This environment carries potential *level stress* (cf. Wettstein 1942, p. 17) in which an increased rhythmic stress may occur on a final unaccented syllable usually at the end of a breath group. When r-lessness occurs under this condition it is quite auditorily prominent.

Table 1: Index scores for (r) for all speakers in 3 phonetic environments

Environment		All speakers
(r)$\{^\#_{\#\#}\}$		
	[ɾ]	34
	[ɹ]	38
	[Ø]	28
(r)##V	[ɾ]	70
	[ɹ]	26
	[Ø]	4
(r)##C	[ɾ]	40
	[ɹ]	48
	[Ø]	12
(r) Total	[ɾ]	47
	[ɹ]	38
	[Ø]	15

Table 2: The co-variation of (r) with age and sex

(r) Type	10 year olds		8 year olds		6 year olds	
	Males	Females	Males	Females	Males	Females
[ɾ]	57	45	48	40	59	33
[ɹ]	15	54	37	54	16	50
[Ø]	28	1	15	6	25	17

Table 3: The co-variation of (r) with age

(r) type	10 year olds	8 year olds	6 year olds
[ɾ]	50	44	46
[ɹ]	32	44	33
[Ø]	18	12	21

almost always rhotic. Before we examine this pattern of sex differentiation in greater detail, we will first outline briefly the patterns of age and style differentiation which the study revealed.

2.2.3 The pattern of age-grading

In view of this overwhelming sex differentiation in the use of (r), the age-group differences are not as striking since they are based on group indices which average out the great differences bewteen the boys and girls of each age group. Nevertheless, some general effects of age-differentiation can be observed in the group scores shown in Table 3. The ten-year-olds make the greatest use of [ɾ] of all three age groups; the six-year-olds make the greatest use of Ø and the eight-year-olds make the least use of Ø but equal use of [ɾ] and (ɹ).

2.2.4 The pattern of style differentiation

Table 4 shows the indices for (r) for ten-year-old males and females in the single interview and reading passage styles. The strong pattern of sex differentiation which we found above is also clearly maintained in the reading passage style. Again we note that the girls make greater use of [ɹ] than the boys. The general picture which emerges from looking at the total scores in both styles is that the use of [ɾ] decreases in the reading passage while the use of both [ɹ] and Ø increases. The girls in fact show some decrease in their use of [ɹ] in the reading passage, but they show a corresponding increase in r-lessness. The boys generally become more frequent [ɹ] users in the reading passage, but they are also more often non-rhotic.

Table 4: The co-variation or (r) with style: 10 year olds

	Single interview		Reading passage	
(r) Type	Males	Females	Males	Females
[ɾ]	57	45	43	36
[ɹ]	15	54	24	48
[Ø]	28	1	33	16

2.2.5 The pattern of sex differentiation
It is now evident that the most important single factor investigated in this study which correlates with (r) use is the sex of the speaker. The following Table 5 with the accompaning figures (1, 2, and 3) shows this sharp differentiation.

Table 5: The co-variation of (r) with sex

Environment		Males	Females
(r){#﹟#}	[ɾ]	38	28
	[ɹ]	18	59
	Ø	44	13
(r)##V	[ɾ]	77	63
	[ɹ]	19	32
	Ø	4	5
(r)##C	[ɾ]	49	28
	[ɹ]	37	64
	Ø	14	8
Total	[ɾ]	54	41
	[ɹ]	24	51
	Ø	22	8

The figures illustrate clearly that the greatest single feature (in terms of frequency) of sex differentiation is the use of [ɹ] by the girls. This 'crossover' pattern is shown in Figure 4. The main difference between the boys and the girls in the use of (r) is that girls are almost always rhotic and most frequently use [ɹ], while boys are less frequently rhotic and tend to use [ɾ] more frequently than the girls. This finding is another quantitative confirmation of an earlier report, namely, Speitel's (personal communication) observation that [ɹ] is a marker of female speech in Edinburgh.

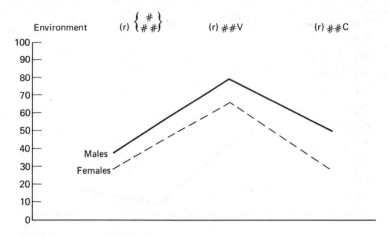

Figure 1. The co-variation of (r) with sex: [ɾ]

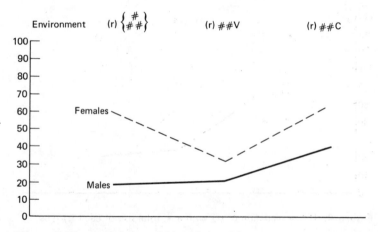

Figure 2. The co-variation of (r) with sex: [ɹ]

3 Interpretation of the results and the issue of sound change in progress

In the introductory remarks about /r/ in Scotland we mentioned the possibility of uncovering evidence which might indicate a linguistic change taking place. From Labov's (1966; 1972a) and Trudgill's work we now know that several factors may point to a sound change in progress. Among the most important of these are: irregularities of class and style variation or unusual patterns of age and sex differentiation. Since no information about possible social-class differences in the use of (r) has been collected, we will be basing the

152   *Susanne Romaine*

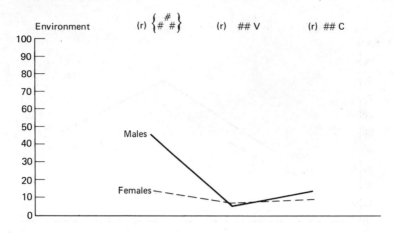

Figure 3. The co-variation of (r) with sex: Ø

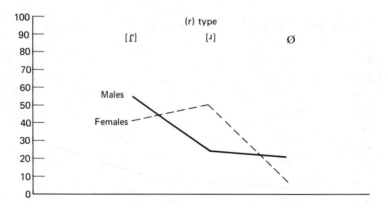

Figure 4: The co-variation of (r) with sex: total use of each (r) type

following remarks on the observed irregularities in the pattern of age, style and in particular, sex differentiation.

3.1 The evidence from age-differentiation

The simplest evidence which can be offered in favour of the existence of a linguistic change is differing behaviour between two successive stages of a language with regard to a particular feature. Such evidence would be indicative of a *change in real time*, as opposed to a *change in apparent time* (cf. Labov 1972a). In other words, differences in the linguistic behaviour in different age groups at a single point in time may be only a manifestation of age-grading and not sound change in progress. We recognize that there are characteristic linguistic behaviours which are appropriate for different stages in a speaker's life span; thus the same change may repeat itself in each new generation of speakers.

Many linguists would deny the possibility of observing sound change in progress (cf. for example, King 1969, pp. 84, 119 for an orthodox generativist view of language change) and argue that what the linguist does observe is dialect mixture or the propagation of a change rather than the change itself. Weinreich, Labov and Herzog (1968) however, have taken the position that no useful distinction can be made between a change and its propagation. In other words, contemporary variation is viewed as a stage in long-term linguistic change. Working from this premise, it is possible to 'observe' sound change in progress by comparing change in apparent time, i.e. the fluctuating language behaviour of different generations of speakers in a population at a given point in time, with change in real time, i.e. usage reported by earlier investigations.

In 1929 Hermann established that Gauchat (1905) had obtained a record of sound change in progress in his observations of age-grading differences in the Swiss village of Charmey by comparing the difference between these two points in time. In like manner, Labov's (1963) study of sound change in progress on Martha's Vineyard relied on a comparison of his data with the Linguistic Atlas of New England records obtained 30 years earlier.

As we mentioned earlier, there is no evidence from earlier records (in this case we are relying on such sources as Grant, Williams, Grant and Dixon, and Murray) of r-lessness in Scots speech or of [ɹ] as a feature of working-class speech in Edinburgh. However, since the latter variant has been a part of the Lowland Scottish linguistic scene since at least the turn of the century, it is highly unlikely that the use of [ɹ] by these speakers is a change which has been repeating itself in each new generation of working-class speakers. This would also seem to be the case with r-lessness which was first observed as a feature of *adult* speech in Edinburgh.

The pattern of age differentiation obtained in this study is interesting in that we do not find a clear linear progression of the usual type: 'The older/younger the speaker, then the greater/lesser his use of feature X.' Instead, we find that the six and ten-yeard-olds behave similarly.[11] Considering the small difference in age between the groups, i.e. two years, it is tempting to dismiss the absence of the classic pattern by predicting that it would in fact be more unusual to find very clearly marked gradient differences of this type between them. However, five of the seven variables in this same study did produce such patterns;[12] more specifically, four variables showed the familiar pattern: 'The younger the speaker, the greater his use of the more stigmatized variant', while the other variable produced the opposite result, namely: 'The older the speaker, the greater his use of the more stigmatized form.'

How can we account for this difference? A more plausible explanation of this irregularity can be found, I think, in the nature of the variable (r) which does not share the same characteristics as the other variables in this study. The

---

[11]The scores for Ø in the six-year-olds could of course reflect a developmental process, i.e. /r/ is acquired late.

[12]One variable, (ing), did not show any significant variation in the interview style which could be correlated with age or sex.

variable (r) stands apart because it is not an overt stereotype, although the results obtained for (r) in the more formal style seems to indicate that there is some awareness of this feature.

3.2 The evidence from style differentiation

The pattern of style differentiation for (r) is again different from that which emerged in conjunction with the other variables in this study. In the reading-passage style the use of both [ɹ] and Ø increased. From previous studies we know that in the case of socially diagnostic variables there is generally a monotonic relationship between the variable in question and style. Stigmatized variants usually decrease in frequency or disappear altogether in more formal styles while a prestigious variant will often increase in frequency. We could speculate that the observed fluctuation in the use of (r) in the two styles (although nowhere is this difference greater than 15 per cent) indicates that there is some low-level awareness of this feature and that the increase in the use of [ɹ] and Ø is accountable to their perceived prestige. This, however, is not to conclude that [ɾ] is a stigmatized variant. The presence of a prestigious feature does not necessarily imply that the alternate form is stigmatized; conversely, the 'avoidance' of [ɾ] in the reading-passage style does not necessarily mean that the other two variants are prestigious.

Trudgill (1974a, pp. 99–115) speculates as to why some variables are subject to little or no stylistic variation and are therefore 'irregular' in this sense. Of the reasons he suggests, the one which is most applicable to the case of (r) is that social consciousness is being directed towards the variable (r) by virtue of the fact that it is undergoing linguistic change.[13] We will clarify and strengthen this argument in the discussion of the evidence from the pattern of sex differentiation.

3.3 The evidence from sex differentiation

A number of American sociolinguistic studies have revealed the finding that women consistently produce forms nearer to the prestige form or produce these forms more frequently than men (cf. e.g. Fischer's 1958 study of New England schoolchildren). This is so because the difference between men's and women's speech, in Western societies at any rate, is believed to be related to women's greater consciousness of social status and awareness of the prestige associated with certain forms of speech. Men, on the other hand, are more favourably disposed to non-standard or less prestigious forms of speech which carry the connotation of 'toughness' or masculinity. This difference in values presumably reflects the different roles which men and women play in the

[13]Certainly (r) is not a stereotyped feature of the magnitude of the glottal stop, for example, but it seems safe to conclude from the discussion on page 145 that social consciousness is being directed towards [ɹ]. This however seems not to be the case with Ø which has gone largely unnoticed (cf. also p. 156). Labov's (1966) work subjective reaction and self-evaluation tests has shown that the use of linguistic features proceeds before their stigma, i.e. people can produce language forms before they are consciously aware of them, and that different rules obtain for using language than for observing it.

society and hence what is expected as appropriate linguistic behaviour by society.

This normative behaviour of women has since been well attested in other studies. In particular, Trudgill's (1974a) and Macaulay and Trevelyan's (1973) work in Britain have shown that this highly replicable pattern is not a linguistic idiosyncrasy of the American social structure but is characteristic of Britain as well. Nordberg (1971; 1973) confirmed this same phenomenon in Sweden; from his own work he concluded that this pattern of sex differentiation seemed to be so general in western societies today that it could almost serve as a criterion for determining which speech forms are stigmatized and which carry prestige in a given community.

It is now also believed that sex differentiation of speech often plays a major role in the mechanism of linguistic change and that women quite frequently have an important part to play in initiating and furthering such change. For example, Levine and Crockett's (1966) study of postvocalic /r/ in Hillsboro, North Carolina shows women in the vanguard of change from the older prestige norm to a new national norm. They (1966; pp. 97–8) report that:

> If we assume that the respondents' concepts of correct speech are also positive
> indicators of directions of linguistic change, we may see the community's march
> towards the national norm as spear-headed by women, young people, short-term
> residents of the community, and by those who are near but not quite at the top of
> the 'white-collar' class. . . . women, young people, the newer residents and higher
> status persons take the national *r* norm as their speech model, while the linguistic
> behaviour of males, older people, long-term residents and blue-collar respondents
> is referred to a Southern prestige norm- the r-less pronunciation of the coastal
> plain.

Trudgill (1972, p. 179) has recently emphasized the importance of sex differentiation as an agent in linguistic change. He claims that: 'Patterns of sex differentiation deviating from the norm indicate that a linguistic change is taking place.' From the indications which we have so far, r-lessness and the use of [ɹ] would appear to be simultaneous trends which are examples of two different types of linguistic change: *change from above* and *change from below* (Labov, 1966, p. 328), each of which is associated with social factors of a different nature.

R-lessness would seem to be an example of change from below which is manifested as a gradual shift in the behaviour of successive generations well below the level of conscious awareness of the speakers. This shift typically begins with a particular group in the social structure and becomes more generalized in the speech of other groups; this initiating group typically has low social status. All observations to date on the loss of postvocalic /r/ in Edinburgh, admittedly few and made largely by Abercrombie and myself, seem to indicate that it is a feature adopted by the younger generation of working-class speakers in a particular area of Edinburgh. Labov (1966) has commented that change from below is usually accomplished without much public attention and will usually become subject to overt pressure from above later. It is not uncommon in sound changes of this type for social reaction to fasten on to such a change and force a reversal in whole or in part by pressure from the upper groups in the social hierarchy. And it is indeed likely that social reaction will attach itself to this feature since r-lessness belongs to prestigious speech in Britain, most notably to RP.

The use of [ɹ] on the other hand seems to indicate a change from above already in operation, i.e. overt social pressure from the top of the hierarchy, since [ɹ] has been associated with middle-class, and particularly female, speech in Scotland (and, we might also add, with Highland English which is one of the few, if not the only, English accent(s) native to Scotland which does have prestige both in and outwith Scotland). In addition, [ɹ] has long been endorsed for teaching purposes in teacher training colleges in Scotland (cf. MacAllister, 1963). However, since Speitel first drew attention to its presence in the speech of teenage girls in Edinburgh fee-paying schools, there has been no mention of its use among young working-class girls.

Both males and females seem to be innovating in this Scottish instance and the females are quite clearly the innovators in a prestige form. The males, interestingly enough, are innovating in a direction away from the local educated Scots prestige norm, but in accepting r-lessness their usage happens to coincide with a much larger national norm. This pattern of differentiation in fact suggests that r-lessness is a separate competing development in Scots and is *not* being adopted in conscious imitation of a Southern English prestige model such as RP. If the latter had been the case, then we would have expected the females to lead the shift of the norm in this direction. The females, however, are clearly more concerned with the pressure exerted by local norms and asserting their status within the Edinburgh social structure.

The unusual pattern of style differentiation deserves some final comment. It suggests that the two variants have roughly equal prestige though of two different types. The males' higher scores for [ɹ] in the reading passage lend support for the assertion that there is overt prestige associated with [ɹ]. However, the females' increased use of Ø in the same instance could indicate that there is some *covert prestige* attached to Ø. Trudgill (1972, p. 10) has cited an instance where it is not only the male speakers who attach covert prestige to certain linguistic features, but also younger female speakers.

Trudgill (1974a) has reported a similarly complex change at work in Norwich in which overt and covert prestige coincide in the case of the variable (o) as in *top*, *dog* etc. In RP this vowel is realized as a rounded [ɒ] while the non-RP vowel, [ɑ], is unrounded. The rounded vowel is being introduced into Norwich English by middle-class women and also by working-class men in imitation of the local working-class speech in Suffolk.

3.4 Conclusion

Recent studies of linguistic variation have illuminated some of the mechanisms which govern the phonetic direction and social location of phonological change, but we still know very little about why such linguistic change proceeds as it does. Since no investigations to date have attempted to rely solely on a sample of young speakers for the purpose of investigating sound change in progress, we do not know if these same patterns, i.e. unusual or irregular patterns of sex, style, age and social-class differentiation, which indicate possible sound change in progress in the adult speech community, are reliable indicators of the same in a sample of younger speakers. Conclusive evidence must await a survey of adults of different ages and social-class backgrounds.

If the evidence which we have presented here should find support in subsequent systematic investigations of the adult population, we may find ourselves in an excellent position to document the incipient stages of a complex linguistic change which will enable us to offer answers to such questions as: What features are selected and eventually adopted by a given speech community? And how are these changes propagated and learned by successive generations? These are certainly some of the most important questions in the study of linguistic change. The case of postvocalic /r/ in Scotland may provide some interesting answers when evidence from more speakers is available.

12

Social and stylistic variation in the speech of children: some evidence from Edinburgh

Euan Reid

Comparatively little is known about how patterns of variation common in the adult speech community develop in the language of children and adolescents. The major studies in the United Kingdom have either not focused on children in particular, as in Trudgill's work in Norwich (Trudgill, 1974a), or have come to rather tentative and surprising conclusions, as in the Glasgow investigation (Macaulay and Trevelyan, 1973, p. 83), which suggests that: 'the pattern is by no means clear at the age of ten, although fairly well-established at fifteen. . . .' The implication here that it is only between ten and fifteen that adult-type patterns of sociolinguistic variation become established corresponds with the model proposed earlier by Labov (1964a, p. 91) for six 'levels in the acquisition of Standard English', based on his New York work. He too suggested that, for example, there is for the child a third stage of '*social perception*', in which: 'the social significance of the dialect characteristics of his friends becomes gradually apparent to him as he becomes exposed to other speech forms, even while he himself is still confined to the single style of his own vernacular.' and a fourth stage of '*stylistic variation*', where: 'the child begins to learn how to modify his speech in the direction of the prestige standard, in formal situations, or even to some extent in casual speech.' According to Labov these stages are not reached until early adolescence, the great turning point being the first year of high school.

However, the results of a study recently undertaken (Reid, 1976) of some aspects of the speech of sixteen eleven-year-old boys in Edinburgh suggest that sociolinguistic development of this kind may in fact take place at the pre-adolescent stage. These results alone cannot of course determine the age at which such variation first appears, but they can suggest whether this kind of linguistic development is established by the age of eleven, or whether it does not clearly emerge until adolescence, as Macaulay and Trevelyan, and Labov appear to be proposing. The methodology used in the study was adapted from that pioneered by Labov in New York (Labov, 1966), and used also in the Norwich and Glasgow studies mentioned. Initially two socially contrasting schools were chosen on the basis of data assembled about the 77 Edinburgh Corporation primary-school catchment areas, and six eleven-year-olds were chosen from each school to represent a range of fathers' occupations. Four boys from a fee-paying day school were later added to the sample. The sixteen informants are grouped on two different, but related, bases: school affiliation and father's occupation. 'School 1' serves one of the bottom eight catchment areas mentioned above, 'School 2' serves one of the top eight, and 'School 3' is the fee-paying day school, which was included so that the investigation would cover the children of those social groups in Edinburgh who did not use the publicly supported schools. Father's occupation is indicated in such a way as to facilitate comparison with the Norwich and Glasgow studies. The letters represent groupings of occupations, of the kind used by the Office of Population Censuses and Surveys (formerly Registrar General's Classification).

A: professionals, managers and employers: socioeconomic groups 1, 2, 3, 4 and 13.
(Macaulay and Trevelyan's I; Trudgill's I + II)
B: Intermediate and junior non-manual workers: socioeconomic groups 5 and 6.
(Macaulay and Trevelyan's IIa; Trudgill's III) none of the 16 informants reported here in fact come into this group.
C: foremen, skilled manual workers, and 'own account workers other than professionals': socioeconomic groups 8, 9, 12 and 14.
(Macaulay and Trevelyan's IIb; Trudgill's IV)
D: personal service workers, semi-skilled and unskilled manual workers: socioeconomic groups 7, 10, 11 and 15.
(Macaulay and Trevelyan's III; Trudgill's V and VI).

Tape-recordings of all sixteen boys were made in four different contexts, as follows:

1 reading aloud a passage specially prepared to concentrate a number of linguistic variables: *RP style*.
2 in a one-to-one interview with the investigator, intended to be fairly formal: *IV style*.
3 talking with two class-mates about topics of mutual interest with minimal participation by the investigator: *GP style*.
4 in playground interaction, where the boy wore a radio-microphone and transmitter while playing with friends between school lessons, and was recorded via a receiver inside the school: *PG style*.

The occurrence of two phonological variables has been charted. In the results which follow (t) represents the variation between alveolar and glottal stops, medially and finally in the word, high indices indicating high incidence of glottalization. Similarly, (ng) represents the variation between velar and alveolar nasals in -*ing* suffixes, high indices representing high incidence of the alveolar nasals. In both cases a simple two-point scale of values for the variables was used:

For (t) a value of 0 is assigned to [t] and [t']
a value of 1 is assigned to [ʔ] and [ʔt]
For (ng) a value of 0 is assigned to [ŋ]
a value of 1 is assigned to [n]

Table 1: Indices for 16 individual informants: (t)

Name	Social Group and School		variable (t) – all environments			
			RP	IV	GP	PG
Alistair	A	3	20	18	43	71
Jim	A	3	18	28	55	65
Douglas	A	3	20	53	66	80
Hamish	A	3	23	48	69	88
George McF	A	2	18	30	63	85
Roddie	A	2	20	53	83	89
Kenneth	A	2	25	78	95	60
Ian M.	A	2	25	90	83	85
Michael	C	2	18	75	85	80
Craig	C	2	23	80	100	90
Stephen	C	1	18	98	100	100
John	C	1	20	95	100	100
Ian G.	C	1	23	100	100	30
George W.	C	1	28	100	100	100
Kevin	D	1	35	93	100	69
Paul	D	1	60	100	100	69

Table 2: Indices for 16 individual informants: (ng)

Name	Social Group and School		variable (ng)			
			RP	IV	GP	PG
Alistair	A	3	0	0	0	0
Jim	A	3	0	0	0	0
Douglas	A	3	0	13	0	13
Hamish	A	3	0	7	(0)	38
George McF	A	2	13	20	0	79
Roddie	A	2	20	9	20	(100)
Kenneth	A	2	0	13	80	0
Ian M.	C	2	7	33	42	67
Michael	C	2	0	20	27	(25)
Craig	C	1	0	33	100	100
Stephen	C	1	21	100	100	(50)
John	C	1	20	93	100	(100)
Ian M.	C	1	100	100	100	100
George W.	C	1	0	100	100	100
Kevin	D	1	33	80	100	88
Paul	D	1	7	100	100	80

The (t) indices are based on a maximum of the first 40 tokens for each speaker in RP, IV and GP styles, and a maximum of the first 20 in PG style. Only instances of (t) in post-tonic position in stressed words are considered. The (ng) indices are based on a maximum of the first 15 tokens in each style. All groups indices are means of the individual informants' indices.

Tables 1 and 2 present indices for the 16 individual informants, in the four styles, and for both variables. Brackets around figures in this and later tables indicate an index based on fewer than five tokens. My general interpretation of these figures is implied by the arrangement of the tables. It seems quite clear that the speech of these Edinburgh informants is related to the same factors of stylistic context and social status already established as relevant by the studies discussed earlier from the USA, from Norwich and from Glasgow. Before considering these factors and the data bearing on them in more detail, however, some attention is given to the question of phonological constraints on the (t) variable.

Phonological constraints

In the random sample of ten of his sixty Norwich informants that Trudgill considered with reference to phonetic environment, in all except his Word List style there were noticeably higher indices for (t) in word-final position than in word-internal positions (Trudgill 1974a, p. 95). And Macaulay and Trevelyan (1973, p. 62 ff) illustrate, using unfortunately a slightly different sub-categorization of environments for their equivalent (gs) variable, that in all their social-class groups a higher proportion of glottal stops is found 'before a consonant' than 'before a vowel' or 'before pause'. (Their 'before a vowel' environment presumably subsumes my 'medial' and my 'final before an initial vowel in the following word' environments.) Their figures also suggest that, for all except their Social Class III, pre-pausal position is the least likely of their three to favour glottal stops. Table 3 below presents my data on these points.

The overall pattern is even more evident when Table 4 is considered. The pattern revealed by Table 3 is highly regular. All but one of the informants in one style (if we leave aside indices based on fewer than five tokens) have lowest proportions of glottal stops in medial position. All but three informants, one

Table 3: (t) variable – individuals' indices for four phonetic environments, two styles.

Name	IV Style					GP Style				
	M	FV	F+	FC	AllF	M	FV	F+	FC	AllF
Alistair	0	0	0	100	22	0	0	13	100	49
Jim	0	0	0	100	35	0	0	(0)	100	67
Douglas	0	29	22	100	64	(25)	0	(33)	100	71
Hamish	0	(0)	33	89	61	40	(50)	(50)	100	82
George McF.	0	0	22	83	33	(33)	38	45	100	65
Roddie	0	42	17	94	62	33	91	71	100	91
Kenneth	29	71	71	100	88	(75)	100	89	100	97
Ian M.	(100)	63	83	100	89	71	50	100	94	85
Michael	20	43	82	100	83	60	79	83	100	89
Craig	(100)	50	64	100	79	100	100	100	100	100
Stephen	86	100	100	100	100	100	100	100	100	100
John	(50)	100	100	100	100	100	100	100	100	100
Ian G.	100	100	100	100	100	100	100	100	100	100
George W.	100	100	100	100	100	100	100	100	100	100
Kevin	86	92	100	93	94	100	100	100	100	100
Paul	100	100	100	100	100	100	100	100	100	100

Notes:
(i) Environments: M = word-medial e.g. 'wa*t*er'; si*tt*ing'
   FV = word-final before initial vowel in following word e.g. 'lo*t* of'; 'righ*t* over'
   F+ = word-final before pause e.g. 'fell-ou*t*.'; 'a minu*t*e.'
   FC = word-final before initial consonant in following word e.g. 'tha*t* would'; 'qui*t*e soon.'
   AllF = All word-final tokens.
(ii) Macaulay and Trevelyan's 'before a vowel' position is equivalent to my M plus my FV environments.

of these in both styles included here, have the same or a lower proportion of glottal stops in FV than in F+ position. And all but one have the highest proportion of glottal stops in FC positions.

Table 4: (t) variable – group indices for four phonetic environments, two styles (all informants).

Environments	M	FV	F+	FC	AllF
IV Style	48	55	62	97	76
GP Style	61	69	74	100	87

Tables 3 and 4 would certainly support the picture Trudgill gives, in making word-final a more likely position for glottal stops than word-medial, but my figures suggest a reversal of the order of the 'before pause' and 'before a vowel' environments given by Macaulay and Trevelyan. With three exceptions, my Edinburgh informants had a higher proportion of glottal stops before pauses than before vowels, either medially or in following words. Wolfram and Fasold (1974) discuss how 'before pause' position sometimes has the effect of 'following vowel', and sometimes of 'following consonant' environments. The discrepancy between the Glasgow and Edinburgh data may then arise from different definitions of the environments, or indeed from differences between Glasgow and Edinburgh speakers. On the basis of the data just presented, I would propose this ordering for Edinburgh at least:

least favouring	↑	word-medial
glottal stops		word-final/following vowel
		word-final/following pause
most favouring		word-final/following consonant
glottal stops	↓	

Although I have insufficient data to support the suggestion fully, there are in addition indications that my medial environment at least might be subdivided into two groups of lexical items—the more 'learned' e.g. *athletic, hospital* are less likely to have glottal stops than the more familiar e.g. *little, better.*

If then we consider the individual's progress through a series of styles, or rather his definition of a series of relationships, in terms of speech styles from formal to informal, the mechanism for the process can be thought of as a series of barriers to be penetrated. The first environment to weaken as far as (t) is concerned is before a following consonant: virtually everyone in IV style has already nearly 100 per cent glottal stops there. The next step is to introduce a few glottal stops before following pauses; then, perhaps only in GP style, glottal stops are produced finally when the next word begins with a vowel. The last step, not taken at all by some of the boys in my sample, is to use glottal stops medially. For the boys of highest social status, this will certainly only be in the most informal stylistic contexts.

Although then there appears to be little significant variation between individuals in FC and F+ environments in the styles considered, a pattern of variation arising principally from the remaining environments is apparent, and needs to be accounted for.

Stylistic context

Tables 5 and 6, and the associated Figures 1 and 2, illustrate the effect of varying stylistic contexts on the two variables. The group indices here, as elsewhere, are means of the individual indices for all sixteen informants. With the exception of the index for PG style, variable (t), it is clear that the process represented by the moves from reading aloud a passage into a tape-recorder, through answering questions posed by an adult stranger, to talking with friends in the presence of an adult, and finally to playing with friends in the playground, is reflected systematically in the increase in indices for both variables, especially when the informants are considered as a single group.

The Reading Passage provoked, as expected, everyone's 'best' linguistic behaviour. It was also very similar behaviour as far as (t) was concerned, with 14 of the 16 individual indices between 18 and 28, and only the two boys at the bottom of the list noticeably higher. Everyone seemed to be aware that glottal stops were not expected, and it is virtually only in FC environments that they occur at all. The (ng) variable offers more of a spread, but only Ian G. appears to make no concessions at all to (or to be quite unaware of ?) the

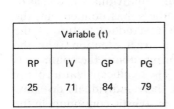

Variable (t)			
RP	IV	GP	PG
25	71	84	79

Table 5

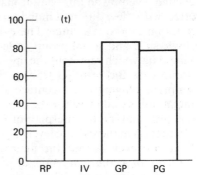

Figure 1

Group indices for (t), 4 styles, all informants

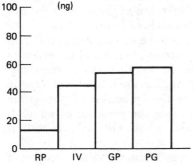

Figure 2

Variable (ng)			
RP	IV	GP	PG
14	45	54	59

Table 6

Group indices for (ng), 4 styles, all informants

F*

conventionally recognized higher status of the written word, staying as he does at (ng)–100 throughout all styles.

The interview situation represents for all but Alistair and Roddie, in (t) and (ng) respectively, an apparently more relaxed setting. (They were, in their general behaviour too, probably the most assured of the boys right from the start of the recording session, when the reading passage was taped.) For nearly everyone else the (t) indices in IV style are noticeably higher, but most dramatically so for those at the bottom of my list. There is therefore a much greater range of scores in the IV style than in RP—from 18 to 100. Similarly for (ng) the scores spread out considerably, ranging in this case from 0 to 100.

In IV then there is the most marked contrast for any style between the informants at either end of my list. I shall suggest in the next section that this is basically a reflection of the social contrast between them, but there may also be a factor at work to do with the informants' perception of the interview situation from which the data were collected. It was quite clear that different individuals saw the interview in different ways. For some it was the fairly formal situation which 'interview' suggests, but others were very relaxed and selfconfident indeed. One must assume therefore that the speech-styles elicited, even by an interviewer making a conscious effort to create a similar effect with these different individuals, were not necessarily from an equivalent point on everyone's range. These differences between speakers even within a single style and social group underline the need to include in studies of this kind data which represent the linguistic behaviour of individuals as well as of groups. As Bickerton (1975b, p. 301), among others, has pointed out, the simple averaging of percentage scores which is a standard feature of the methodology adapted for the present study does distract attention from: 'the complex and subtle interplay of forces which brings about the continuous fluctuation in the stylistic levels of actual speech.' The significant feature of my data, however, is that the figures suggest that these individuals do show evidence of a common tendency to move along the stylistic continuum in the same direction, even if their rates of progress are different.

The movement in the (t) variable indices from IV to GP style is slight for those near the bottom of the list, since they were at near 100 in IV already, but it is quite marked again for those at the top. (ng) presents a similar, though not so clear-cut situation. The major obvious difference in the context for this style was the change in addressees from the researcher as sole addressee to the two classmates involved in the discussion. It has to be said again that different group sessions achieved different degrees of 'success', in terms of the extent to which the researcher's presence was ignored or forgotten completely. Nevertheless, only one (t) index and two (ng) indices are lower in GP than in IV styles. It appears highly likely therefore that presence of peer-group members almost always overrides in importance the presence of an adult stranger, in terms of effect on speech-style. And GP style overall is significantly more relaxed than IV.

'PG' style presented special difficulties in connection with the collection of data, and there have to be particular reservations in interpreting it. These difficulties are reflected in my Table 4 and Figure 1, which show for (t) an actual *drop* in the group index for PG, rather than the rise which might have been expected. This material was after all recorded, albeit with the speaker's knowledge, outside the physical presence of the researcher. Interestingly, the change in the physical situation alone was enough to increase, or at least maintain, the (t) indices for ten individuals, and the (ng) indices for eleven.

The difficulty which arose with the remaining informants derived from a device used to encourage a flow of speech into the microphone in the slightly inhibiting circumstances involved in the radio-recording sessions. The researcher rashly seized on the suggestion made by one of the informants that the speaker wearing the radio-microphone should act as a commentator, while the other two participants ran races, played football, fought boxing matches etc. This certainly produced a more ample flow of speech—but in several cases this speech was obviously a quite close imitation of TV commentators, Scottish, English or American. This was particularly reflected in the (t) indices of, for example, Paul, Kevin, Kenneth and Ian G. This last boy in fact, having had indices of 100 for both IV and GP styles, makes a remarkable drop to 30 for PG, entirely as a result of his mastery of Harry Carpenter-style boxing commentary. Although the commentary device backfired as far as the immediate design of this investigation was concerned, and the limited availability of the equipment did not allow any re-recording, these 'accidental' effects produced by some of the informants are suggestive of a greater flexibility in speech styles, given appropriate models, than might have been expected.

There is no reason, either, to think that PG style is in any absolute sense the end of the range for some at least of these boys. There were hints of something 'further down', that is to say even more relaxed, in brief passages where the recording equipment was temporarily forgotten, or where someone addressed the microphone-wearer without realizing that he was 'wired up'.

The phenomenon of style-shifting, and its relationship to factors in the environments having to do with the speaker's perception of the formality of the situation, seems then quite clearly demonstrated for the eleven-year-olds in this investigation, manifest in all informants, and for both variables.

Social variation

The systematic increases in the indices of Tables 1 and 2 from left to right then appear to be quite clearly related to 'stylistic' variation of the kind just described. The less closely associated with the teacher-figure's controlling position, the more likely is the context to provoke glottal stops and 'dropped gs'. The second striking feature of these tables is the pattern revealed by the top-to-bottom increases in indices for both variables. These may be more clearly seen if we ignore for the moment the stylistic differences just discussed, and average out each individual's scores into a single figure, as in Table 7. Indices range from 38 to 82 for (t), and from 0 to 100 for (ng), and the scores correspond quite closely to position on the list of informants, more obviously with the (t) than with the (ng) variable. The list is once again ordered according to school affiliation and social group membership, as described earlier.

	(t)	(ng)
Alistair	38	0
Jim	42	0
Douglas	55	7
Hamish	57	11
George McF.	49	28
Roddie	61	37
Kenneth	65	23
Ian M.	71	57
Michael	65	18
Craig	73	58
Stephen	79	68
John	79	78
Ian G.	63	100
George W.	82	75
Kevin	74	75
Paul	82	72

Table 7: Individual indices – all styles averaged

If these 'polystylistic' indices for individuals are further averaged into social group indices, or into school indices, as in Tables 8 and 9, and the associated Figures 3 and 4, the pattern is once again even more regular. Whether we group the individuals in this study according to father's occupation, or by school affiliation, the basic relationship between high indices and low social status, low indices and high social status, remains. The expectations derived from previous studies of adult speakers are confirmed for these boys.

If we now consider the combined effect of style and social class, grouping the figures either by social class or by school again supports the position established for mature language-users, as Tables 10 to 13, with associated Figures 5 to 8, demonstrate. With the reservation already made about PG style for Social Groups C and D, and for Schools 1 and 2, where the fall in indices would seem to result from weakness in the design of the investigation rather than anything more significant, there are two major features to note in these graphs and tables. Firstly, the behaviour of each sub-grouping considered reflects the same stylistic tendencies as did the 16 informants

	A	C	D
(t)	55	74	78
(ng)	18	66	74

Table 8

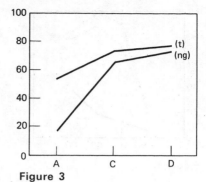

Figure 3

Group indices by social class, 'polystylisic', (t) and (ng)

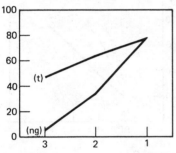

Figure 4

	3	2	1
(t)	48	64	77
(ng)	5	34	78

Table 9

Group indices by school, 'polystylistic', (t) and (ng)

	RP	IV	GP	PG
A	21	50	70	78
C	22	91	98	83
D	48	97	100	69

Table 10

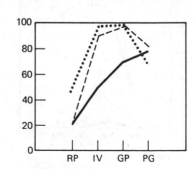

Figure 5

Group indices for 4 styles, 3 social groups, (t)

Social group A———— C————D . . . . . .

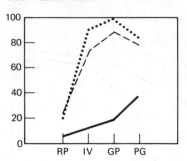

Figure 6

	RP	IV	GP	PG
A	5	12	18	37
C	24	74	88	79
D	20	90	100	84

Table 11

Group indices for 4 styles, 3 social groups, (ng)

	RP	IV	GP	PG
School 3	20	37	58	76
School 2	22	68	85	82
School 1	31	98	100	78

Table 12

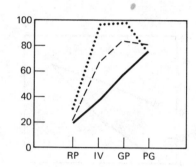

Figure 7

Group indices for 4 styles, 3 schools, (t)

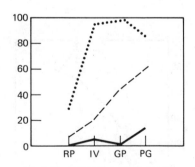

Figure 8

	RP	IV	GP	PG
School 3	0	5	0	13
School 2	7	21	45	61
School 1	30	96	100	86

Table 13

Group indices for 4 styles, 3 schools, (ng)

School 1 . . . . . . 2 – – – – – – 3 ———

considered as a single group: they all have a substantial range. Secondly, there is a significant distance between the lines representing the different groups, indicating a noticeable difference in linguistic behaviour between the groups, especially in the more central styles of IV and GP, and more markedly in (ng) than in (t). It is as true of these eleven-year-old Edinburgh boys then as of older informants investigated previously in a similar way in the United States and in Britain that there are features of their speech which relate in a systematic way to their social status and to the social context in which their speech is produced.

Awareness of variation

The relationship suggested by the correlational evidence so far offered can be complemented in an informal way by some explicit comment from the boys made in the course of the individual interviews recorded. It became particularly evident that there was considerable awareness of stylistic variation. Most of the boys claimed to have noticed examples of this, either in themselves, or in other people. The examples given of 'upward' variation included, from Paul:

> '. . . some girls . . . when they talk to their teacher they talk sort of posh . . . and when they talk to their pals . . . they just talk normal . . .'

and from Douglas:

> '. . . if you've got parents who want you to be brought up very well . . . you'd speak in a . . . better sort of way . . . and then if you've got friends who aren't so . . . well-spoken . . . then perhaps you'd change when you got out with your friends, and when you went into the house with your parents.'

A likely setting for variation suggested by George W. was 'in a hotel', and Ian G. offered:

> '. . . when they go to a party, they talk . . . kind of posh . . . and then when they're ootside they talk a' funny . . .'

Kevin agreed that children were generally more careful about their speech in somebody else's house, adding:

> '. . . especially when their mother's wi them . . . ken[1] . . . they just gie them a wee flick . . . [indicating with his foot] . . . to tell them to talk nice . . .'

There were also examples of stylistic movement in the opposite direction. George McF. quoted one from a TV comedy which he had recently seen (*Rising Damp*), whose central character, a socially ambitious landlord:

---

[1] *Ken* is the Scots equivalent of English *know* and here functions as *you know*.

'talked to the students in a common way but when the . . . Conservative candidate came in . . . started talking more politely . . .'

Michael recounted a personal experience at a neighbouring, tougher, school:

'. . . up at X school once, playing backetball . . . they started to take the micky out of all of us . . . because of the way we speak . . .'

When asked if this led to a change in accent, he replied:

'. . . not a case of changing . . . you just keep your mouth shut and you don't say much . . .'

Ian M., a boy who had the year before moved out of Edinburgh to Fauldhouse, a town in West Lothian, but continued to attend his old school, had first-hand experience of the pressures of moving between two socially-different communities. He gave this description of his adaptation:

'. . . I talk with a bit of a Scottish accent when I'm out in Fauldhouse.'

and when asked if he changed when he came to school in Edinburgh:

'. . . slightly . . . I don't really go from . . . clean . . . straight to dirty . . . it's just a slight change in the way I talk . . .'

It is these last two boys again who point to the vital factor at work here, linking this kind of variation with that considered earlier. First Michael:

'I don't exactly like to be the odd one out . . . maybe speaking like some posh person . . . and maybe they're tougher . . .'

and then Ian M:

'. . . if I talk to them with a sort of clean accent . . . they'll think . . . a bit of a bore . . . if you talk with the same accent as they do they'll just think . . . you're one of us in a way . . .'

Finally, in answer to a question which was an attempt to enquire in terms accessible to eleven-year-olds about the implicit policy of the school in promoting accent change, Kevin thought it was a good idea within certain limits, since:

'. . . that's what we're really here for . . . to talk nice and that . . .'

but his classmate, George W. laughed off the idea, on the grounds that:

'. . . you'd get battered off a' the pals . . .'

Most of the other boys agreed that it was, quite apart from anything else, impractical. Once again the pressure of the peer-group would be much stronger than anything that the school might promote.

Taken together, the answers just exemplified to these groups of questions offer support for the suggestion that, already at the age of eleven, not only are patterns of social and stylistic variation well-established, but there is also a considerable degree of conscious awareness of variation. Many of these eleven-year-old boys in Edinburgh can at least begin to explain what the functions of social and stylistic variation are. Some have experience in using the possibilities offered to assume through their speech different identities in different situations. Naturally enough, however, most of them also seem to share adult society's at best ambivalent attitude towards variation. They would not all accept Hamish's straightforward view of the situation:

'. . . different kinds of people . . . just have to talk differently.'

References

AITKEN, A. J. 1962: *Vowel length in Modern Scots*. University of Edinburgh, mimeo.

ALLGEIER, E. R. 1975: Beyond sowing and growing: the relationship between sex typing to socialization, family plans, and future orientation. *Journal of Applied Social Psychology* 5, 217–26.

AGHEYISI, R. and FISHMAN, J. A. 1970: Language attitude studies: a brief survey of methodological approaches. *Anthropological Linguistics* 12, 137–57.

d'ANGLEJAN, A. and TUCKER, G. R. 1973: Sociolinguistic correlates of speech style in Quebec. In Shuy, R. W. and Fasold, R. W., editors, *Language attitudes: Current trends and prospects*, Washington DC: Georgetown University Press, 1–27.

ATKIN, R. H. 1974: *Mathematical structure in human affairs*. London: Heinemann.

BACH, A. 1950: *Deutsche Mundartforschung*. Heidelberg: Winter.

BAILEY, C. J. N. 1973a: *Variation and linguistic theory*. Arlington, Va: Centre for Applied Linguistics.

1973b: The patterning of language variation. In Bailey, R. W. and Robinson, J. L., editors, *Varieties of present-day English*, New York: Macmillan, 156–86.

BAILEY, C. J. N. and SHUY, R. W. 1973: *New ways of analysing variation in English*. Washington: Georgetown University Press.

BARRON, N. 1971: Sex-typed language: the production of grammatical cases. *Acta Sociologica* 14, 24–41.

BAUMAN, R. and SHERZER, J. 1974: *Explorations in the ethnography of speaking*. London: Oxford University Press.

BEM, S. L. 1975: Sex role adaptability: one consequence of psychological androgyny. *Journal of Personality and Social Psychology* 31, 634–43.

BERDAN, R. H. 1975: *On the nature of linguistic variation*. University of Texas at Austin: unpublished PhD dissertation.

BICKERTON, D. 1971: Inherent variability and variable rules. *Foundations of Language* 7, 497–502.

1973a: The nature of a Creole continuum. *Language* 49, 640–69.

1973b: Quantitative versus dynamic paradigms: the case of Montreal *que*. In Bailey, C. J. N. and Shuy, R. W., editors, *New ways of analysing variation in English*, Washington: Georgetown University Press, 23–43.

1975a: *Dynamics of a Creole system*. London: Cambridge University Press.

1975b: Review of P. Trudgill: 'Social differentiation of English in Norwich'. *Journal of Linguistics* 11, 299–307.

BLAKAR, R. 1974: Sex roles are represented, reflected and conserved in the Norwegian language. University of Oslo. (Mimeo.)

BLOCH, B. 1948: A set of postulates for phonemic analysis. *Language* 24, 3–46.

BLOCK, J. H. 1973: Conceptions of sex role: some cross-cultural and longitudinal perspectives. *American Psychologist* 28, 512–27.

BLOOMFIELD, L. 1926: A set of postulates for the science of language. *Language* 2, 153–64.

BOAL, F. W. et al. 1974: *The spatial distribution of some social problems in the Belfast urban area*. Belfast. (Research Paper for the N.I. Community Relations Commission.)

BOISSEVAIN, J. 1974: *Friends of friends: networks, manipulators and coalitions*. Oxford: Basil Blackwell.

BOTT, E. 1971: *Family and social network*. London: Tavistock.

BOUGHEY, A. S. 1969: *Contemporary readings in ecology*. Belmont: Dickenson Publ. Co.

BOURHIS, R. Y. and GILES, H. 1976: The language of cooperation in Wales: a field study. *Language Sciences* 42, 13–16.

1977: The language of intergroup distinctiveness. In Giles, H., editor, *Language, ethnicity and intergroup relations*, London: Academic Press, 119–35.

BOURHIS, R. Y., GILES, H. and LAMBERT, W. E. 1975: Social consequences of accommodating one's style of speech: a cross-national investigation. *International Journal of the Sociology of Language* 6, 55–72.

BOURHIS, R. Y., GILES, H., LEYENS, J. P. and TAJFEL, H. (in press). Psycholinguistic distinctiveness: language divergence in Belgium. In Tajfel, H., editor, *Studies in Intergroup Behaviour*, London: Academic Press.

BOURHIS, R. Y., GILES, H. and TAJFEL, H. 1973: Language as a determinant of Welsh identity. *European Journal of Social Psychology* 3, 447–60.

BURTON, D. and STUBBS, M. 1975: On speaking terms: analysing conversational data. *Journal of the Midlands Association for Linguistic Studies*, Autumn 1975.

CALLARY, R. J. 1975: Phonological Change and the Development of an Urban Dialect in Illinois. *Language in Society* 4, 155–70.

CHASE, I. D. 1975: A comparison of men's and women's intergenerational mobility in the United States. *American Sociological Review* 40, 483–509.

CHEYNE, W. 1970: Stereotyped reactions to speakers with Scottish and English regional accents. *British Journal of Social and Clinical Psychology* 9, 77–9.

CHOMSKY, N. 1965: *Aspects of the theory of syntax*. Cambridge, Mass.: MIT Press.

CHOMSKY, N. and HALLE, M. 1968: *The sound pattern of English*. New York: Harper and Row.

CONSTANTINOPLE, A. 1973: Masculinity-femininity: an exception to a famous dictum. *Psychological Bulletin* 80, 389–407.

COOK, S. 1969: *Language change and the emergence of an urban dialect in Utah.* University of Utah: unpublished PhD dissertation.

COOMBS, C. H. 1964: *A theory of data.* New York: Wiley.

CRYSTAL, D. 1966: *Studies in the prosodic features of educated British English with special reference to intonation.* University of London: unpublished PhD thesis.

1969: *Prosodic systems and intonation in English.* London: Cambridge University Press.

1971: Prosodic and paralinguistic correlates of social categories. In Ardener, E., editor, *Social anthropology and language*, London: Tavistock, 185–206. (=ASA Monograph 10.)

1975: *The English tone of voice.* London: Edward Arnold.

CRYSTAL, D. and DAVY, D. 1969: *Investigating English style.* London: Longmans.

CRYSTAL, D. and QUIRK, R. 1964: *Systems of prosodic and paralinguistic features in English.* The Hague: Mouton. (Janua Linguarum Series Minor 39.)

FASOLD, R. and SHUY, R. 1975: *Analysing variation in language.* Washington: Georgetown University Press.

FISCHER, J. L. 1958: Social influences on the choice of a linguistic variant, *Word* 14, 47–56.

FISHMAN, J. 1970: *Sociolinguistics: a brief introduction.* Rowley, Mass.: Newbury House.

1972: *The sociology of language.* Rowley, Mass.: Newbury House.

FRANCIS, W. N. 1968: Modal 'daren't' and 'durstn't' in dialectal English, *NS* II.

FRANKENBERG, R. 1969: *Communities in Britain.* Harmondsworth: Penguin.

FRIED, M. 1973: *The world of the urban working class.* Cambridge, Mass.: Harvard University Press.

GARFINKEL, H. 1968: The origins of the term 'ethnomethodology'. In Hill, R. and Crittenden, K., editors, *Proceedings of the Purdue symposium on ethnomethodology.* Institute for the Study of Social Change: Purdue University.

GARVEY, C. and DICKSTEIN, E. 1972: Levels of analysis and social class differences in language. *Language and Speech*, 15, 375–84.

GAUCHAT, L. 1905: L'unité phonétique dans le patois d'une commune. Halle.

GILES, H. 1970: Evaluative reactions to accents. *Educational Review* 22, 211–27.

1971a: Ethnocentrism and the evaluation of accented speech. *British Journal of Social and Clinical Psychology* 10, 187–8.

1971b: Patterns of evaluation in reactions to RP, South Welsh and Somerset accented speech. *British Journal of Social and Clinical Psychology* 10, 280–81.

1972a: The effects of mildness-broadness in the evaluation of accents. *Language and Speech* 15, 262–9.

1972b: Evaluation of personality content from accented speech as a function of listeners' social attitudes. *Perceptual and Motor Skills* 34, 168–70.

1973a: Communicative effectiveness as a function of accented speech. *Speech Monographs* 40, 330–31.

1973b: Accent mobility: a model and some data. *Anthropological Linguistics* 15, 87–105.

1977: Social psychology and applied linguistics: towards an integrative approach. ITL: *A Review of Applied Linguistics* 33.

GILES, H., BAKER, S. and FIELDING, G. 1975: Communication length as a behavioural index of accent prejudice. *International Journal of the Sociology of Language* 6, 73–81.

GILES, H. and BOURHIS, R. Y. 1973: Dialect perception revisited. *Quarterly Journal of Speech* 59, 337–42.

1976a: Black speakers with white speech—a real problem? In Nickel, G., editor, *Proceedings of 4th International Congress of Applied Linguistics.* Stuttgart: Hochschulverlag.

1976b: Methodological issues in dialect perception: a social psychological perspective. *Anthropological Linguistics* 18 (in press).

GILES, H., BOURHIS, R. Y. and TAYLOR, D. M. 1977: Towards a theory of language in ethnic group relations. In Giles, H., editor, *Language, ethnicity and intergroup relations.* London: Academic Press, 307–48.

GILES, H. and POWESLAND, P. F. 1975: *Speech style and social evaluation.* London and New York: Academic Press.

GILES, H., TAYLOR, D. M. and BOURHIS, R, Y. 1973: Towards a theory of interpersonal accommodation through language: some Canadian data. *Language in Society* 2, 177–92.

GLAUSER, B. 1974: *The Scottish-English linguistic border: lexical aspects.* Bern: Francke Verlag.

GOFFMAN, E. 1976: Replies and responses. *Language in Society* 5.

GRANT, W. 1914: *The pronunciation of English in Scotland.* Cambridge: at the University Press.

GRANT, W. and DIXON, J. 1921: *Manual of Modern Scots.* Cambridge: at the University Press.

GREGG, R. J. 1972: The Scotch-Irish boundaries in Ulster. In Wakelin, M. F., *Patterns in the folk speech of the British Isles.* London: Athlone Press.

GUMPERZ, J. 1971: *Language in social groups.* Stanford: Stanford University Press.

GUMPERZ, J. and HERNANDEZ, E. 1971: Bilingualism, bidialectalism, and classroom interaction. In Gumperz (1971).

HALLIDAY, M. A. K. 1967: Intonation and grammar in British English. The Hague: Mouton. (*Janua Linguarum Ser. Practica* 48.)

1973: *Explorations in the functions of language.* London: Edward Arnold.

HEMPEL, C. G. 1965: *Aspects of scientific explanation.* New York: The Free Press.

HERMANN, M. E. 1929: Lautveränderungen in der Individualsprache einer Mundart. *Nachrichten der Gesellschaft der Wissenschaften zu Göttingen. Philosophisch-historische Klasse* XI, 195–214.

HERZLER, J. 1965: *The sociology of language.* New York: Random House.

HOLMER, N. M. 1942: *The Irish language in Rathlin Island, Co. Antrim.* Dublin.

HOLTER, H. 1970: *Sex role and social differentiation.* Boston: Boktrykkeri.

HONIKMAN, B. 1964: Articulatory settings. In Abercrombie, D. *et al.,* editors, *In honour of Daniel Jones.* London: Longman.

HYMES, D. 1974: *Foundations in sociolinguistics.* Philadelphia: University of Philadelphia Press.

JAKOBSON, R. and HALLE, M. 1956: *Fundamentals of language*. The Hague: Mouton.

KETT, J. 1975: *Tha's a rum'un, tew!* Woodbridge: Baron Publishing.

KING, R. D. 1969: *Historical linguistics and generative grammar*. Englewood Cliffs, N.J.: Prentice Hall.

— 1975: Integrating linguistic change. In Dahlstedt, K. H. *The Nordic languages and modern linguistics* 2. Stockholm: Almqvist and Wiksell.

KINGDON, R. 1958: *Groundwork of English intonation*. London: Longman.

KIPARSKY, P. and KIPARSKY, C. 1968: Fact. In Bierwisch, M. and Heidolph, H., editors, *Recent advances in linguistics*. The Hague: Mouton, 143–73.

KNOWLES, G. 1974: *Scouse: the urban dialect of Liverpool*. University of Leeds: unpublished PhD thesis.

KRAMER, C. 1974: Women's speech: separate but unequal? *Quarterly Journal of Speech* 60, 14–24.

— 1975a: Sex-related differences in address systems. *Anthropological Linguistics* 17, 198–210.

— 1975b: Stereotypes of women's speech: the word from cartoons. *Journal of Popular Culture* 8, 622–38.

— (in press). Female and male perceptions of female and male speech. *Language and Speech*.

KRETSCHMER, E. 1925: *Physique and character*. Trans. from 2nd German edn. by W. J. H. Sprott. New York: Harcourt, Brace.

KURATH, H. 1964: *A phonology and prosody of modern English*. Heidelberg: Winter.

LABOV, W. 1963: The social motivation of a sound change. *Word* 19, 273–309.

— 1964a: Stages in the acquisition of Standard English. In Shuy, R. W., editor, *Social Dialects and Language Learning*, NCTE.

— 1964b: Phonological correlates of social stratification. In Gumperz, J. J. and Hymes, D., editors, *The ethnography of communication*, Menasha, Wisc.: American Anthropological Association, 164–76. (Special Publication *American Anthropologist* vol. 66, 6 (2).)

— 1966: *The social stratification of English in New York City*. Washington DC: Center for Applied Linguistics.

— 1969: Contraction, deletion, and inherent variability of the English copula. *Language* 45, 715–62.

— 1970: The study of language in its social context. *Studium Generale* 23, 30–87.

— 1972a: *Sociolinguistic patterns*. Philadelphia: University of Pennsylvania Press.

— 1972b: *Language in the inner city*. Philadelphia: University of Pennsylvania Press.

— 1972c: Negative attraction and negative concord in English Grammar. *Language* 48, 773–818.

— 1975: On the Use of the Present to Explain the Past. *Proceedings of the Eleventh International Congress of Linguists*. Bologna.

— (forthcoming). Locating the frontier between social and psychological factors in linguistic variation. *Proceedings of conference on individual differences in language ability and language behaviour*, Monterey, 1976. London: Academic Press.

LABOV, W., COHEN, P., ROBINS, C. and LEWIS, J. 1968: A study of the non-standard English of Negro and Puerto Rican speakers in New York City. *Final Report, US Office of Education Cooperative Research Project* no. 3288, vols I and II. Washington DC: Office of Education.

LABOV, W., YAEGER, M. and STEINER, R. 1972: *A quantitative study of sound change in progress.* Vols I and II. National Science Foundation Contract NSF-GS-3287. University of Pennsylvania. US Regional Survey.

LADEFOGED, P. 1960: The value of phonetic statements. *Language* 36, 387 ff. 1971: *Preliminaries to linguistic phonetics.* Chicago: University Press.

LAKOFF, R. 1973: Language and woman's place. *Language in Society* 2, 45–80.

LAMBERT, W. E. 1967: The social psychology of bilingualism. *Journal of Social Issues* 23, 91–109.

LAMBERT, W. E., GILES, H. and ALBERT, G. 1976: Language attitudes in a rural community in Northern Maine. *La monda lingvoproblemo* 5, 129–44.

LAMBERT, W. E., GILES, H. and PICARD, O. 1975: Language attitudes in a French American community. *International Journal of the Sociology of Language* 4, 127–52.

LANGER, S. 1942: *Philosophy in a new key.* Cambridge: Harvard University Press.

LAVER, J. D. M. 1968: Voice quality and indexical information. *British Journal of Disorders of Communication* 3, 43–54.

LEE, R. R. 1971: Dialect perception: a critical review and re-evaluation. *Quarterly Journal of Speech* 57, 410–17.

LE PAGE, R. B. 1969: Problems of description in multilingual communities. *Transaction of the Philological Society* 1968.

LE PAGE, R. B., CHRISTIE, P., JURDANT, B., WEEKES, A. J. and TABOURET-KELLER, A. 1974: Further report on the sociolinguistic survey of multilingual communities: Survey of Cayo District, British Honduras. *Language in Society* 3, 1–32.

LEVINE, L. and CROCKETT, H. J. 1966: Speech variation in a Piedmont community: postvocalic r. In Lieberson, S., editor, *Explorations in sociolinguistics,* Bloomington: Indiana University Press, 76–98.

LOWMAN, G. and KURATH, H. 1973: *The dialectal structure of southern England: phonological evidence.* American Dialect Society: University of Alabama Press.

MACALLISTER, A. H. 1963: *A Year's course in speech training.* (9th edn). London: University of London Press.

MACAULAY, R. K. S. 1976: Social class and language in Glasgow. *Language in Society* 5, 173–88.
(forthcoming). *Language, social class, and education: a Glasgow study.* To be published by University of Edinburgh Press.
(forthcoming). The myth of female superiority in language. *Journal of Child Language.*

MACAULAY, R. K. S. and TREVELYAN, G. D. 1973: *Language, education, and employment in Glasgow.* (Report to the Social Science Research Council.) Edinburgh: Scottish Council for Research in Education.

MCINTOSH, A. 1952: *Introduction to a survey of Scottish dialects.* Edinburgh: Nelson.

MACKINNON, K. 1974: *The lion's tongue.* Inverness: Highland Book Club.

MACLARAN, R. 1976: The variable (ʌ), a relic form with social correlates. *Belfast Working Papers in Language and Linguistics,* 1(2).

MARTINET, A. 1963: Preface. In Weinreich (1963).

MARTYNA, W. (in press). Beyond the he/man approach: the case for linguistic change. *Signs: Journal of Women in Culture and Society.*

MATHER, J. Y. 1975: Social variation in present-day Scots speech. In McClure, J. D., editor, *The Scots language in education.* Association for Scottish Literary Studies Occasional Papers 3, 44–54.

MILROY, J. 1976: Length and height variations in the vowels of Belfast vernacular. *Belfast Working Papers in Language and Linguistics* 1(3).
(in preparation). Vowel alternations in Belfast vernacular. (To appear in *Belfast Working Papers.*)

MILROY, L. 1976: Phonological correlates to community structure in Belfast. *Belfast Working Papers in Language and Linguistics* 1(1).

MURRAY, J. 1873: *The dialect of the southern counties of Scotland.* London: Asher.

MUTSCHMANN, H. 1909: A phonology of the Northeast Scotch dialect on a historical basis. *Bonner Studien zur englischen Philologie I.* Bonn.

NORDBERG, B. 1971: En undersökning av språket i Eskilstuna. *Språkvard* 3, 7–15.
1973: Contemporary social variation as a stage in long-term phonological change. In Dahlstedt, K. H., editor, *The Nordic languages and linguistics,* Stockholm: Almquist and Wiksell International, 587–608.

NUNBERG, G. 1975: A falsely reported merger in 18th century English. *Pennsylvania working papers in linguistic change and variation,* 1, 2.

O'CONNOR, J. D. and ARNOLD, G. F. 1973: *Intonation of colloquial English.* London: Longman.

OLLER, D. K. and EILERS, R. E. 1975: Phonetic expectation and transcription validity. *Phonetica* 31, 288–304.

OPPENHEIM, A. N. 1966: *Questionnaire design and attitude measurement.* London: Heinemann.

ORTON, H. 1962: *Introduction to survey of English dialects.* Leeds: E. J. Arnold.

ORTON, H. and TILLING, P. 1969: *Survey of English dialects vol 3: the East Midland counties and East Anglia.* Leeds: E. J. Arnold.

PALMER, F. R. 1974: *The English verb.* London: Longman.

PATTERSON, D. 1860: *The Provincialisms of Belfast pointed out and corrected.* Belfast.

PELLOWE, J. 1967: *Studies towards a classification of varieties of spoken English.* University of Newcastle upon Tyne: unpublished M.Litt. thesis.
1970: Establishing some prosodic criteria for a classification of speech varieties. Newcastle University. (Mimeo.)
1973: A problem of diagnostic relativity in the Tyneside Linguistic Survey. *Class. Soc. Bull.* 3(1), 2–8.
1976: The Tyneside Linguistic Survey: aspects of a developing methodology. In Viereck, W., editor, *Sprachliches Handeln—Soziales Verhalten: ein Reader Zur Pragmalinguistik und Soziolinguistik,* Munich: Wilhelm Fink, 203–17, 365–7.

PELLOWE, J. (ed.) (forthcoming). Studies in unity and variety: collected papers of the Tyneside Linguistic Survey. To appear as a special publication of the Philological Society.

PELLOWE, J. and JONES, V. (forthcoming, a). Varietal variability of prosodic systems and its correlates.

(forthcoming, b). Establishing intonationally variable systems in a multi-dimensional linguistic space.

PELLOWE, J., NIXON, G. and MCNEANY, V. 1972a: Some sociolinguistic characteristics of phonetic analysis. In Rigault, A. and Charbonneau, R., editors, *Proceedings of the VII International Congress of Phonetic Sciences* (Montreal 1971), The Hague: Mouton, 1172–8.

PELLOWE, J., NIXON, G., STRANG, B. and MCNEANY, V. 1972b: A dynamic modelling of linguistic variation: the urban (Tyneside) linguistic survey. *Lingua* 30, 1–30.

PETYT, K. M. 1977: 'Dialect' and 'accent' in the industrial West Riding. University of Reading: unpublished Ph.D. thesis.

PIELOU, E. C. 1969: *An introduction to mathematical ecology*. New York: Wiley.

POSTAL, P. 1968: *Aspects of phonological theory*. New York: Harper and Row.

POWESLAND, P. F. and GILES, H. 1975: Persuasiveness and accent-message incompatibility. *Human Relations* 28, 85–93.

QUIRK, R. 1965: Descriptive statement and serial relationship. *Language* 41, 205 ff.

QUIRK, R. and CRYSTAL, D. 1966: On scales of contrast in connected English speech. In Bazell, C. E., Catford, J. C., Halliday, M. A. K. and Robins, R. H., editors, *In memory of J. R. Firth*, London: Longmans, 359–69.

QUIRK, R. and GREENBAUM, S. 1973: *A university grammar of English*. London: Longman.

QUIRK, R., SVARTVIK, J., DUCKWORTH, A. P., RUSIECKI, J. P. L. and COLIN, A. J. T. 1964: Studies in the correspondence of prosodic to grammatical features in English. In *Proc. IX International Congress of Linguists* (Boston 1962), The Hague: Mouton, 679–91.

REID, E. 1976: *Social and stylistic variation in the speech of some Edinburgh schoolchildren*. University of Edinburgh: unpublished M.Litt. thesis.

ROBINSON, W. P. 1972: *Language and social behaviour*. London: Penguin.

ROMAINE, S. 1975: *Linguistic variability in the speech of some Edinburgh schoolchildren*. Edinburgh University: M.Litt. thesis.

SACKS, H., SCHEGLOFF, E. and JEFFERSON, G. 1974: A simplest systematics for the organization of turn-taking in conversation. *Language* 50.

SANKOFF, G. 1974: A quantitative paradigm for the study of communicative competence. In Bauman and Sherzer, editors (1974).

SANKOFF, G. and BROWN, P. 1976: The origins of syntax in discourse. *Language* 52.

SCHEGLOFF, E. 1968: Sequencing in conversational openings. *American Anthropologist* 70.

SCHULZ, M. R. 1975: How serious is sex bias in language? *College Composition and Communication* 26, 163–7.

SINCLAIR, J. and COULTHARD, R. 1974: *Towards an analysis of discourse*. London: Oxford University Press.

SMELSER, N. J. and LIPSET, S. M. (editors) 1966: *Social structure and mobility in economic development*. London: Routledge, Kegan Paul.

SPEITEL, H. 1969a: *Some studies in the dialect of Midlothian*. Edinburgh University: PhD thesis.

1969b: A typology of isoglosses: isoglosses near the Scottish-English border. *Zeitschrift für Dialektologie und Linguistik* 7, 49–66.

SPENCE, J. T., HELMRICH, R. and STAPP, P. 1974: The personal attributes questionnaire: a measure of sex-role stereotypes and masculinity-femininity. *Catalog of Selected Documents in Psychology* 4, 43–4.

STRANG, B. M. H. 1968: The Tyneside Linguistic Survey. *Zeitschrift für Mundartforschung*, 788–94.

1970: *A History of English*. London: Methuen.

STRONGMAN, K. and WOOSLEY, J. 1967: Stereotyped reactions to regional accents. *British Journal of Social and Clinical Psychology* 6, 164–7.

TAJFEL, H. 1959: A note on Lambert's 'Evaluational reactions to spoken language'. *Canadian Journal of Psychology* 13, 86–92.

TAYLOR, MARY VAIANA, 1974: The great Southern Scots conspiracy. In Anderson, John M. and Jones, C. *Historical linguistics* vol II, Amsterdam: North Holland, and Oxford.

THORNE, B. and HENLEY, N. 1975: *Language and sex: difference and dominance*. Rowley, Mass.: Newbury House.

TRUDGILL, P. 1972: Sex, covert prestige and linguistic change in the urban British English of Norwich. *Language in Society* 1, 179–96.

1974a: *The social differentiation of English in Norwich*. London: Cambridge University Press.

1974b: *Sociolinguistics*. London: Penguin.

TRUDGILL, P. and GILES, H. 1977: Sociolinguistics and linguistic value judgements: correctness, adequacy and aesthetics. In Coppieters, F. and Goyvaerts, D., editors, *The functions of language and literature studies*, Ghent: Story-Scientia.

TURNER, R. 1970: Words, utterances and activities. In Douglas, J., editor, *Understanding everyday life*. Chicago: Aldine.

WAKELIN, M. F. 1972: *English dialects: an introduction*. London: Athlone press.

WEINREICH, U. 1963: *Languages in contact*. The Hague: Mouton.

WEINREICH, U., LABOV, W. and HERZOG, M. 1968: Empirical foundations for a theory of language change. In Lehmann, W. P., editor, *Directions for historical linguistics*, Austin: University of Texas Press, 95–195.

WETTSTEIN, P. 1942: *The phonology of a Berwickshire dialect*. Biel: Schuler S.A.

WELLS, J. C. 1970: Local accents in England and Wales. *Journal of Linguistics* 6, 231–52.

WIJK, AXEL. 1937: *The orthography and pronunciation of Henry Machyn*.

WILKINS, D. 1977: *Notional syllabuses*. London: Oxford University Press

WILLIAMS, I. F. 1912: *Phonetics for Scottish students: The sounds of polite Scottish described and compared with those of polite English* (2nd edn). Glasgow: James Maclehose and Sons.

WILLIAMS, J. A. 1977: Psychological androgyny: some implications for life stress and psychopathology. University of Bristol. (Mimeo).

WILLIAMS, J. E. and BEST, D. L. 1977: Sex stereotypes and trait favourability on the adjective checklist. *Educational and Psychological Measurement,* in press.

WILLIAMS, J. E., GILES, H., EDWARDS, J. R., BEST, D. L. and DAWS, J. T. (in press). Sex trait stereotypes in England, Ireland and the United States. *British Journal of Social and Clinical Psychology.*

WILSON, R. M. 1963: The orthography and provenance of Henry Machyn. In Brown, A. and Foote, P. editors, *Early English and Norse studies,* London:

WÖLCK, W. 1965: *Phonematische Analyse der Sprache von Buchan.* Heidelberg: Carl Winter Universitätsverlag.

WOLFRAM, W. 1969: *A sociolinguistic description of Detroit Negro speech.* Washington DC: Center for Applied Linguistics.

WOLFRAM, W. and FASOLD, R. W. 1974: *The study of social dialects in American English.* Englewood Cliffs, N.J.: Prentice-Hall, Inc.

WOLFRAM, W. and CHRISTIAN, D. 1976: *Appalachian speech.* Washington: Center for Applied Linguistics.

WOLFRAM, W. and WOLFRAM, T. (forthcoming). How come you asked how come? In NWAVE III. Washington: Georgetown University Press.

WRIGHT, J. 1892: *A Grammar of the dialect of Windhill.* London: English Dialect Society.

WYLD, H. C. 1920: *A history of modern colloquial English.* London: Unwin.

Index

school, truancy from, in Reading 53, 65; speech, in Reading 67; and Edinburgh children's speech 165–71
Schulz, M. R., cited 125
Scotland, regional accent 123, 125; RP in 139; border isoglosses 142; postvocalic /r/ 144–57; *see also* individual towns
Scots pronunciation, in Ulster 34
Scottish Standard English (SSE) 145
Scouse dialect, phonological variables in 80–90
secular linguistics 11–12, 16
segmental phonology 101, 104
self-esteem 127
sex differentiation, in linguistic change 155
Sinclair, J. *and* Coulthard, R., cited 5, 10
'sing-song' 81
Smelser, N. J. *and* Lipset, S. M., cited 131
social attractiveness traits 126
social factors, and varieties in N. Ireland 37–51; in Reading speech 63–4; in Glasgow speech 138, 140; and speech categories 143; in Edinburgh speech 164; *see also* ambition (social)
social perception 158
social psychology of language 9–10, 17
sociolinguistics, defined and classified 1–3, 10–11
sociology of language 9, 10
Somerset 123
sound change 69, 74–6, 78–9, 151–3, 155
space, and varietal association 104
speech *see* articulatory setting
Speitel, H., cited 142, 145, 148, 150, 156
Spence, J. T., Helmreich, R. *and* Stapp, P., cited 127, 129
standard deviations (SD), in Glasgow 139
Strang, B. M. H., cited 91n
Strang, Barbara, cited 101n
Strongman, K. *and* Woosley, J., cited 123
structured variability 148
Stubbs, M., cited 1n
stylistic variation, in Edinburgh children 158, 163–71
Suffolk 77, 156
summons-answer sequences 5
Survey of English Dialects 70–71, 73–4, 97
Survey of English Usage 108n
Sutcliffe, D., cited 70n
Swarbrick, M. *and* Swarbrick, J., cited 122n
Sweden 155
syntactic complexity, in Glasgow 141
syntax, varietal features 101, 104

Tajfel, H., cited 122n, 123
talk, defined 2–3
'talking down your nose' 81
'talking far-back' 81
Taylor, D. M., cited 122n
Taylor, M. V., cited 34
Tilling, P. M., cited 39n
telephone conversations, rules of 5, 7, 8
Thorne, B. *and* Henley, N., cited 125
Tok Pisin 10
tone, in Tyneside analysis 106, 108–12; *see also* intonation
tone-units 101, 105, 109, 111
toughness 64–6, 130

transfer, and vocalic mergers 72–5, 77–8
Trudgill, P., on social evaluations of language 10; on a-verbing 15; cited 37, 40, 67–8, 70, 72, 74, 76, 89, 95, 104, 125, 130, 133, 136, 146, 151, 154–6, 158–9, 161–2
Turner, R., cited 2, 3
Tyneside, intonational variability 103, 105, 109
Tyneside Linguistic Survey 103–4, 106, 108, 121

Ulster Scots 19, 34
United States of America, postvocalic /r/ in 144
upward accent convergence 124

variability, in linguistic description 12; and intuitions 13–14; constraints on 14–16, 18; social 18; in Belfast vernacular 19–36; in N. Ireland village 37–51
variation theory 12
varietal variability 102–5, 117
variety space 104, 108, 121
verbs, vernacular meanings in Reading 60–61; *see also* auxiliary verbs; perfect tense; present tense
vernacular speech, defined 53
vowels, Belfast variables 24–36; N. Ireland village variables 41–3, 45–7; mergers in E. Anglia 69–79; in Liverpool 82–6, 89; hypercorrection of 86–7; Glasgow variables 134, 137–8; Edinburgh variables 147

Wakelin, M. F., cited 58
Wales, reactions to RP in 123–4
Watford 70
Weinrich, U., cited 10
Weinrich, U., Labov, W. *and* Herzog, M., cited 133, 153
Wells, J. C., cited 70
West Yorkshire *see* Yorkshire (West)
Wettsetein, P., cited 148n
Wijk, A., cited 20n
Wilkins, D., cited 10
Williams, I. F., cited 144, 145, 148, 153
Williams, J. E. *and* Best, D. L., cited 126
Williams, J. E. *et al.*, cited 126
Wilson, R. M., cited 20n
Wölck, W., cited 145
Wolfram, W., cited 67, 125, 133
Wolfram, W. *and* Christian, D., cited 15
Wolfram, W. *and* Fasold, R. W., cited 15, 61, 162
Wolfram, W. *and* Wolfram, T., cited 6–7
women, RP speech and perception of 122–31; and prestige speech 155–6; *see also* femininity
Women's Institutes 39n
work *see* occupations
working classes, slow adoption of mergers 71; and Liverpool speech 82–3, 85; secondary negative contractions 91, 95, 98–100; Edinburgh speech 146, 153, 155
Wright, J., cited 94
Wyld, H. C., cited 20

yes/aye variable 43
Yorkshire 88, 123
Yorkshire (West), secondary negative contractions 91–100